FOOD FOR SPORT COOKBOOK

THE ULTIMATE NUTRITIONAL GUIDE FOR PEAK PERFORMANCE

To our children, Naomi, Jacqueline, Natasha and Richard.

Karen Inge, Consultant Sports Dietitian, is a director of the Institute of Health and Fitness, McKinnon Sports Medicine Centre, in Melbourne, and Consultant Dietician to the Hawthorn Football Club, the Melbourne Magic basketball team, the Australian Ballet Company and School, and the Victorian Institute of Sport. She is a consultant to various commercial organisations and is a well-known television and radio personality. Karen is co-author of the award-winning book *Food for Sport*, and author of *Food, Fitness and Feeling Good*.

Christine Roberts is Director of the Melbourne Dietetic Centre, and Consultant Dietitian to hospitals and commercial organisations. She is Chief Dietician at St Georges Hospital, Kew, and is in private practice. Her focus is on sports nutrition, diabetes, weight-control and cardiology. Christine has co-authored a number of books for people with special dietary needs, including the best-selling book *Eat & Enjoy* for diabetes. She has a high profile in her profession, and is frequently called upon to lecture before both professional and public interest groups.

FOOD FOR SPORT COOKBOOK

THE ULTIMATE NUTRITIONAL GUIDE FOR PEAK PERFORMANCE

New edition. Fully revised and updated.

Karen Inge • *Christine Roberts*

This edition first published in 1996 by
New Holland (Publishers) Ltd
London • Cape Town • Sydney • Singapore

24 Nutford Place
London W1H 6DQ
UK

P.O. Box 1144
Cape Town 8000
South Africa

3/2 Aquatic Drive
Frenchs Forest, NSW 2086
Australia

ISBN 1 85368 616 6 (pbk)

Editors: Alison Leach and Coral Walker

Typeset by Ace Filmsetting Ltd, Frome, Somerset
Reproduction by Hirt & Carter (Pty) Ltd
Printed and bound in Hong Kong by Everbest

All meal plans in this book have been presented as samples only. Anyone
wishing to follow these meal plans should first seek the advice of a qualified
dietician.

In all the recipes, quantities are given in both metric and imperial
measurements. As these are not interchangeable, follow one system in each
case. Nutritional data is expressed only in grams in accordance with current
dietetic practice.

CONTENTS

ACKNOWLEDGMENTS

There are several people we would like to thank for their great help to us in producing this new edition of the *Food for Sport Cookbook*.

First, our sincere thanks to Noel Roberts, a consultant dietician who combined his artistic ability and cookery skills with his extensive knowledge of nutrition and food to help create the recipes in this book.

We would like to express our appreciation to Lorna Garden, for her invaluable contribution and support in the nutritional analysis and development of the Menu Plans.

Our thanks go also to Naomi Roberts and Susannah Gibson for their help with the nutritional data and to Lisa Grennan and Allison Politi, who gave generously of their time and advice for the microwave adaptations in the book.

The Publishers would also like to thank The Rice Bureau and the Sports Nutrition Foundation at St Bartholomew's Hospital for their advice and help.

We would like to thank our families, most specially our husbands, George Janko and Noel Roberts, for their support, understanding and for suffering with us during the production of the *Food for Sport Cookbook*. Finally, we would like to thank all the sportspeople who have inspired us to write this book and who have enthusiastically sampled many of the recipes.

Karen Inge and Christine Roberts

EAT WELL, PERFORM WELL

What you eat can and does make a difference to your performance. Put quite simply, the better your nutritional status, the better you perform.

This applies to anyone who is seriously committed to sport. The nutritional guidelines we set out in this book apply, however, to anyone who wants to maintain fitness and good health, and the recipes suit a modern, active way of life.

If you play sport, you probably know that you should eat more carbohydrate and less fat. But research into sports nutrition is developing so quickly that you may be confused as to what really works.

You may know Carbohydrate Loading increases endurance, but what is involved in using this dietary regime?

You may know that vitamins and minerals are important, but what do they really do and how can you ensure that you are taking in enough?

There is so much myth and misunderstanding about the role of fluids and salt, you would be forgiven for feeling bewildered. And then there is the matter of incorrect information, wild promises, rumour and changing-room gossip, all of which add to the confusion.

We believe that the first things to understand are the principles of nutrition. But knowing the principles is only part of the answer; you need to understand how to translate them into a nutritious Eating Plan, and into dishes which are quick to prepare and taste delicious.

To help bridge the gap between theory and the kitchen, we have shown you how to devise an Eating Plan suited to you and your sport. The chapter 'Your Eating Strategy' deserves time and attention. In it you will find the tools you need to build your diet – and your performance.

We also explain how to structure an effective Training Diet, what to eat in preparation for competition, and what to eat to recover after a strenuous training session or event. This information is backed up by Meal Plans, which include foods that require little or no preparation.

Another possible stumbling block between you and peak nutritional status may simply be that you feel uncertain in the kitchen and therefore need general information on how to choose, store and cook food so it retains its nutritional value.

We cover all these aspects in the following chapters.

WHAT YOU NEED IS ENERGY

Energy and endurance are the prime factors in peak performance. With greater energy you can run faster, jump higher, exercise more rigorously. You can also sustain your sporting activity more easily.

You could describe energy as the fuel on which our bodies run. Our bodies create energy by breaking down carbohydrate, fat and, to a lesser extent, protein.

Each of these three nutrients breaks down into a different energy-giving substance. Carbohydrate is stored as glycogen and breaks down into glucose, fats break down into fatty acids and proteins break down into amino acids.

Neither vitamins nor minerals give you energy. Their role is to keep your body working efficiently and to help in the transfer of energy from carbohydrates, fats and proteins.

The athlete's most precious fuel is glycogen (stored carbohydrate), for it is the key to endurance. At any time, you have only about 8,375 kJ (2,000 cal) stored in this form, most of it in your muscles and a smaller amount in your liver. By comparison, the energy stored as fat in your body is considerable. Even a person carrying little excess body fat has about 7 kg (16 lb) of it, representing about 251,200 kJ (60,000 cal).

The exhaustion of glycogen stores is the limiting factor in sporting performance. When your glycogen stores are exhausted, you are exhausted and your performance falters.

One of the benefits of training is that your muscles develop an increased capacity to store glycogen. The right training diet will not only provide enough carbohydrate to fill your glycogen stores to enable you to exercise longer and harder, but will also provide you with enough of all the essential nutrients you need to maximise your health, and therefore, your performance.

THE GOLDEN RULES OF SPORT NUTRITION

Our experience with tailoring diets for athletes has led us to evolve The Golden Rules of Sport Nutrition, based on current research. We list them below and then explain why these Golden Rules are important and how they work:

- Eat plenty of carbohydrate.
- Limit the fat in your diet.
- Be sure to eat enough protein.
- Eat plenty of dietary fibre.
- Cut down on salt.
- Eat a variety of foods to make sure you are getting enough minerals and vitamins.
- Include plenty of fluids, especially when exercising.
- Cut back on alcohol.

EAT MORE CARBOHYDRATE

Carbohydrate-rich foods are the preferred source of energy for athletes and you should eat plenty of them.

In simple terms, carbohydrates can be broadly divided into starches and sugars.

You should include more starchy foods such as bread, rice, pasta, potatoes and pulses in your diet, as these provide other important nutrients. Sugar-rich foods such as honey, confectionery, soft drink and sugar itself provide less nutrients but are useful for athletes with high carbohydrate needs. Foods such as fruit, milk and yoghurt contain sugar rather than starch but at the same time they provide an excellent source of valuable nutrients, and so should be considered exceptions.

Different carbohydrate foods have different effects on blood glucose levels, even when they provide the same amount of carbohydrate. Foods have been rated according to this effect. This is known as the glycaemic index (GI). Some carbohydrate-rich foods cause a quicker and higher rise in blood glucose levels than others, i.e. they have a high GI. Many factors affect the rise in blood glucose (sugar) levels such as the type of fibre, starch or sugar, the amount of fat and the processing and cooking of foods. The following chart gives some examples of high and low glycaemic index foods.

Foods which cause a quicker rise in blood glucose (i.e. high glycaemic index)

Glucose, glucose confectionery (e.g. jelly beans/babies), honey
Some breakfast cereals: e.g. cornflakes, puffed rice
Wholemeal and white bread
Rice noodles
Rice: brown and white
Some fruits: tropical, stewed fruits, ripe bananas
Some vegetables: parsnip, potato and pumpkin
Sports drinks, soft drinks and cordials

Foods which cause a slower, more sustained rise in blood glucose, i.e. low glycaemic index

Pulses: dried beans, baked beans, peas and lentils
Oat, barley and bran cereals: porridge, muesli, bran flakes
Breads with large amounts of wholegrains
All pastas
Basmati rice
Some fresh fruits: apples, cherries, grapefruit, oranges, peaches, pears, plums and firm bananas
Some vegetables: sweet potato, sweet corn
Barley, buckwheat, bulghur (e.g. tabbouleh)

All high carbohydrate, low fat foods are beneficial to athletic performance; however, there are times when one group may be more beneficial than the other. Current research suggests that high glycaemic index foods speed recovery after strenuous exercise and low glycaemic index foods result in sustained energy release.

Your Training Diet should consist of:

Carbohydrate   55–60%
Protein   12–15%
Fat   25–30%

It is worth pointing out that the recommended intake of carbohydrate for everyone, whether you play sport or not, is 55–60%. The main difference between a normal healthy diet and one geared for sporting performance is in the total quantity of kilojoules (calories) consumed.

However, if you are involved in particularly rigorous training, you may need to draw as much as 65–70% of your total energy from carbohydrate. You will need 7–10 g carbohydrate per kilogram of bodyweight per day.

Many of the recipes in this book feature complex carbohydrates (see following listing), and the Meal Plans (see pages 17–19) offer the recommended levels of carbohydrate. Then in the chapter 'Your Eating Strategy' we show you how to tailor your diet so that you can ensure that you eat enough carbohydrate for training and competition.

The carbohydrate-rich foods – pasta, pulses and rice – make excellent bases for many dishes, and you will find them scattered throughout the chapters. This may make them a little difficult for you to find, so we have compiled a list of dishes using these foods.

Pasta	Page	Rice	Page
Macaroni Cheese	156	Hawaiian Chicken & Rice	136
Noodle & Poppyseed Salad	167	Kitchri (Savoury Rice & Lentils)	155
Pasta Marinara	146	Salmon, Potato & Rice Bake	112
Silver & Jade Salad	164	Cheesy Peppers	97
Spinach Fettuccine	148	Conqueror's Curry Pie	162
Vegetable Lasagne	149	Fish & Rice Ratatouille	110
Suitable Pasta Sauces		Meal-in-one Rice Salad	167
Classic Tomato Sauce	176	Rice, Cheese & Spinach in Filo Pastry	161
Low-fat Cheese Sauce	179	Beef à la Pizzaiola	132
Meat Sauce	128	Spicy Liver with Rice	135
Neapolitan Sauce	176	Skewered Lamb with Vegetables	125
Quick Vegetable Sauce	178	Sweetcorn & Salmon Rissoles	105
Pulses		**Suitable Rice Sauces**	
Adzuki Bean Simmer	154	Sweet & Sour Sauce	175
Divine Lentil & Pumpkin Loaf	154	Satay (Peanut) Sauce with Chilli	177
Zoom Burgers	157		

Other particularly high carbohydrate recipes not listed here are found throughout the recipe chapters, and especially appear in 'Carbohydrate & Protein Alternatives' and 'Breads, Cakes, Biscuits, Scones & Muffins'. Any recipe with more than 20 g carbohydrate per serving can be considered high in carbohydrate.

EAT LESS FAT

No more than 25–30% of your total energy should come from fat. This is not as much as it sounds, and represents a low-fat diet.

There is no need to cut red meat and dairy foods from your diet. It is simply a matter of knowing what the fat content is and how to prepare these foods to minimise it.

Fats – The Facts

- For athletes, all fats should be limited.

- Saturated fats (e.g. butter), and unsaturated fats (e.g. oils and margarines) have the same kilojoule (calorie) value.

- Use mono-unsaturated (e.g. olive oil) or polyunsaturated oils and margarines when needed.

Red Meat

- Lean red meat (with all visible fat removed) is:
  - no higher in fat than chicken or turkey (without the skin) or non-oily types of fish
  - a valuable source of protein for athletes, although, like all high-protein foods they should be eaten in moderation
  - the richest source of iron in your diet.

Dairy Products

- Athletes need dairy products as a source of calcium.
- By choosing low-fat, fat-free or skimmed milk dairy products you get the nutritional advantages and minimise your fat intake.

Fatty Foods

Because fat is a flavour enhancer, it is hidden in much of the processed food we eat, making it easy for your fat intake to soar above the recommended level if you don't watch out; so you should eat less:

- fried fast foods (e.g. chicken in batter, fried fish and chips, etc.)
- pies, pastries, cakes and biscuits, chocolates and snack foods (e.g. potato crisps)
- cream, butter, margarine, cooking and salad oils.

You will find small quantities of fat in some of the recipes and the Meal Plans, reflecting the wisdom of a properly balanced diet.

EAT ENOUGH PROTEIN

Protein is the substance from which all our body tissues, muscles, skin, hair and blood cells are made. Hormones, enzymes and antibodies are also created from protein.

The protein in your food is broken down in your digestive tract to make basic units called amino acids, of which there are 23 different kinds. Most of these can be manufactured by your body from elements in your diet. The remainder can't, and are called essential amino acids; you need to consume these amino acids every day and know which foods contain them.

Approximately 12–15% of your total energy intake should come from dietary protein.

Note: There is no need to take amino acids supplements. All amino acids are readily available from high protein foods.

Animal Proteins

These contain all the essential amino acids and are complete proteins.

Good Sources of Animal Proteins

- Lean red and white meats, poultry (without skin) and fish
- Low-fat dairy products
- Eggs.

Plant Proteins

These do not contain all the essential amino acids, and are incomplete proteins.

Good Sources of Plant Protein

- Cereals (rice, corn, wheat, rye, oats and barley)
- Pulses (dried beans, peas and lentils)
- Nuts and seeds.

If you are a vegetarian athlete or enjoy some meals without animal protein, you need to know how to combine vegetable proteins to give a balanced intake. We discuss this further in the chapter 'Special Groups, Special Needs'.

EAT PLENTY OF DIETARY FIBRE

Dietary fibre

- Regulates your rate of digestion and absorption and helps you eliminate waste.
- Bulks up your food without adding kilojoules (calories).

Athletes, particularly those trying to lose weight, should eat plenty of high-fibre foods. The best sources of dietary fibre are often foods which are good for you for other reasons as well. For instance (in addition to fibre), wholegrain bread, brown rice, fruit and wholemeal pasta are all excellent sources of complex carbohydrates, essential vitamins and minerals.

Good sources of dietary fibre

- Fruit (especially if eaten with skin on, e.g. apples and pears)
- All vegetables, preferably unpeeled
- Nuts (e.g. almonds and pecans)
- Pulses, such as dried beans, peas and lentils
- Wholegrain cereals (e.g. brown rice, wholemeal pasta, corn, oats, wholemeal breads, biscuits and breakfast cereals).

CUT DOWN ON SALT

We need salt, and it occurs naturally in many of the foods we eat. However, there is no need to add any extra salt to your food, or to use salt tablets, even if you sweat a lot. There is evidence that cramp is caused by too much salt, rather than the lack of it, as so many people believe. Excessive salt increases the load on your kidneys and, if you don't compensate by drinking enough fluids, you may find yourself becoming dehydrated.

Ways to Cut Down the Salt in Your Diet

- Cut down on salt gradually and your taste buds will adjust.
- Try using herbs and spices in your cooking (as we have done in many of our recipes). You will be amazed at how little salt you really need for flavour.
- Always taste your food before adding salt.
- Choose low-salt packaged foods (check labels).

EAT ENOUGH VITAMINS AND MINERALS

Whether or not to take vitamin and mineral supplements is one of the most controversial areas in sports nutrition. It reflects the increasing pressure on athletes and coaches to perform well – at any cost.

There are only two possible reasons for taking extra vitamins and minerals: as a legitimate supplement to your diet if it is inadequate; and as an attempt to boost performance.

One of the apparent benefits of mega-doses of vitamins and minerals may be the placebo effect (where your performance improves simply because you believe that something you are taking will help you). While this effect cannot be under-estimated, unless you understand exactly what particular vitamins and minerals do, taking large doses is potentially dangerous.

Most people who exercise and eat a nutritionally adequate diet will not need any vitamin or mineral supplements. However, if you train hard (or belong to a vulnerable group, as described below) it is important that your nutritional status is professionally assessed by a dietitian or doctor to determine if you need additional vitamins or minerals. If you belong to any of the risk groups, improve your diet before you look to supplements.

Athletes Who May Not Have an Adequate Diet

- those existing on very restricted vegetarian regimes
- those who survive on convenience or fast foods
- those who smoke and drink alcohol excessively
- those whose diet is high in refined carbohydrates
- those on weight reduction diets
- those who take oral contraceptives or other drugs such as diuretics or laxatives.

Improve the Nutrient Value of Your Food

- Buy fresh food that hasn't been stored for long periods.

- Don't over-cook food as this destroys certain vitamins.

- Cook vegetables using just a little water and in the quickest way possible. Steam over, or drop into, boiling water, or cook in the microwave.

- Use unprocessed food wherever possible. Buy wholegrain products and cut back on foods high in sugar and fat.

- Be aware of the effects of your environment and lifestyle on your nutrition, for instance: alcohol, cigarettes, drugs, oral contraceptives, some food additives, rushed or missed meals, over-eating and over-training.

DRINK, DON'T DEHYDRATE

The human is the only animal for whom thirst is not an accurate indicator of fluid needs. By the time you feel thirsty, you are already partly dehydrated. Normally active people should drink 2 litres (3½ pints) of fluid per day for healthy body function; athletes need more, especially before, during and after training sessions or games. Under normal circumstances, it is easy to maintain the balance between fluid intake and output; however, athletes often lose a great deal of fluid while exercising and, if they only drink when thirsty, risk dehydration – to the point of heat exhaustion.

Maintaining fluid levels and the effects of dehydration are discussed in detail on pages 26–8.

CUT BACK ON ALCOHOL

Through sponsorship, alcohol has come to be closely associated with sport, and for many people a social drink after the game is an important part of the sporting life. Nevertheless, alcohol has a detrimental effect on your performance:

- It interferes with co-ordination.

- It dilates the blood vessels, which delays recovery.

- It may affect blood glucose levels and body temperature control.

- It adds greatly to your kilojoule/calorie intake, which could make you gain excessive fat.

- It dehydrates you.

This last effect, dehydration, is particularly damaging. Drinking alcohol before an event (even social drinking) puts you at a severe competitive disadvantage.

YOUR EATING STRATEGY

We appreciate that it is not enough just to give you the theory of sports nutrition, nor does it help simply to present recipes. What you will need is a strategy that lets you combine this knowledge with the recipes to create an Eating Strategy that meets your specific needs.

In order to create your own Eating Strategy, you will need to refer to three parts of this book:

- In the chapter 'Eat Well, Perform Well' you will find a detailed description of The Golden Rules of Sports Nutrition. Read this chapter carefully, it will explain what your sports Eating Strategy should aim to achieve.

- This chapter, 'Your Eating Strategy', gives the tools for you to create your own Eating Strategy: charts, tables, ready-reckoners and examples.

- The recipe section of this book provides delicious, easy-to-prepare dishes. We give the kilojoule (calorie) counts and the amounts of carbohydrate, fat and protein for each recipe.

Because every athlete is different, it is not possible to set down a single Eating Strategy for peak performance. Male athletes have different requirements to female athletes, your weight, height and fitness will affect your needs, and each sport makes its own nutritional demands, whether you train hard or simply play for pleasure.

The most important variable in working out your Eating Strategy is what we have termed the 'You Factors'. Begin by using the various tables and formulae in this chapter to work out what your own needs are.

The Meal Plans we have specially created for this book are intended as a guide; use the one best suited to you as a guide for your own Eating Strategy.

By using the information in this chapter, including the Meal Plans, it is simple to take the recipes and work out an Eating Strategy for peak performance.

DESIGNING YOUR TRAINING DIET

In this section, we set out the steps you need to follow in order to tailor your Training Diet to meet your individual needs. Combine your Eating Strategy with effective training, and you are likely to surpass your performance expectations. Follow each of these steps, and you are also on the path to good health.

Step 1 – Assessing the You Factors

In order to take the first step towards creating your Training Diet, you need to assess the You Factors. Here are the questions you need to ask yourself. (Write down the answers.)

- Are you male or female?
- How old are you?
- Are you still growing? (Most of us have stopped by the time we are 19 years old.)
- How tall are you?
- What do you weigh?
- Are you happy with your weight? Trying to lose body fat or trying to bulk up?
- Do you know your body fat levels, or skinfold thickness?
- Are you pregnant?
- Do you menstruate?
- What is your sport?
- If you participate in a team sport, what position do you play?
- How heavy is your training programme?
- How often do you compete?
- What is your occupation, and other daily activities?

Example – 'Richard J'

To help you understand what to do with your answers, we have given an example for you. Consider Richard J's answers to the You Factors questionnaire:

He is male, 28 years old, 182 cm (6 ft) tall and weighs 81 kg (178 lb). He is happy with his weight; although he recently lost 5 kg (12 lb), his weight is now stable.

The total of his skinfolds is 53 (measured at eight sites on his body), and his major sport is hockey (he plays left back position). During the season, he trains three times a week and plays one match a week.

His only other exercise is a short daily work-out with weights, although his occupation as a sales representative means that he also does a fair amount of walking. He occasionally gardens and mows the lawn.

Step 2 – Estimating Your Energy Needs

The next step is to calculate your energy needs. This can be done in two ways:

- Method A – Food Record
- Method B – Using Charts.

Both methods are only approximate – the only way you can really fine-tune your energy intake with your energy requirements is by watching what happens to your body fat levels. If you begin putting on fat, you know that you need to cut back on your kilojoule (calorie) intake. If you unintentionally begin to lose fat (or, even worse, muscle), you know that you need to increase your kilojoule (calorie) intake.

Method A – Food Record

The most accurate way to estimate your energy needs is to record what you eat each day and then analyse it for energy value. If your body composition is stable, then you know that your kilojoule (calorie) intake is adequate.

(a) Record your food and fluid intake for 7 days.

This will take into account the difference in your eating and drinking pattern during training and while competing. The more accurate and honest your record, the more valuable the result. It is best for you to write down your intake immediately after you have eaten; if you don't, you will discover how easy it is to forget.

(b) Use the ready reckoners we have given you on pages 14–16 and pages 214–15 to work out your kilojoule (calorie), carbohydrate, protein and fat intake over these seven days.

If you want to have a more exact account, you should purchase Food Composition Tables or consult a Dietitian.

Method B – Using Charts

Another way of estimating your energy needs is to use the following charts, together with the You Factors.

(a) Predict Basal Metabolic Rate (BMR) using Chart I on the next page.

(b) Consider your occupation and determine approximate activity level (expressed as a multiple of BMR) using Chart II on the next page.

Note: Exclude your sporting activity when determining your level of activity; this is dealt with below.

(c) Determine Daily Energy Expenditure by multiplying BMR by Level of Activity as shown in Chart II.

(d) Determine the time (in minutes) spent each week in training and competing. Use Chart III (on page 213) to calculate energy needs of your total sporting activity. Divide this by 7 to obtain a daily energy need for this factor.

(e) Add the figures obtained in (c) and (d) above to give your estimated daily energy needs:

Est. Daily Energy Needs = (BMR x Daily Activity Level) + (Energy Cost of Sporting Activities ÷ 7)

Special Energy Needs

If you are growing, pregnant or lactating, your energy requirements are increased as shown:

	Age (yrs)	Additional energy requirement per day
Growth	10–14	8 kJ/kg bodyweight
	15	4 ''
	16–18	2 ''
Pregnancy	—	850–1,100 kJ (3,570–4,620 kcal)
Lactation	—	2,000–2,400 kJ (8,400–10,080 kcal)

Chart I – Equations for Estimating Basal Metabolism Rate (BMR)

Sex	Age (yrs)	Equation = BMR (kJ per day)	
Males	10–18	[(0.074 x wt) + 2.754] x 1000	
	18–30	[(0.063 x wt) + 2.896] x 1000	
	30–60	[(0.048 x wt) + 3.653] x 1000	
	60 +	[(0.049 x wt) + 2.459] x 1000	
Females	10–18	[(0.056 x wt) + 2.898] x 1000	Notes:
	18–30	[(0.062 x wt) + 2.036] x 1000	(a) 'wt' is bodyweight in kg.
	30–60	[(0.034 x wt) + 3.538] x 1000	(b) To convert kJ to cal ÷ by 4.2.
	60 +	[(0.038 x wt) + 2.755] x 1000	(c) To convert lb to kg x 0.45.

Chart II – Average Daily Energy Expenditure (shown as multiples of BMR)

Activity Level	Males Average (Range)		Females Average (Range)	
Bed rest	1.2	(1.1–1.3)	1.2	(1.1–1.3)
Very sedentary	1.3	(1.2–1.4)	1.3	(1.2–1.4)
Sedentary/ Maintenance	1.4	(1.3–1.5)	1.4	(1.3–1.5)
Light	1.5	(1.4–1.6)	1.5	(1.4–1.6)
Light–moderate	1.7	(1.6–1.8)	1.6	(1.5–1.7)
Moderate	1.8	(1.7–1.9)	1.7	(1.6–1.8)
Heavy	2.1	(1.9–2.3)	1.8	(1.7–1.9)
Very heavy	2.3	(2.0–2.6)	2.0	(1.8–2.2)

Both charts modified from *Recommended Nutrient Intakes, Australian Papers*, ed. A. S. Truswell, Australian Professional Publications, 1990.

Example – Richard J

We have used Richard J as an example to show you how to work out energy requirements.

Method A – Food Record

Using the Food Record Method, we analysed Richard J's 7-day record and found that he took in about 14,250 kJ (3,400 cal) daily.

Method B – Using Charts

Using Richard J's You Factors and Charts I–III, we can determine his total energy needs per day. See page 213 for Chart III, which provides the information needed to complete the 'sporting activity' section.

Richard J's Estimated Energy Needs

You Factors	Calculation	Energy needs (kJ)
Sex/age: Male, 28 years **Weight:** 81 kg (178 lb)	**Basal Metabolism Rate:** [(0.063 x 81) + 2.896] x 1000 =	7,999
Occupation: Sales representative **Level of Activity:** Light–moderate	7,999 x 1.7 =	13,598
Sporting activity: Hockey Training x 3/wk (270 min) Games x 1/wk (+ 120 min) Weights x 1/wk (90 min)	**Energy needs per week:** (270 + 120) x 29.3 = 11,427 90 x 28.5 = <u>+ 2,565</u> 13,992 **Energy needs per day:** 13,992 ÷ 7 =	 1,999
Special energy needs (e.g. pregnancy)	NIL	NIL
Total Energy Needs Per day	13,598 + 1,999 =	15,597*

* To convert kJ to cal ÷ 4.2

When we compared Richard J's actual energy intake from his food record with the energy intake we estimated he needed (worked out using the tables and charts), there was some discrepancy as neither method is exact. However, when we completed this step, we had a reasonable starting point.

Step 3 – Calculating Your Carbohydrate Intake

The next step is to calculate your carbohydrate intake. You should be taking in about 60% of your total energy from carbohydrate. One gram carbohydrate will give you about 16 kJ (4 cal). 150 g carbohydrate will give you about 2,400 kJ (600 cal).

Therefore, to achieve a 60% carbohydrate intake, for every 4,200 kJ (1,000 cal), you will need to eat (or drink) 150 g carbohydrate. To help you estimate your carbohydrate intake, we have included a carbohydrate count with each recipe. The following table gives you a quick kilojoule (calorie)/carbohydrate ready reckoner.

Kilojoule (Calorie)/Carbohydrate Ready Reckoner

kJ	cal	Grams carbohydrate for 60% energy	kJ	cal	Grams carbohydrate for 60% energy
6,300	1,500	225	16,800	4,000	600
8,400	2,000	300	18,900	4,500	675
10,500	2,500	375	21,000	5,000	750
12,600	3,000	450	23,100	5,500	825
14,700	3,500	525	25,200	6,000	900

*Because the figure 15,597 is only an estimate, we have chosen the closest kJ value (14,700kJ) from the Ready Reckoner (above) to make it easier to estimate carbohydrate, protein and fat requirements.

Food for Sport Cookbook

Example – Richard J

Richard J's energy requirement is about 14,700 kJ (3,500 cal) per day. Therefore, he needs 525 g carbohydrate a day.

Step 4 – Calculating Your Protein Intake

The next step is to calculate your protein intake. Recent studies suggest that the following protein intake is appropriate.

Protein Requirements of Athletes

Athlete	Grams protein per kg (2.2 lb) bodyweight
Endurance	1.2–1.6
Power strength	1.2–1.7
Extra protein needs (i.e. growth, pregnancy, lactation)	2.0

P. W. R. Lemon, 'Effects of Exercise on Protein Requirements', *Journal of Sports Science,* 1991 (9), 53.70.

Approximately 12–15% of your kilojoule (calorie) intake should come from protein. One gram protein will give you about 17 kJ (4 cal). Therefore, to achieve a 12–15% protein intake you will need to eat 30–37 g protein for every 4,200 kJ (1,000 cal).

The following table gives you a quick kilojoule (calorie) protein ready reckoner.

Kilojoule (Calorie)/Protein Ready Reckoner

kJ	cal	Grams protein for 12–15% energy	kJ	cal	Grams protein for 12–15% energy
6,300	1,500	45–56*	16,800	4,000	120–150
8,400	2,000	60–75	18,900	4,500	135–169
10,500	2,500	75–94	21,000	5,000	150–188
12,600	3,000	90–113	23,100	5,500	165–206
14,700	3,500	105–131	25,200	6,000	180–225

* Depending on bodyweight, for most athletes this protein level will be inadequate. Rather than compromise your protein intake, you should decrease your fat and increase your protein intake to no more than 20% of total energy.
To help estimate your protein intake, refer to the nutritional data we supply with each recipe.

Example – Richard J

Richard's energy requirement is about 14,700 kJ (3,500 cal) per day, so he needs 105–131 g protein per day (which is 1.2–1.6 g protein per kg [2.2 lb] of bodyweight).

Step 5 Calculating Your Fat Intake

You should derive about 25–30% of your total energy intake from fat. 1 g fat will give you about 37 kJ (9 cal), therefore, to achieve a 25–30% fat intake, you will need to eat 28–33 g fat per day for every 4,200 kJ (1,000 cal). The following table gives you a quick kilojoule (calorie)/fat ready reckoner.

Kilojoule (Calorie)/Fat Ready Reckoner

kJ	cal	Grams fat for 25–30% energy	kJ	cal	Grams fat for 25–30% energy
6,300	1,500	42–50	16,800	4,000	111–133
8,400	2,000	56–67	18,900	4,500	125–150
10,500	2,500	69–83	21,000	5,000	139–167
12,600	3,000	83–100	23,100	5,500	153–183
14,700	3,500	97–117	25,200	6,000	167–200

When you design your Eating Strategy, use the nutritional data with each of the recipes to work out how much fat your diet contains.

Example – Richard J

His energy requirement is about 14,700 kJ (3,500 cal) per day, so he needs 97–117 g fat daily.

A Note About Alcohol

Ideally, athletes should not drink alcohol at all (see pages 24–25 where we discuss this). One standard drink (e.g. a glass of wine) holds about 10 g alcohol and 335 kJ (80 cal), so you can see how quickly the kilojoules (calories) will add up.

Putting It All Together

Example – Richard J

Now we can take the information gained from the first five steps and show how these combine to form an Eating Strategy for Richard J. Our calculations show that Richard needs about 14,700 kJ (3,500 cal) per day. This energy should be made up of: carbohydrate 525 g (60% of energy), protein 105–131 g (12–15% of energy), fat 97–117 g (25–30% of energy). When we translate this into food you can see how this relationship works. Meal Plan A on page 17 is ideal for Richard J.

THE MEAL PLANS

We have formulated three suggested Meal Plans that allow you to see how the nutritional information gained by following the five Eating Strategy steps translates into actual meals.

Remember that these Meal Plans serve only to give you ideas on meal planning; you need to adapt the appropriate one to your individual lifestyle and training programme.

Although these Meal Plans do not include water, remember to drink plenty.

Meal Plan A – 144,700 kJ (3,500 cal) *(For 'Richard J')*

Protein – 20%; Fat – 20%; Carbohydrate – 60%

Suitable for male athletes involved in full training schedules, and female athletes with high energy needs or who are trying to bulk up.

Breakfast

- 60 g (2 oz) wholegrain breakfast cereal with 250 ml (8 fl oz) low-fat milk
- 1 piece of fresh fruit, or 185 g (6 oz) canned unsweetened fruit
- 2 slices wholemeal toast, or 2 slices raisin bread, or 1 muffin, spread with 2 tsp jam/honey/fruit spread
- 1 glass 100% fruit juice

Snack

- 185 g (6 oz) fresh fruit salad, or 1 piece fresh fruit
- 1 carton low-fat, fruit flavoured yoghurt

Lunch

- 2 wholemeal rolls or sandwiches, or 1 large pitta bread, filled with one of the following:

30 g (1 oz) lean chicken or meat, or 1 slice low-fat cheese, or 1 egg, or 45 g (1½ oz) tuna or salmon, or 1 tbsp hummus, or 2 slices avocado, plus mustard/chutney/pickles, plus fresh salad

- 1 low-fat energy bar, or 1 small piece low-fat fruit cake
- 1 piece fresh fruit

Pre-training Snack

- 1 crumpet, or 3 rice cakes, or 2 slices raisin bread, with 1 tbsp honey/jam/fruit spread

Post-training Snack

- 2 rice cakes or dry biscuits, or 1 slice raisin bread or fruit loaf spread with 4 tsp jam/honey/fruit spread, or 2 tsp peanut butter

Dinner

- 150 g (5 oz) lean beef/lamb/pork or chicken, or 200 g (6½ oz) fish, or 200 g (6½ oz) cooked pulses: stir-fried in non-stick pan brushed with 1 tsp olive oil and low-salt soy or teriyaki sauce
- 345 g (11 oz) cooked brown rice, or 440 g (14 oz) pasta, or 4 jacket potatoes
- 315–470 g (10–15 oz) steamed or stir-fried vegetables
- low-fat dessert (fruit or milk-based)

Snack

- Low-fat smoothie: Blend together 250 ml (8 fl oz) low-fat milk, 1 tbsp low-fat yoghurt and 1 piece fresh fruit (e.g. banana). Drink cold.

Meal Plan B – 8,400 kJ (2,000 cal)

Protein – 20%; Fat – 20%; Carbohydrate – 60%

Suitable for female athletes, or for male athletes who want to lose weight and still have enough energy for their full training schedule.

Breakfast

- 30 g (1 oz) wholegrain breakfast cereal with 185 ml (6 fl oz) low-fat milk
- 1 piece of fresh fruit, or 185 g (6 oz) canned unsweetened fruit
- 1 slice wholemeal toast, or ½ muffin spread with 2 tsp peanut butter
- 1 glass 100% fruit juice

Snack

- 1 slice fruit loaf or raisin bread, or 2 rice cakes with 1 tsp honey/jam/fruit spread

Lunch

- 2 slices wholemeal bread, or 1 roll, or 1 small pitta bread, filled with one of the following:

30 g (1 oz) lean turkey or chicken, or 45 g (1½ oz) tuna or salmon, or 1 slice low-fat cheese, or 1 tbsp hummus, or 2 slices avocado, plus mustard/chutney/pickles, plus fresh salad

- 1 low-fat energy bar, or 1 small slice low-fat fruit cake/muffin
- 1 piece fresh fruit

Pre-training Snack

- 1 carton low-fat fruit yoghurt, or 1 glass low-fat flavoured milk

Post-training Snack

- 1 rice cake or wholemeal dry biscuit topped with 1 tbsp ricotta cheese and 1 tsp jam/fruit spread, or 1 piece fresh fruit

Dinner

- 100 g (3½ oz) lean beef/lamb/pork or chicken, or 150 g (5 oz) fish, or 100 g (3½ oz) pulses (cooked without added fats/oils, e.g. grilled/baked/stir-fried)
- 185 g (6 oz) cooked brown rice, or 2 baked potatoes, or 220 g (7 oz) pasta
- 315 g (10 oz) steamed or stir-fried vegetables
- low-fat dessert (fruit or milk-based)

Snack

- 1 piece fresh fruit

Meal Plan C – 6,300 kJ (1,500 cal)

Protein – 20%; Fat – 20%; Carbohydrate – 60%
Suitable for female athletes who wish to lose weight.

Breakfast

- 30 g (1 oz) wholegrain breakfast cereal with 185 ml (6 fl oz) low-fat milk
- 1 piece of fresh fruit, or 250 ml (8 fl oz) canned unsweetened fruit
- 1 glass 100% fruit juice

Snack

- 185 g (6 oz) fresh fruit salad, or 1 piece fresh fruit

Lunch

- 1 wholemeal roll, or 1 small pitta bread, filled with one of the following:

30 g (1 oz) lean chicken or meat, or 45 g (1½ oz) tuna or salmon, or 1 slice low-fat cheese, or 1 tbsp hummus, or 2 slices avocado, plus mustard/chutney/pickles, plus fresh salad

- 1 piece fresh fruit

Pre-training Snack

- 1 carton low-fat, diet fruit yoghurt, or 2 rice cakes, or 1 slice raisin bread with 1 tsp jam/honey/fruit spread

Post-training Snack

- 1 piece fresh fruit

Dinner

- 100 g (3½ oz) lean beef/lamb/pork or chicken, or 150 g (5 oz) fish, or 100 g (3½ oz) pulses (cooked without added fats/oils, e.g. grilled/baked/stir-fried)
- 125 g (4 oz) cooked brown rice, or 2 baked potatoes, or 150 g (5 oz) pasta
- 315 g (10 oz) steamed or stir-fried vegetables
- small serving of low-fat dessert (fruit or milk-based)

Snack

- 1 piece fresh fruit, or 2 rice cakes, or 1 slice raisin bread/fruit loaf, topped with 2 tsp jam/honey/fruit spread or 1 tsp peanut butter

TIMING YOUR MEALS

When you have your meals is very important. On one hand, you don't want to exercise feeling loaded down with a meal; on the other, you need to ensure that you are eating frequently enough to maintain a good blood glucose level while you are exercising. Another issue is that if you train early in the morning, there is often not enough time to eat and leave a decent gap before you actually begin training. If you train in the early evening, again there may not be enough time to eat before you train and you may be too tired to eat a full meal after training.

This is where planning and the use of nutritious snacks and beverages is important. By making quick nutritious drinks (see the 'High Protein Drinks' chapter for wonderful recipes) and eating healthy snacks during the day, you can avoid feeling low in energy when you train.

The You Factors should also be considered. Sit down and draw up a plan for yourself showing when you train, work, or do other things on a regular basis. Consider when you are most likely to have time to prepare proper meals and to eat them in comfort. Once you have this information, work out when to eat snacks or meals so that you can train comfortably and with maximum energy.

As for when you compete, we have dealt with the whole issue of the pre-event and between-event meals elsewhere in this book. You may find it to your advantage to discuss this and all other matters relating to your dietary needs with a dietician.

THE COMPETITION DIET

Today we know that what you eat in the days leading up to, and during, a competition can affect your performance. The pre-competition and competition diets are the subject of continuing research and are an important focus among top-ranking sportspeople.

Because of their differing energy demands, the pre-competition and competition diets are best discussed by categorising sport as endurance, short duration and intermittent sports.

For all three, the groundwork should be laid by your Training Diet, where the emphasis is on high carbohydrate intake combined with effective training. During training, your regimen should allow you to recover between sessions by rebuilding your energy reserves and replacing fluid lost during exercise.

Everyone has their own energy requirements and tastes, but the following recommendations serve as a basis for all athletes.

Endurance Sport

Any continuous event lasting more than about 90 minutes is termed an endurance event. In endurance events, fat is your chief energy resource. Even the leanest athlete carries enough fat to supply them with energy for several days. The body of an endurance athlete will draw its energy from fat while conserving its precious muscle glycogen. However, the critical factor is muscle glycogen supply – once this runs low you experience fatigue. When you completely exhaust muscle glycogen supplies, you can no longer perform. Endurance athletes often describe this drastic situation as 'hitting the wall'.

It has been shown that a combination of proper training and dietary manipulation can build up your muscle glycogen to twice its normal level. The key to this dietary manipulation is Carbohydrate Loading (see below).

Short Duration Sports

Carbohydrate Loading, as such, is not suited to short-duration events and could even be to your disadvantage if you are involved in short, high-speed and explosive events. Carbohydrate Loading can lead to weight gains of as much as 1.5 kg (3 lb) and you may find this extra weight a liability, or even be disqualified for it.

If you compete in events such as weight-lifting, sprint events or boxing, it is highly unlikely that you will exhaust your body's normal glycogen store. Your training schedule should have built up your body's ability to store sufficient glycogen. But, it is still vitally important that you replenish your glycogen stores before competition. In the 24–36 hours before the event, you should taper off your normal training regimen, but maintain your normal diet with its carbohydrate emphasis.

Intermittent Sports

If you play sports such as squash, hockey, football, soccer, rugby, basketball, netball or tennis you will need short intermittent bursts of energy. How active are you? What position do you play? Are you on the go all the time, or do you play in short energetic bursts? Depending on what you find, tailor your diet according to either the endurance or short duration regimes we have described.

Carbohydrate Loading

Carbohydrate Loading is a relatively new concept. Introduced by Swedish researchers in the 1930s, it was not until the 1960s that the Swedes developed the concept into a week-long regime. Their method combined diet and training in such a way that the body built up 2–3 times its normal stores of glycogen, which gave athletes significantly greater endurance.

Athletes who repeatedly practised the early form of Carbohydrate Loading found that they suffered depression, lethargy, loss of muscle tissue, and some experienced chest pains and abnormal electrocardiographs.

The Modern Carbohydrate Loading Technique

Recently, American physiologists have modified the Carbohydrate Loading regime and have overcome some of the side-effects. Begin the regime early in the week prior to competition:

Stage 1: Gradually reduce your level of training while maintaining your normal (moderate-to-high) carbohydrate diet. This holds your glycogen level relatively steady.

Stage 2: For the three or four days prior to competition, reduce your training even further. At the same time, increase your carbohydrate intake to 70–85% of energy.

Carbohydrate Loading does not mean that you should stuff yourself with food. What it does mean is that you should be extremely conscious of what you eat and should mainly eat foods that contain carbohydrate. Carbohydrate-rich drinks give you extra carbohydrate in an easily digestible form.

As competition day draws closer, your diet should contain more refined carbohydrate (including simple sugars), and you should cut down on foods high in fibre (see also the information we give below about the pre-event meal). This will help you reduce the bulk of your diet while allowing your carbohydrate intake to rise.

Remember, it is vital that you 'fluid load' as well, and drink as much fluid (not alcoholic!) as you can in the few days leading up to competition.

By following this regime your glycogen stores should be at least doubled by the time you are ready to compete – and you should not experience the side-effects connected with earlier loading techniques.

Should I Use Carbohydrate Loading?

Carbohydrate Loading is only recommended and is only beneficial if you participate in endurance events lasting longer than about 90 minutes, or if you take part in multiple-event competitions over a sustained period.

The Pre-event Meal

We know of no magic food or meal you can eat before a competition to ensure that you win. There are, however, some important guidelines you can follow to enhance your performance and certain diet-related disadvantages and complications you can avoid.

Essentially, your pre-event meal should be fairly light and easy to digest, but should contain enough food to satisfy your hunger and prevent hunger pangs or weakness when you compete.

If you are involved in endurance sports, the pre-event meal can make a significant contribution to your energy levels. In the weeks and days prior to competition, your diet should be planned to build up muscle glycogen reserves. Your pre-event meal will add little to these reserves, but it can replenish your blood glucose level, and this is important.

Guideline 1: High in carbohydrate, low in fat

We advise you to eat a minimum amount of fat as it is difficult to digest. You certainly do not want your body diverting blood supply to your stomach when you need blood for your muscles.

Many athletes, knowing the importance of carbohydrate, mistakenly eat large quantities of sugar and sugar-rich foods before they compete. Research shows that athletes who eat large amounts of sugars immediately before competing, without adequate fluid, increase their risk of dehydration.

For your pre-event meal, therefore, you should eat a range of carbohydrates. The endurance athlete may find low glycaemic foods an advantage for sustained energy whereas those competing in short duration events may prefer to eat high glycaemic index foods (see pages 3–4).

Guideline 2: Eat at least 2–3 hours before you compete

Ideally, your stomach should be empty by the time you compete, therefore the timing of your pre-event meal is important. Correct timing:

- cuts down on the competition for blood supply between stomach and muscles
- allows the hormones involved in digestion to settle down to normal
- allows you to perform more comfortably on an empty stomach. Two to three hours is adequate for any sensation of bulkiness to subside.

Guideline 3: Your meal should contain 2,100–4,200 kJ (500–1,000 cal)

To assist you in working out the energy value of food, the recipes in this book include kilojoule (calorie) counts per serve.

Guideline 4: Keep the fibre content low to moderate

We normally recommend a diet high in dietary fibre and this certainly applies to your Training Diet. However, it is advisable to cut down on the fibre content in your pre-event meal. Fibre increases faecal bulk, which may increase your need for bowel excretion at a time when you need to focus on competing. In some people, dietary fibre may cause excessive gas production and discomfort. However, if your diet is normally high in dietary fibre, you are less likely to suffer any of these negative effects.

Guideline 5: Maintain hydration (See pages 27–8)

The Psychological Aspect

What you eat before you compete is important to you psychologically. The meal should be familiar and enjoyable; this is not the time for hidden surprises, or for experiments. Don't include anything that gives you indigestion or wind, or makes you feel bloated.

Use your Training Diet to test different foods and work out the ideal components for your pre-event meal.

What If I Feel Nervous?

If you are nervous and find it difficult to eat 2–3 hours before you compete, you may find a liquid meal more acceptable. We have included a number of recipes for liquid meals which are generally low in fat and easy to digest. Another advantage is that they supply beneficial fluids. (See 'High Protein Drinks', pages 43–49.)

Suitable Pre-event Meals

- Breakfast cereals and low-fat milks

- Fruits and fruit juices

- Bread, toast, crumpets, muffins, pancakes

- Suitable toppings – banana, honey, yeast extract spread

- Rice, pasta/noodles, potatoes – with low-fat sauces/toppings

- High Protein Drinks, pages 43–49.

Eating Between Events

Some sports require you to compete several times a day, for instance at athletic meets, or swimming heats. In such cases, your priority is to replace fluids and top up your glucose levels between events.

If you have 2–3 hours between events you can eat solid food as well as fluids. Solid foods will not only restore glucose levels, they will also prevent you being distracted by hunger pangs. If, however, there is too little time to eat and digest properly between events, your priority must be fluids; if the gap is very short, drink plain water or sports drinks. (Read the section 'Maintaining Your fluid Levels' on pages 26–8 for more information.)

Fluids containing carbohydrates, such as sports drinks, can also replenish some of your carbohydrate losses and prevent dehydration.

DIET AND RECOVERY

If you play a strenuous contact sport such as football or hockey – or train hard for endurance events such as triathlons and marathons – you have unique requirements in terms of recovery from training and matches. You are often expected to recuperate from an event or match in a short time, and may have to train at your optimum a day later. Several very important factors can help you enhance your recovery.

Rebuilding Glycogen Stores

Your glycogen stores are the main energy stores in your muscles. The amount of glycogen you have stored depends on the amount of carbohydrate in your diet. A high carbohydrate diet provides large glycogen stores.

Recent studies show that the amount and type of carbohydrate, and when you eat it after exercise, is vital for proper recovery. During a strenuous training session or event, your glycogen stores are used up. Glycogen then takes 24–48 hours to be resynthesised from the carbohydrate you eat. This means that you must keep up your carbohydrate intake *every* day.

If you play a collision sport, you may find that muscle damage after a training session or game reduces your ability to rebuild glycogen stores. It is critical for you to obtain enough carbohydrate in the first 24 hours before swelling and bruising fully develop.

Within 15–30 minutes after an event/session: you need about 1 g carbohydrate per kg bodyweight (preferably from high glycaemic index foods/fluids). This means if you weigh 55 kg (122 lb) you need about 55 g carbohydrate immediately.

Within 24 hours after an event/session: you need between 7–10 g carbohydrate per kg bodyweight. For instance, if you weigh 85 kg (190 lb), you need between 680–850 g carbohydrate. That's a lot of carbohydrate when you consider that 1 banana has 20 g carbohydrate.

Replacing Fluid Losses

As mentioned in The Golden Rules of Sport Nutrition, you should be aware of the importance of drinking enough fluid before and during training sessions and games. Your fluid intake after training and competing is also very important.

Do not rely on thirst as a reliable measure of how much fluid you need. You should have a plan to follow for adequate rehydration following exercise. For example, if you lose 2 kg (4 lb) during a training session or event, aim to replace 2 litres (3½ pints) of fluid during the 2 hours following. You can do this, for example, with 1 litre (1¾ pints) sports drink, plus 1 litre (1¾ pints) water.

What About Alcohol?

There are a number of good reasons why you shouldn't drink alcohol for several hours following strenuous exercise.

First, it is a strong diuretic and makes your body dehydrate. In addition, it is filling and high in kilojoules (calories), yet does not provide significant amounts of carbohydrate.

Drink alcohol only in moderate amounts, and then only *after* you have rehydrated properly. If you have any injuries, avoid alcohol altogether as it will slow down your recovery, particularly when there is bruising.

Repairing the Damage

As well as carbohydrate, your body requires protein to help repair damaged muscle and tissue. At this stage, research has not proven how much and when you need to have protein; however, it is a good idea to try and include protein as soon as possible after a training session or event. This may be in the form of a low-fat milk drink, or commercial liquid meal supplement and/or a cheese sandwich. Your evening meal should also include protein (e.g. meat, fish, chicken, or eggs) to accompany your rice, noodles, potatoes and bread.

Recovery Regime

Immediately following an event or strenuous training session most athletes will require between 50–100 g carbohydrate in addition to replenishing fluid losses. This may be provided by the event organiser or your club or you may need to supply your own recovery snack.

The following groups of high glycaemic index foods contain 50 g of carbohydrate and are ideal for rapid replenishment of your glycogen stores:

- 50 g jelly beans or other glucose confectionery
- 2 large ripe bananas
- 1 ripe banana and honey sandwich
- 1 bowl of low-fat creamed rice
- 1 bowl of breakfast cereal, such as cornflakes
- 4 rice cakes/crackers with honey
- 2 large potatoes
- 750 ml (1¼ pints) sports drink
- 1 can soft drink (not diet nor containing caffeine).

A high carbohydrate meal containing some protein should be eaten within 2–3 hours after the event/training session (for example Savoury Minced Beef [meat sauce] page 128, Satay Chicken and rice, page 138).

For those who can't face large quantities of food after the training session or event, the following 'Recovery Snacks' may be helpful.

Recovery Snacks

Each of the following snacks provides about 100 g carbohydrate. Most male athletes will need 7–9 of these snacks in the following 24 hours; most female athletes will require 4–6. Don't forget to drink lots of water.

- 1 carton fromage frais
  2 bananas
  1 glass orange juice
- 4 slices toast, spread thinly with peanut butter and topped with 2 sliced bananas
- 60 g (2 oz) cereal with milk
  185 g (6 oz) canned fruit
- 315 g (10 oz) Creamy Rice* topped with sultanas and chopped banana
- 3 muffins spread with jam or low-fat cheese
  2 glasses lemonade
- Eggs on toast (4 thick slices)
  1 large glass fruit juice
- 5 wheat biscuits breakfast cereal, spread with honey
  1 bowl fruit salad
- 3 bread rolls filled with tuna, lean meat and salad
  1 banana
- 4 slices fruit bread spread with jam
  1 large glass cordial
- 1 large slice fruit cake
  1 can flavoured mineral water

- 4 medium or 3 large potatoes, filled with 1 small can sweetcorn and melted low-fat cheese
- 1 large bowl of minestrone
  2 wholemeal rolls
  1 bowl fresh fruit salad
- 4 medium or 3 large jacket potatoes topped with 1 large can baked beans
- 4 pancakes topped with 2 tbsp golden syrup
- 2 muesli bars
  1 apple
  1 can soft drink
- 2 packets 2-minute noodles
  1 glass fruit juice
- 2 fruit buns
  1 bowl fruit salad
- 315 g (10 oz) jelly with 185 g (6 oz) canned fruit
  1 carton low-fat fruit yoghurt
- Smoothie, made with:
  250 ml (8 fl oz) skimmed milk, 2 bananas and
  3 scoops ice-cream

* Recipe in this book; see index.

MAINTAINING YOUR FLUID LEVELS

You can survive for weeks without food, but you would be lucky to survive more than a few days without water. Your body is 60% water; if for any reason this percentage drops significantly, you are in danger of dehydration. Your body rids itself of heat by increasing blood circulation to your skin, so that you sweat. As sweat evaporates, you cool down; this is an important survival mechanism. However, in the process of cooling down, you are also losing fluids.

The amount of fluid you lose through sweat depends on how hard you exercise, your body surface area and the temperature and humidity of the environment. It is not unusual for an exercising athlete to lose 1 litre (1¾ pints) of fluid in 1 hour, and athletes playing sport in warm conditions have been known to lose up to 4 litres (7 pints) during a single sporting event. This rate of fluid loss will have an adverse effect on performance and is extremely dangerous because it causes dehydration.

The effects of dehydration are fatigue, lower blood pressure, lowered performance, increased body temperature, reduced urine output, increased pulse rate and circulatory collapse.

The Signs of Dehydration

There are several stages in the development of dehydration, and each stage shows itself through distinct physical reactions. If you are dehydrating, your knowledge of the symptoms should give you an early alert:

Stage 1: You begin to lose concentration and performance drops.

Stage 2: Your muscles begin to cramp, particularly the large muscles of the thighs and buttocks.

Stage 3: You begin to show symptoms of heat distress and exhaustion, these include nausea, vomiting, dizziness and fainting.

By this stage, you should stop whatever exercise you are doing and, if necessary, withdraw from the event or training to tend to your fluid balance.

Up until and including Stage 3, your heat regulation mechanisms are still coping. Beyond this, you suffer heat stroke and your body is out of control. Heat stroke is a medical emergency and requires urgent hospitalisation.

How to Prevent Dehydration

1. Drink before you feel thirsty. Thirst is not an accurate indicator of your fluid needs. By the time you are thirsty, you are already partly dehydrated.

2. The correct way to replace fluid loss and maintain normal body temperature is to drink enough to replace the amount of fluid you estimate you have lost. For every 1 kg (2 lb) of weight lost during exercise, drink 1 litre (1¾ pints) of fluid.

3. Be well hydrated before you begin exercising or participate in sport. The day before you are due to compete, you should be topping up your fluids with a minimum of 250 ml (8 fl oz) of liquid with each meal, and at least 2 drinks between each meal. Obviously, none of these drinks should be alcoholic!

4. Avoid alcohol in any form the day before you exercise and on the day of the event. Alcohol increases fluid loss (it is a diuretic) and aggravates the state of dehydration.

5. Your pre-event meal, taken 2–3 hours before you compete, should include at least 2 drinks (500 ml–1 litre/16–32 fl oz of fluid). Follow up with 125 ml (4 fl oz) of fluid every 15 minutes until your event.

6. Cool fluids are more rapidly absorbed by the body than warm ones. The body tolerates small quantities of fluid better than large, but don't drink more than 1 litre (1¾ pints) per hour since this matches your stomach's emptying rate.

7. Where possible, take sips of fluid during suitable breaks in competitions. Sip and swallow the fluid, rather than merely rinsing out your mouth. Don't guzzle, or your drink will probably come straight back up again.

---

8. Water or sports drinks are ideal to replace fluid. Sports drinks with a carbohydrate concentration of between 5 and 10%, together with small amounts of salts (electrolytes), are beneficial. Avoid drinks with a high sugar/salt concentration; they can cause gastro-intestinal disturbances (e.g. stomach cramping, nausea or vomiting).

9. After competition, don't forget to replenish lost fluids. Drink water or sports drinks to quench your thirst and to replenish nutrient losses (see 'Diet and Recovery', page 24).

A Word on Sports Drinks

Different carbohydrate foods have different effects on blood glucose levels. Advances in research have shown that a sports drink with 5–10% carbohydrate concentration in the form of either glucose, glucose polymer or a mixture of the two with fructose and the addition of electrolytes, in particular sodium, is well tolerated by most athletes. It is now well proven that carbohydrate intake during exercise is beneficial in supplying fuel when muscle glycogen levels are low. The sodium added to sports drinks plays two roles – it assists in fluid absorption and replaces sodium lost in endurance exercise. One of the benefits of sports drinks often overlooked is that most athletes are prepared to drink greater quantities of a flavoured beverage than plain water: the great variety available today is testimony to this.

Internationally Available Commercial Sports Drinks

Drink	Carbohydrate (% = g/100 ml)	Electrolytes (mmol/l)	
Body Fuel 750 (USA)	7.5% – glucose polymer, fructose	Sodium Potassium	12 2
Exceed (USA)	7% – glucose polymer, fructose	Sodium Potassium	10 5
Gatorade (USA)	6% – sucrose, glucose	Sodium Potassium	23 3
Isosport (Australia)	7% – glucose polymer, sucrose, fructose	Sodium Potassium	20 5
Isostar (Europe)	7.5% – sucrose, glucose polymer	Sodium Potassium	24 4
Replace (New Zealand)	8% – glucose, fructose, glucose polymer	Sodium Potassium	10 5
Sport Plus (Australia)	7% – sucrose, glucose	Sodium Potassium	17 7.5
Staminade (Australia)	4% – glucose	Sodium Potassium	10 5
Suntory (Japan)	6.5% – sucrose, glucose	Sodium Potassium	12 5
100 Plus (Singapore)	7% – sucrose, glucose	Sodium Potassium	21 4

Source: Clinical Sports Nutrition, eds L. M. Burke and V. Deakin, McGraw-Hill, Australia 1994. Reproduced with permission.

LOSING WEIGHT, WITHOUT LOSING ENERGY

If you need to lose weight, aim to lose body fat, rather than decreasing your muscle or 'lean body mass', or dehydrating yourself. The Meal Plans on pages 16–19 provide examples of how to go about planning your weight control diet so that you do not suffer nutritional deficiencies.

If you control your food intake, you can lose weight in a sustained and controlled way. Ideally, you should aim to lose 0.5–1 kg (1–2 lb) per week and, by eating a balanced diet, you should remain in good health.

If you are muscular and worry that you weigh more than indicated on the weight/height charts prepared for the general public, be assured that muscle weighs more than fat. You may seem overweight compared with the average – but you may not need to lose any weight. If you are certain that you need to lose weight, it is best to tackle the problem in the off-season.

Guidelines to Losing Weight

- Eat less food that is high in energy and low in food value (e.g. alcohol, biscuits, cakes, chocolates, cordials, ice-cream, pastries, potato and corn crisps, snack foods, soft drinks).

- Never skip meals. You are more likely to binge if you are hungry or tired. If possible, eat small meals frequently.

- Use low-fat dairy products instead of full cream varieties.

- Trim all visible fat from meat before cooking. Remove skin from chicken. Eat more fish.

- Use alternative, low-fat sources of protein such as cottage cheese and pulses (e.g. lentils).

- Grill and steam food rather than frying it in added fat. Roasts should be placed on a rack in a baking dish, so that any melted fat drips away during cooking.

- Avoid crumbed or battered foods.

- Cut down on butter and margarine on bread and toast and avoid gravies, dressings and sauces containing fat.

- Use herbs, spices, lemon juice or tomato juice to flavour your food, instead of fat.

- Make soups, casseroles and stews a day ahead. Allow them to stand overnight, and skim off any fat from the surface. The flavour of these dishes often improves with standing.

- Keep nutritious, low-kilojoule (calorie) snacks, such as carrots, celery and nutritious dips, ready in the refrigerator for when you are hungry.

BULKING UP

There is no magic nutrient, hormone, drug or protein powder that will effectively increase your muscle mass without exercise. The only way you can increase your muscle size is by stimulating growth at a cellular level.

By combining diet and weight training, you can expect to increase your body mass by about 0.5 kg (1 lb) per week.

The best and safest way of bulking up is by following an individually tailored weight training programme, plus a diet that meets your nutrient requirements and gives you a surplus of energy to help create more muscle.

Guidelines for Bulking Up

- Eat a nutritious diet high in energy, and with enough carbohydrate and protein.
- Ensure your energy intake is spread evenly through the day and the week.
- Give priority to arranging meals effectively on weekends, and around training sessions.
- Make the most of low-fat, high-protein foods.
- Use nutritious snacks to help meet your high-energy needs.
- High Protein Drinks (see pages 43–49) and Liquid Meal Supplements are extremely useful as high energy snacks.

Amino Acids

There has been increased interest in taking amino acid supplements recently, because of the suggestion that specific amino acids in large doses can stimulate the production of growth hormone and thus promote muscle growth.

The amino acids arginine and ornithine, in particular, have been implicated in the muscle-building role. Current evidence is based primarily on testimonials from athletes. The few studies that have been carried out suggest that very large doses of these amino acids are required for growth hormone release – many times the amount found in most commercially available amino acid supplements.

Specific amino acid supplements, in large doses, are being tested on humans. To date, the long- and short-term effects of these supplements remain inconclusive.

Clearly, this is still a controversial area, and we eagerly await further scientific studies to confirm or disprove whether amino acid supplements are effective and, if so, which of the amino acids work, in what quantities, and at what risk.

SPECIAL GROUPS, SPECIAL NEEDS

In this chapter we cover the main points relevant to athletes with special needs. Athletes requiring a specially designed eating programme to meet their individual needs should consult a sports dietician. Athletes and non-athletes with diabetes should consult *Eat & Enjoy* by Christine Roberts, Jennifer McDonald and Margaret Cox (New Holland Publishers, 1995).

VEGETARIANISM

For reasons that range from matters of conscience to personal taste, many people embrace vegetarianism. Vegetarian athletes can have a nutritionally adequate diet, provided that they take great care with their meal planning to ensure a balanced intake of protein, iron, calcium, zinc, riboflavin and vitamin B12. This is easier if you eat eggs and dairy products.

Tips for Vegetarian Athletes

1. Protein

Many plant foods contain protein but do not contain all the essential amino acids. These foods are known as incomplete proteins. Protein complementation is the combining of incomplete protein-rich plant foods to provide adequate amounts of all the essential amino acids.

The combination of any of the pulses (e.g. lentils, peas, dried beans) with grain products (e.g. breads, rice, pasta, taco shells), nuts or seeds provides an alternative to animal protein.

2. Iron

An athlete is at greater risk of developing iron deficiency than a non-athlete; vegetarian athletes are at even greater risk, because they are not eating meat – a major food source of iron. On pages 32–34 you will find information on iron deficiency and ways to avoid it.

Have regular blood tests to check on your iron status. If necessary, your dietitian or doctor may recommend iron supplements.

3. Calcium

On pages 34–35 you will find information on the importance of calcium in your diet. If you are a vegetarian who eats dairy products, calcium deficiency is unlikely to be a problem. In the case of vegans, it is cause for concern.

Vegans can obtain calcium from foods such as nuts, dried fruit, sesame seeds and fortified soy milk. However, calcium from these sources is not readily absorbed by the body and it may be necessary for you to increase your calcium intake through supplements. However, only use supplements under direction from your doctor or dietician.

4. Zinc

Zinc assists in the metabolism of protein and carbohydrate. It is also important in the healing process.

The richest source of zinc is oysters, followed by red meat. Zinc is also found in pulses, wholegrain cereals and certain vegetables, but it is poorly absorbed, especially when fibre intake is high.

The first signs of zinc deficiency are generalised fatigue, loss of hair and poor healing. Vegetarian athletes should have a blood test to determine zinc status.

5. Vitamin B12

This vitamin is important for normal blood cell formation, nervous system functioning, and the formation of genetic material.

It is found exclusively in animal foods, therefore, it is better to include eggs and dairy products in your diet to meet your vitamin B12 requirements. Soy milk which has been fortified with vitamin B12 is an alternative to cow's milk.

Vegetarian athletes should have regular blood tests to check their vitamin B12 status.

6. Riboflavin (Vitamin B2)

This is essential for energy production, growth and development.

The richest sources of riboflavin are milk and milk products, yeast extracts, liver, eggs, cereals and green leafy vegetables. Vegans will need to eat plenty of green leafy vegetables to ensure adequate riboflavin intake.

IRON DEFICIENCY

A low level of stored iron in your body is now seen as having an adverse effect on your performance. When the amount of iron your body uses and loses is greater than the amount your diet offers, your iron stores become depleted. Unless set right, the level of iron circulating in your blood may also drop, in which case you may develop anaemia.

When you become anaemic, the level of haemoglobin in your blood drops. And since this is the part of the red blood cells that carries oxygen to your body, your energy levels fall too – and your performance is impaired.

Am I At Risk of Becoming Iron Deficient?

If you belong to any of the following groups, you may be at risk:

- women of childbearing age
- vegetarians
- people on low-energy diets
- endurance athletes, particularly females
- people who sweat heavily.

How Do You Become Iron Deficient?

Everyone loses iron naturally through the bowel, bladder and skin. Women also lose iron through menstruation. If you undergo surgery or suffer injury, you also lose blood and, therefore, iron. If you are a blood donor, every time you give blood you lose a considerable amount of iron. The way in which you can counter the loss is simply through your diet.

Athletes are particularly at risk of iron deficiency because they lose iron through sweat and through the trauma which occurs when the body is jarred in exercise. This iron is lost through the urine, bowel and feet. It is also known that endurance athletes are especially prone to losses through exercise, and their ability to absorb iron may be impaired.

How Do I Know If I Have Iron Deficiency?

If you suffer any of the following symptoms, it is worth having a check-up:

- impaired performance
- tiredness
- headaches
- cramps
- shortness of breath.

Only a blood test will tell if you have iron deficiency (anaemia). It is not enough to measure your haemoglobin levels, you also need to know your serum ferritin (iron store) levels.

How Can I Protect Myself from Becoming Anaemic?

The most important means of preventing anaemia is through diet. Maximise iron absorption by eating the correct combinations of iron-rich foods. These combinations are explained in The Golden Rules for Adequate Iron Intake (following).

Two Types of Iron

Your food provides iron in two forms – haem and non-haem iron.

Haem Iron

This is readily absorbed by your body, and is found primarily in animal products, especially liver, kidneys, red meat, and in the dark flesh of chicken and fish.

Non-haem Iron

This is less readily absorbed by your body than haem iron, and is found primarily in vegetables and plant foods. Especially good sources are dark green vegetables (e.g. broccoli, spinach and Swiss chard), as well as pulses and wholegrain cereals.

The Golden Rules for Adequate Iron Intake

- Eat lean red meat three times a week. This will ensure your haem iron supply.
- Eat liver and kidney. (For delicious recipes, look under 'liver' in the index.)
- Eat poultry and fish; the dark flesh is a good source of haem iron.

- Eat vegetables that contain non-haem iron with your meat meal.

- Eat pulses (dried beans, lentils, peas and wholegrain cereals) if you are not eating meat.

- Vitamin C enhances iron absorption; include foods rich in it in each meal (e.g. citrus/tropical fruit, tomatoes).

- Don't drink tea with your meals – the tannic acid inhibits iron absorption.

- Don't take iron supplements unless instructed by a medical practitioner or your dietician.

CALCIUM AND BONE STRENGTH

Of the body's calcium, 99% is stored in your skeleton where it is critical in bone formation. The remaining 1% is found in various body membranes, soft tissues and body fluids.

Besides its role in bone-formation, calcium is also involved in blood clotting, nerve transmission, muscle contraction and enzyme activity.

Osteoporosis is the term generally used to describe drastic loss of calcium from bones which is often seen in post-menopausal women. The condition leads to lower bone density and to brittle bones. The term osteopenia better describes the condition found in some athletes. With this, there is a reduced bone mass which may be a result of inadequate bone formation during growth or loss of bone mass due to low oestrogen levels.

Who Is At Risk?

Some women, particularly endurance athletes, ballet dancers or gymnasts, may experience delayed menarche or other menstrual irregularities (called sports amenorrhoea). These athletes usually have a low percentage of body fat, exercise rigorously and have low oestrogen levels. Having low oestrogen levels will accelerate bone loss and, as a result, lead to a decrease in bone density.

Other risk categories include athletes with eating disorders, veteran athletes and post-menopausal women.

How Do I Know If I Have Osteopenia?

Other than being susceptible to bone fractures, the only way to find out whether or not you have osteopenia is by having a bone ultrasound.

How Can I Protect Myself?

Today we know that the combination of weight-bearing exercises (such as walking or jogging) and sufficient calcium in your diet, as well as adequate oestrogen levels help to protect you from osteopenia.

If you belong to any of the above groups, you will need 1,000–1,500 mg of calcium daily. This means drinking plenty of low-fat milk, and eating plenty of low-fat cheese, yoghurt and other dairy products.

Best Sources of Calcium

The richest, and most easily absorbed sources of dietary calcium are dairy products. Canned fish with bones, fortified soy beverages, nuts, seeds, and leafy green vegetables are also good calcium sources. For the greatest overall benefit, keep these two points in mind:

- Diets too high in salt, protein, caffeine, phosphorus or fibre will inhibit your body's ability to absorb calcium from your food.

- Full-cream dairy products are also high in fats. Make sure you use skimmed, low-fat or reduced-fat dairy products.

If you eat a well-balanced diet, you should receive enough calcium.

SPORT AND DIABETES

The key issue for athletes with diabetes today is not whether they can continue (or take up) sport, but whether they have the necessary talent! An athlete with diabetes can certainly remain an athlete.

The cornerstones of good management of diabetes are diet, exercise and correct medication (if this is necessary). Dietary principles for people with diabetes match the recommended diet for athletes (i.e. high in carbohydrate and fibre, and low in fats).

Important note: If you have diabetes and you want to play sport, you must have a specially tailored programme designed for you by a sports dietician.

Because most athletes with diabetes fall into the 'insulin dependent' category, we have largely directed our comments to them.

Your main aim is to keep a stable blood glucose level that prevents your blood glucose from dropping too low (hypoglycaemia) or becoming too high (hyperglycaemia). To achieve this, you need to balance the energy you expend, the energy you take in (eat) and your insulin dosage.

If you have only just been diagnosed as having diabetes, you should stop training until you have the diabetes under control. Until you have achieved proper control, exercise may worsen the swings in your blood glucose levels. Even if your diabetes is well controlled, exercise will affect your blood glucose levels, depending on the type and timing of your insulin injections and food intake in relation to the times when you are exercising.

In order for you to maximise your performance, you must monitor your blood glucose levels before, during and after exercise, and then adjust accordingly your food intake, insulin dosage, and when you eat and have your injections.

Points to Consider

- If possible, train when your blood glucose is above fasting level, but not high. Usually 1–2 hours after a meal is best.

- For short duration activities, you might need extra carbohydrate before and/or after.

- For long duration activities, you might need extra carbohydrate during the event as well as before and after.

- If your exercise is broken up, you should take some form of carbohydrate during the breaks to control your blood glucose levels. These foods will also satisfy your hunger. For instance, eat fruit which gives sugar, fibre and fluid – as well as being filling.

After exercise, your body continues to need extra carbohydrate to replenish your glycogen stores. Just as important, however, is the need to replace your fluid losses.

Exercise may speed up absorption of insulin from exercising limbs. You can counter this to some extent by injecting into parts of your body away from the exercising muscle – for instance, into the abdomen.

Carbohydrate Loading is not recommended if you have diabetes; it leads to excessive fluctuations in blood glucose levels.

In terms of adjusting your food intake, there is no simple answer to this question because individuals vary. Only by monitoring blood glucose levels before, during and after training will you be able to determine your needs.

TIPS AND TRAPS FOR TRAVELLING

Individuals and Groups Competing Away from Home

When you compete you may well find yourself having to travel and eat away from home in an unfamiliar environment. This calls for careful advance planning. The following tips (and traps) will help you avoid many of the common problems that occur.

Tips

- If you are travelling with a group, ask your group co-ordinator to telephone ahead to motels and arrange for suitable snacks to be provided in your rooms (e.g. fresh fruit and juice, mineral water, energy bars and low-fat yoghurt).

- The group co-ordinator should contact motels, hotels and restaurants in advance and organise a special group menu for your meals. For instance, pasta with low-fat sauces, or rice and vegetable dishes and, most importantly, the pre-event foods with which you are most familiar.

- Individuals in your group should each bring particular snack foods (see the chapter 'Nutritious Snacks'), to keep their carbohydrate levels up while travelling.

- Contact your airline several days in advance and request low-fat, high-carbohydrate meals during your flight. Most airline companies now cater for special dietary requirements.

- If you take along healthy snacks to eat on the aeroplane, check custom regulations first, as some foodstuffs may not be taken across national boundaries.

- Ensure you drink plenty of fluids. Don't drink tea, coffee, cola drinks and alcohol on the flight. Drink one glass of water every hour to minimise the effect of jet-lag and dehydration.

Traps

- Beware of the 'holidaying athlete syndrome'. When staying at athletes' villages, the large self-serve cafeteria can be seductive. Faced with such variety and abundance, there is a real risk of athletes overeating, especially just before competition when training will have tapered off. The result can be unwanted weight gain – with disastrous consequences.

- In less developed countries, or areas where the water supplies may not agree with you, always boil or sterilise your drinking water, or use bottled water and beverages.

- If you are concerned that you may not like the food in the country you are visiting, take some canned foods and supplements such as liquid meals (Complan) with you.

Diarrhoea

To limit your chances of contracting traveller's diarrhoea, avoid: tap water and ice cubes; eating unpeeled fruit and uncooked vegetables (such as salads); undercooked meat; unpasteurised milk products; and highly spiced foods if you aren't used to them.

If you do develop diarrhoea, it is vital that you rehydrate yourself immediately by drinking bottled, treated beverages or electrolyte replacement liquids. Avoid milk until your symptoms settle. Drink weak tea, apple juice or clear soups. Once your stomach settles, begin eating light solids (e.g. dry biscuits, boiled white rice or pasta).

QUICK AND EASY MEAL IDEAS

- **Plan meals ahead** – try a week at a time.

- **Make sure your pantry is well stocked.** Shop for a week using this menu as a guide. Basic ingredients include rice, pasta, bottled tomato purée or pasta sauce, canned fish, canned pulses (e.g. red kidney beans, lima beans, mixed beans, chick peas, baked beans), canned or frozen vegetables, canned fruit, herbs, spices, soy and tomato sauces.

- **Prepare meals ahead** and in bulk when time permits – cook more than one serving, divide into portions and refrigerate or freeze for another day. Casseroles, soups and low-fat sauces can be frozen easily and will reheat quickly in a microwave.

- **Take short cuts** wherever possible (e.g. use canned tomatoes instead of fresh, dried herbs instead of fresh, frozen vegetables and commercial sauces, such as pasta sauce, in bottles or cans).

- **Forget the fat** – use quick and healthy low-fat cooking methods such as grilling, microwaving and stir-frying with a stock cube and water.

- **Increase your carbohydrate** – rice, pasta, potatoes and pulses can be pre-cooked or used from a can and heated or mixed into casseroles or other dishes.

- **Cook your meal while you train** – consider placing a casserole or other slow-cooking meal and vegetables into a low temperature oven while you are out training.

- **Choose the best time of day to eat** – if your work and training schedule allows you more time during the day, have your main meal at midday and a lighter evening meal when you have less time.

LIGHT MEAL SUGGESTIONS

- Sandwiches, rolls, bagels, pittas, biscuits (e.g. rice cakes, wholemeal or rye crackers), *no* butter/margarine, *with* lean red or white meat, salmon, tuna, egg, low-fat cheese, beans, lentil burgers, peanut butter and salad vegetables

- Pasta, rice or potato salad with extra salad

- Baked beans or egg or sweetcorn and tomatoes/asparagus/mushrooms on toast

- Thick soup and bread

- Toasted sandwiches and salad

- Omelette, scrambled or poached eggs on toast

- Jacket potatoes with low-fat cheese and chives/salmon and onion/baked beans/ sweetcorn/onion, parsley and a sprinkling of pepper and parmesan cheese

- Pancakes with sweet or savoury fillings

- Two-minute noodles

- Filo pastry rolls, made with low-fat milk and filled with grated vegetables and lean meat or spinach and ricotta or fruit
- Butternut pumpkin baked in the oven with a tablespoon of honey and a tablespoon of sesame seeds
- A can of kidney beans mixed with sliced spring onions, chopped red pepper and mung beans served with yoghurt spiced with garlic
- Microwaved cobs of corn, sprinkled with lemon juice and black pepper
- Toasted muffins topped with baked beans
- Pre-chopped frozen vegetables mixed with cooked rice, topped with low-fat cheese and baked in the oven.

MAIN MEAL SUGGESTIONS

- Home prepared cooked meal *with*:
  - lean red or white meat, fish, pulses (dried beans, peas, lentils), eggs or cheese
  - large serving of potato, rice or pasta
  - vegetables (cooked and raw) combined to give variety as grills, roasts, burgers, casseroles, curries, stir-fries, pasta dishes (spaghetti, tortellini, lasagne, ravioli, fettuccine, noodles etc.), rice dishes, risotto. Add bread/roll (*no* butter/margarine)
- Dessert: fruit (e.g. fruit salad, baked apple, jellied peaches), low-fat milk dessert (e.g. custard, yoghurt, ice-cream, creamy rice).

MEALS 'ON-THE-RUN'

- Try commercially prepared 'healthy' frozen meals with extra high carbohydrate foods and cooked frozen vegetables.
- Reheat pre-prepared frozen meals (e.g. pasta dishes, casseroles made with meat/chicken/pulses) and lots of vegetables, potatoes, rice or noodles.
- Try canned fruits, commercially prepared creamy rice, custards, low-fat yoghurt.
- A liquid meal – blend any combination of: milk/low-fat milk, yoghurt/low-fat yoghurt, fruit, fruit juice, eggs, ice-cream/low-fat ice-cream, wheatgerm, bran, skimmed milk powder, flavourings, sugar/sweetener.

MEAL CHOICES WHEN OUT

- As for home prepared meals when available
- Pasta with low-fat sauce and salad
- Hamburgers – low-fat

- Chicken (no skin), grilled fish or seafood, lean meat, jacket potatoes and salad/vegetables
- Soup and roll
- Jacket potato, low-fat or grated cheese and salad
- Souvlaki.

SNACK SUGGESTIONS

- Dry biscuits and cheese
- Dried fruits and nuts
- Carrot/fruit/banana/wholemeal cake
- Oatmeal/wholemeal/shredded wheat sweet biscuits
- Muffins/crumpets/rice cakes/toast/roll and toppings
- Milk and fruit drinks
- Yoghurt/fromage frais/creamy rice or macaroni/custard
- Fruit bread/buns.

USE THE FOLLOWING RECIPE IDEAS TO HELP YOU GET STARTED:

Country style or 'bottom of the fridge' soup

Bring 500 ml (16 fl oz) of beef, chicken or vegetable stock to the boil. Stock cubes or commercially prepared broth may be used. Add 315 g (10 oz) of roughly chopped vegetables (any will do, e.g. celery, broccoli, cauliflower, courgette, leek, mushrooms, pumpkin, carrot, green beans), 2 tsp tomato paste and 100 g (3½ oz) cooked or canned beans and simmer for about 30 minutes, or until soft. Season with salt and ground black pepper to taste. Serve in a large bowl with wholegrain toasted bread.

Fish/chicken/veal/lamb ratatouille

Place fish or chicken fillet or veal/lamb cutlet into a casserole dish, add a little water to prevent sticking and top with a can of ratatouille (or roughly cut onion, tomato, green pepper, mushrooms, courgette, aubergine, black pepper and herbs). Cover and bake. Place jacket potatoes into the oven and cook at the same time, or serve with cooked rice.

Stir-fry vegetables with egg, chicken or pork

Heat 1 tbsp of soy sauce and 3 tbsp chicken stock in a wok or pan. Add 315–470 g (10–15 oz) of frozen stir-fry vegetables or freshly chopped vegetables (any combination of: onion, bell pepper, celery, green beans, mushrooms, Chinese or plain cabbage, cauliflower/broccoli florets and courgette). Stir through and cover. Cook until they can be pierced with a fork but are still crisp, stirring occasionally. In a separate pan make an egg omelette, slice and add to vegetables or alternatively add diced cooked chicken or lean cooked pork.

Foiled fish

Take a piece of foil, spray with cooking oil or lightly brush with oil. Place a fillet of white, fleshy fish on foil and top with sliced tomato, onion and mushroom. Sprinkle with ground black pepper and lemon juice and wrap around with the foil. Bake in the oven for 15–20 minutes.

Kebabs

Thread wooden or metal skewers alternatively with bite-sized dices of lean pork or lamb fillets, mushrooms, pepper, tomato and onion. Marinade for 3 hours in a mixture of 1 tsp grated fresh or dried ground ginger, 1 tbsp each of soy sauce and Worcestershire sauce and 2 tbsp lemon juice. Drain and grill slowly until meat is tender (about 12 minutes). Serve on a bed of rice.

Chicken and pineapple casserole

Spray pan lightly with cooking oil or brush lightly with oil. Add 180 g (6 oz) diced chicken and brown in the pan. Add 65 g (2½ oz) canned crushed pineapple, 2 tsp Worcestershire sauce, 1 tbsp lemon juice, 1 tsp soy sauce and pepper to taste. Cover and cook for about 1 hour (or until tender) in a moderate oven. Serve with rice or noodles.

Pitta pizza

Spread pitta bread with tomato paste or purée and top with sliced tomato, onion, pepper, mushrooms, pineapple and grated low-fat cheese. Sprinkle lightly with dried oregano or mixed herbs and black pepper and bake in a moderate oven.

Mexican at home

Brown minced meat in a non-stick pan with chopped onion and garlic. Drain off fat and add canned Mexican chilli beans, tomato purée and canned corn kernels. Simmer for 15–20 minutes. Heat taco shells in microwave or oven for 1–2 minutes. Fill with hot meat mixture and serve with shredded lettuce, diced onion and tomato, grated low-fat cheese and low-fat natural yoghurt.

Jacket potatoes

Scrub potatoes (do not peel) and bake in oven until soft through.

- Serve with cottage cheese or low fat, plain yoghurt and chives.
- Mix centre with chopped tomato, onion and cheese, refill skins and reheat.
- Mix centre with salmon, chopped spring onion and low-fat milk, refill skins and reheat.
- Split open and top with baked beans to which has been added a little minced chilli.

Serve with salad or coleslaw.

Risotto

Sauté 1 sliced onion, 3 sliced leeks and 1 crushed garlic clove in a little olive oil until the onion becomes transparent. Add 440 g (14 oz) uncooked rice and a variety of vegetables. Add 1.5 litres (2½ pints) of chicken stock and stir well. Bring to the boil and allow to cook slowly, stirring occasionally (for about 15–20 minutes if using white rice). Season with black ground pepper and a little grated parmesan cheese if desired.

Savoury rice

Mix cooked rice with canned salmon and frozen cooked corn and peas or canned asparagus.

Toasted open sandwiches

Top bread with:

- pineapple or asparagus and with low-fat cheese (and ham if desired)
- tomato, onion and low-fat cheese.

Grill. Serve with side salad.

Easy pasta sauce

Place 100 g (3½ oz) each of tomato purée, canned ratatouille (or sautéed/cooked combination of pepper, tomato, onion and mushrooms) and canned red kidney beans (or 90 g/3¼ oz lean, sautéed/cooked minced meat) in a saucepan. Heat thoroughly and serve on a bed of pasta. *Note:* To sauté vegetables and meat toss gently in a little water, chicken or beef stock until cooked.

Rice salad

Toss pre-cooked rice with corn kernels, some champignons, sliced spring onions, red pepper, toasted pinenuts and some no-oil dressing.

Deluxe salad

Mix together a handful of spinach leaves, 8 cherry tomatoes, 1 chopped spring onion, 8 lightly cooked asparagus spears, 4 quartered hard boiled eggs, ½ avocado and 1 x 200 g (7 oz) can drained tuna. Sprinkle lightly with freshly ground black pepper and a no-oil dressing or balsamic vinegar. Toss.

HIGH PROTEIN DRINKS

FORTIFIED MILK

Fortified Milk is a home-made mixture of low-fat or skimmed milk combined with skimmed milk powder or canned evaporated skimmed milk. It contains twice as much protein and calcium, is no higher in fat than other milk and is recommended for athletes with high energy needs.

Fortified Milk has high energy value and may be used wherever you would usually take milk in your diet. It can also be used as the base for a variety of energy drinks. However, for those athletes trying to control body fat, we recommend that you use low-fat or skimmed milk, instead of Fortified Milk.

Fortified Milk using Skimmed Milk Powder

Makes: approximately 1.15 litres (2 pints)

1 litre (1¾ pints) low-fat (fat-reduced or skimmed) milk

1 cup skimmed milk powder

This is best prepared the day before use.

Method:

1. Combine ingredients in a bowl. Use a whisk or fork to blend until smooth. Pour mixture into a jug.
2. Cover and keep in refrigerator until required.

Nutritional data per serving: 900 kJ (215 cal), Carbohydrate 26 g, Fat 4 g, Protein 18 g.

Preparation time: 5 minutes – chill overnight before using.

Fortified Milk using Evaporated Skimmed Milk

Makes: approximately 1.4 litres (2½ pints)

500 ml (16 fl oz) low-fat (fat-reduced or skimmed) milk

4 cups canned, evaporated skimmed milk

Method:

1. Combine ingredients. Pour into a jug.
2. Cover and keep in refrigerator until required.

To store: Both can be kept, covered in the refrigerator, for up to 2 days.

Nutritional data per serving: 1,279 kJ (300 cal), Carbohydrate 37 g, Fat 6 g, Protein 25 g.

Preparation time: 5 minutes.

Banana Booster

Serves: 2

250 ml (8 fl oz) skimmed
   milk or 2% fat milk or
   Fortified Milk (page 43)
1 ripe banana
pinch of ground cinnamon
1 tbsp honey
pinch of allspice
125 ml (4 fl oz) low-fat
   yoghurt

Method:

1. Place all ingredients in a blender, and process until smooth.
2. Drink as is, or chill before serving, with a sprinkling of extra cinnamon on top.

Nutritional data per serving (using 2% fat milk): 1,618 kJ (387 cal), Carbohydrate 65 g, Fat 7 g, Protein 20 g.
Preparation time: 5 minutes.

QUICK TIP: If your fruit is getting overripe, blend with low-fat milk and yoghurt to make a quick snack. Add 1 tbsp of rice bran for a nutritious breakfast on the run.

Egg Flip

Serves: 1

1 egg
2 tbsp skimmed milk
185 ml (6 fl oz) skimmed
   milk or 2% fat milk or
   Fortified Milk (page 43)
vanilla essence
caster sugar and ground
   cinnamon or nutmeg, to
   taste

A great breakfast-time energy food.

Method:

1. Separate the egg yolk and white.
2. Whisk the egg white until soft peaks form.
3. In a bowl, beat the egg yolk, skimmed and fortified milks.
4. Add vanilla essence and sugar to taste. Beat well.
5. Carefully fold in the beaten egg white.
6. Serve the Egg Flip in a bowl or glass, topped with a sprinkling of cinnamon or nutmeg.

Easy Egg Flip

Blend all ingredients at once, except cinnamon or nutmeg. Serve as above.

Nutritional data per serving (using 2% fat milk): 1,095 kJ (261 cal), Carbohydrate 23 g, Fat 10 g, Protein 22 g.
Preparation time: 10 minutes.

Citrus Whisk

Serves: 1

---

250 ml (8 fl oz) orange juice

3 tsp lemon juice

1 tbsp caster sugar

1 egg

Method:

1. Whisk or blend all the ingredients together.
2. Drink as is, or chill before serving.

Nutritional data per serving: 927 kJ (222 cal), Carbohydrate 35 g, Fat 6 g, Protein 8 g.

Preparation time: 5 minutes.

Iced Coffee

Serves: 1

---

1 tsp instant coffee

1 tsp caster sugar

60 ml (2 fl oz) hot water

185 ml (6 fl oz) skimmed
  milk or 2% fat milk or
  Fortified Milk (page 43)

1 tbsp ice-cream (optional)

Method:

1. Dissolve instant coffee and sugar in 2 tbsp hot water.
2. Add cold milk and stir to blend.
3. If desired, top with the scoop of ice-cream.

Nutritional data per serving (using 2% fat milk): 746 kJ (178 cal), Carbohydrate 23 g, Fat 6 g, Protein 10 g.

Preparation time: 5 minutes.

Pineapple Flip

Serves: 2

---

250 ml (8 fl oz) skimmed
  milk or 2% fat milk or
  Fortified Milk (page 43)

1 egg

90 g (3 oz) unsweetened,
  crushed pineapple

crushed ice

Method:

1. Place all ingredients in a food processor blender.
2. Process until smooth. Serve at once.

Nutritional data per serving (using 2% fat milk): 1,141 kJ (273 cal), Carbohydrate 28 g, Fat 11 g, Protein 17 g.

Preparation time: 5 minutes.

Banana Milk Shake

Serves: 1

250 ml (8 fl oz) skimmed
  milk or 2% fat milk or
  Fortified Milk (page 43)
1 ripe banana
30 ml (2 tbsp) ice-cream

Method:
1. Place all ingredients in a blender.
2. Process until smooth. Serve at once.

Nutritional data per serving (using 2% fat milk): 1,166 kJ (279 cal), Carbohydrate 42 g, Fat 7 g, Protein 13 g.
Preparation time: 5 minutes.

Chocolate Delight

Serves: 2

250 ml (8 fl oz) skimmed
  milk or 2% fat milk or
  Fortified Milk (page 43)
2 tsp cocoa
½ banana
2 tsp honey
30 ml (2 tbsp) ice-cream

Method:
1. Place all the ingredients in a food processor or blender.
2. Process until smooth. Serve at once.

Nutritional data per serving (using 2% fat milk): 837 kJ (200 cal), Carbohydrate 3 g, Fat 6 g, Protein 8 g.
Preparation time: 5 minutes.

Lemon Honey Milk

Serves: 1

250 ml (8 fl oz) skimmed
  milk or 2% fat milk or
  Fortified Milk (page 43)
1 tbsp clear honey
1 tbsp lemon juice

Method:
1. Place ingredients in food processor. Process for 10 seconds.
2. Pour into a small saucepan and heat gently – do not boil. Serve at once.

To vary: Add a handful of crushed ice at Step 1. Blend until smooth and serve at once.

Nutritional data per serving (using 2% fat milk): 944 kJ (225 cal), Carbohydrate 36 g, Fat 5 g, Protein 11 g.
Preparation time: 3 minutes.

Pine Cooler

Serves: 1

*250 ml (8 fl oz) unsweetened
pineapple juice*
*60 g (2 oz) celery, including
the leaves, chopped*
1 egg
crushed ice

Method:
1. Place all ingredients in a blender or food processor. Process until smooth.
2. Serve at once.

Nutritional data per serving: 811 kJ (194 cal), Carbohydrate 28 g, Fat 6 g, Protein 8 g.
Preparation time: 5 minutes.

Apple Awakener

Serves: 2

*125 ml (4 fl oz)
unsweetened apple juice*
*125 ml (4 fl oz) skimmed
milk or 2% fat milk or
Fortified Milk (page 43)*
*1 medium apple, peeled
and chopped*
*60 ml (2 fl oz) low-fat,
natural yoghurt*
crushed ice
*pinch of nutmeg or ground
cinnamon*

Method:
1. Place all ingredients, except the nutmeg or cinnamon, in a food processor or blender. Blend until smooth.
2. Pour into glasses. Sprinkle with nutmeg or cinnamon and serve at once.

Nutritional data per serving (using 2% fat milk): 835 kJ (199 cal), Carbohydrate 34 g, Fat 3 g, Protein 9 g.
Preparation time: 5 minutes.

QUICK TIP: If your work and training schedule allow more time during the day than in the evening, change your meal structure to have your main meal at midday, with a light snack in the evening.

Peach–apricot Supreme

Serves: 3

440 g (14 oz) unsweetened,
   canned peaches
250 ml (8 fl oz) low-fat
   apricot yoghurt
125 ml (4 fl oz) skimmed
   milk or 2% fat milk or
   Fortified Milk (page 43)
1 tbsp crystallised ginger,
   roughly chopped
1 tbsp wheatgerm
   (optional)

Method:

1. Place peaches and yoghurt in a food processor or blender. Blend until smooth.
2. Add milk and all remaining ingredients. Process until smooth.
3. Chill before serving.

Nutritional data per serving (using 2% fat milk): 1,126 kJ (269 cal), Carbohydrate 49 g, Fat 3 g, Protein 12 g.

Preparation time: 5 minutes.

Melon Cream

Serves: 2

½ small cantaloupe melon,
   skinned and de-seeded
125 g (4 oz) ice-cream
125 ml (4 fl oz) low-fat,
   natural yoghurt
pinch of ground cinnamon

Method:

1. Place all ingredients in a food processor or blender.
2. Process until light and fluffy.
3. Serve at once.

Nutritional data per serving: 659 kJ (79 cal), Carbohydrate 23 g, Fat 5 g, Protein 7 g.

Preparation time: 5 minutes.

QUICK TIP: Use low-fat milks in making sauces, soups and custards. Substitute evaporated skimmed milk or low-fat yoghurt for cream in recipes. Add yoghurt to hot dishes just before serving to avoid curdling.

Orange-apple Cup

Serves: 2

1 orange, peeled
1 apple, peeled
125 g (4 oz) ice-cream
125 ml (4 fl oz) low-fat,
    natural yoghurt
125 ml (4 fl oz) skimmed
    milk or 2% fat milk or
    Fortified Milk (page 43)
125 ml (4 fl oz) apple juice
pinch of nutmeg or ground
    cinnamon

Method:

1. Purée the fruit in a blender or food processor.
2. Add ice-cream and yoghurt and blend.
3. Add milk and apple juice, combine well.
4. Pour into glasses and sprinkle with nutmeg or cinnamon.
5. Serve at once.

Nutritional data per serving (using 2% fat milk): 1,061 kJ (254 cal), Carbohydrate 41 g, Fat 6 g, Protein 8 g.

Preparation time: 10 minutes.

Fast Fruity Fluff

Serves: 4

1 small banana
2 apricots, peeled
6 strawberries, hulled
½ small cantaloupe melon,
    seeded and skinned
1 passion fruit
250 ml (8 fl oz) skimmed
    milk or 2% fat milk or
    Fortified Milk (page 43)
1 tbsp honey
125 ml (4 fl oz) orange
    juice, fresh or
    unsweetened
250 ml (8 fl oz) low-fat,
    natural yoghurt
ground allspice

Method:

1. Place all fruit in a food processor or blender and process until smooth.
2. Add milk, honey, orange juice and yoghurt. Blend well.
3. Chill in the refrigerator.
4. Pour into glasses and serve topped with a sprinkling of ground allspice.

Nutritional data per serving (using 2% fat milk): 1,171 kJ (280 cal), Carbohydrate 47 g, Fat 4 g, Protein 15 g.

Preparation time: 10 minutes.

BREAKFAST, EGGS &
EGG-BASED DISHES

THE MEAL YOU CAN'T BEAT

What you eat for breakfast and how much are determined by your training schedule. However, don't underestimate the importance of this early meal.

A properly balanced breakfast restores blood glucose levels after the night's fast. This gives you energy and heightens your concentration during the first few hours of your day.

Foods for your morning meal are virtually limitless. Use your imagination to break free from the standard ideas about breakfast menus.

As a general rule, breakfast should include foods high in carbohydrates and fibre, as well as some foods high in protein.

Cereals & Breads

When choosing cereals and breads, look for wholegrain, wholemeal or multigrain products. Wholegrain products contain the extra fibre and nutrients that are lacking in processed and refined cereals.

Cereals can include untoasted muesli, wheat flakes, wheat biscuits, bran cereals, porridge or many of the mixed commercial products that are available.

Making Your Own Muesli

- Muesli is rich in fibre and nutrients. It also makes a fresh-tasting, palate-cleansing start to the day.

- Making your own muesli can be more economical than buying ready-made products – and you can choose the flavours and textures you like best. Serve with yoghurt, stewed or fresh fruits or plain milk.

Light Protein Foods

If you find it difficult to organise a proper eating plan during the day, you should try to include some light protein foods at breakfast time. The most common breakfast protein foods are eggs, low-fat cheese or dairy products. However, there is no reason why you should not include lean meat, chicken, fish or baked beans.

Fruits

Not only do fruits add variety, flavour and colour to breakfast, their vitamin, mineral, sugar and fibre content improve the nutritional value of your morning meal.

You can eat fruits fresh, stewed or canned. Try different combinations on a platter or as a fruit salad. A mixture of dried fruits, as in Dried Fruit Compote (page 184), is ideal for breakfast or dessert.

Fruit Suggestions for Breakfast

- Sliced melon and berry fruits
- Cantaloupe melon and kiwi fruit
- Cantaloupe melon with lemon juice or passion fruit pulp
- Pawpaw (papaya) and mango slices
- Orange and grapefruit segments
- When cooking porridge, add sultanas or, when almost cooked, grated apple
- Unsweetened canned or fresh peaches with mango slices
- Unsweetened canned or fresh apricots and orange segments
- Stewed Fruit (page 187) e.g. apples, or apple and rhubarb, cooked with cloves, cinnamon or sultanas
- Dried Fruit Compote (page 184)
- Try cottage or ricotta cheese or low-fat natural yoghurt as toppings.

Vegetables

Favourites like grilled tomato, asparagus, sweetcorn or mushrooms on toast add variety and nutrients to this important meal.

No-time-to-cook Breakfasts

There are some excellent ideas for quick, delicious and nutritious breakfasts – they also make good snacks.

Liquid Breakfasts

- If you have early training sessions or are short of time in the morning, a nutritious beverage is an excellent option.
- Some people find it difficult to face food first thing in the morning, but *remember:* you don't have to eat solids; instead, try any of the delicious liquid meals containing Fortified Milk suggested in the chapter 'High Protein Drinks' (pages 43–49).

Starter's Muesli

Makes: approximately 280 g (9 oz)

---

150 g (5 oz) oatmeal

1 tbsp brown sugar

15 g (½ oz) desiccated coconut

45 g (1½ oz) mixed dried fruit
(apple, apricot, sultanas)

1 tbsp chopped nuts

30 g (1 oz) wheatflakes

30 g (1 oz) bran granules

The benefits of making your own muesli extend to cost savings and control of refined sugars and fats.

Method:

1. Combine oatmeal and sugar. Spread out on a baking sheet. Place under a medium grill.
2. Grill the oatmeal mixture, stirring frequently, until lightly browned.
3. Add coconut, stir, and continue grilling until mixture is an even golden colour.
4. Remove muesli from the grill. Leave to cool.
5. Add remaining ingredients.
6. Serve with milk or low-fat natural yoghurt. Use stewed or chopped fresh fruit as a topping.

To vary: Add toasted sesame, pumpkin or sunflower seeds at Step 5.

To store: Keep in an airtight jar or tin.

Nutritional data per 30 g serving: 493 kJ (118 cal), Carbohydrate 14 g, Fat 6 g, Protein 3 g.

Preparation time: 15 minutes. Cooking equipment: baking sheet. Grill temperature: medium.

QUICK TIP: Make sure you have a good supply of basic ingredients in your store cupboard – set aside a regular time to go shopping. Basic ingredients include rice, pasta, bottled tomato-based pasta sauces, canned vegetables and fruit, as well as herbs, spices, soy and tomato sauces. With these ingredients, you can always put together a quick nutritious meal.

Custom-made Cereal

Makes:
approximately 625 g (1¼ lb)

Basic ingredients:
wheatflakes
puffed wheat or *puffed rice*
bran granules

Extra ingredients:
Choose from:
chopped nuts (any variety
  or mixed)
chopped, mixed fresh fruits
dried sultanas, raisins,
  banana slices, dates,
  apricots or *apple* or
  mixed dried, chopped,
  fruit (sold ready to use)
desiccated coconut
toasted sesame seeds
sunflower or *pumpkin*
  seeds
raw sugar
rolled oats
sprinkling of cinnamon
low-fat yoghurt

Rather than pay a high price for a blended cereal, mix your own at the breakfast table. With a few screw-top jars of your favourite ingredients you can quickly put together a personal blend. The nutritional value depends on the combination of cereals you choose.

Method:

1. Combine all your ingredients.
2. Add hot or cold skimmed milk to your cereal.

Nutritional data per 90 g (3 oz): 545 kJ (130 cal), Carbohydrate 28 g, Fat 1 g, Protein 1 g.

Note: This data was analysed using 185 g (6 oz) of dried fruit per total quantity.

Toppings for Wholemeal Toast, Muffins or Crumpets

Lower your fat intake by using tasty toppings instead of butter and margarine:

- banana (mashed or sliced) and cinnamon
- low-fat hard cheese or cottage cheese with slices of fresh apple or pear
- use peanut butter instead of butter or margarine and top with sliced celery or cucumber
- instead of butter or margarine, use Chicken Liver Pâté (page 70) and top with sliced tomato, celery or cucumber
- low-fat hard cheese, on top of yeast extract spread, honey or jam
- toasted tomato or asparagus and low-fat cheese, with a sprinkle of oregano
- use avocado sprinkled with lemon juice instead of butter or margarine.

Cooked Breakfast Suggestions

Microwaved or Grilled Tomatoes

Cut the tomato in thick slices and top with grated mozzarella or low-fat hard cheese. Sprinkle with oregano or basil and black pepper to taste. Serve on toasted wholemeal bread or muffins.

Corn-on-the-cob

Boiled and served with freshly ground black pepper. To make your own **Creamed Corn,** use fresh, frozen or canned baby corn or kernels, combined with Savoury White Sauce (page 177). Serve on toasted wholemeal bread or muffins.

Mushrooms

Sauté or microwave finely chopped onion in very little water. Add sliced mushrooms, and sauté/microwave until tender. Season with oregano and black pepper. Make **Creamed Mushrooms** by adding Savoury White Sauce (page 177) or Low-fat Cheese Sauce (page 179). Serve on wholemeal toast or muffins.

Eggs

Can be poached, boiled, scrambled or in an omelette (page 54–58). As a change from the usual savoury fillings, try omelettes with sweet fillings, such as stewed apple and cinnamon.

Baked Beans on Toast

Add extra flavour to this old favourite with a little chilli sauce or with chopped parsley, onion or basil.

Pancakes (page 159)

With savoury (page 160) or sweet (page 191–2) fillings. For a special breakfast, make a pancake filling of canned salmon mixed with Savoury White Sauce (page 177).

Eggs

Eggs are a useful protein food for athletes; they can be cooked quickly and in many cases make an excellent alternative to meat and other protein foods. They are also a rich source of iron. Eggs are very versatile; try them for light meals, snacks, nourishing drinks and desserts.

A fresh egg: has a slightly rough shell and feels heavy.

Store eggs: in a cool place – not necessarily in the refrigerator, although this helps prolong their freshness.

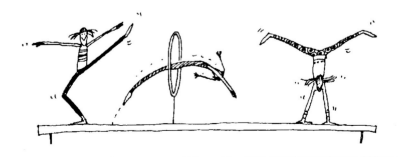

Boiled Eggs

Serves: 1

*1 or 2 eggs, at room
temperature*

Add 1 tsp of salt to the boiling water. Eggs cooked in salt water will leak less if they crack during cooking.

Method:

1. Fill the saucepan with enough cold water to cover the egg(s). Bring to the boil.
2. Remove saucepan from the heat. Use a tablespoon to lower the eggs gently into the hot water. Return to heat.

Soft-boiled: Bring to the boil, and simmer for 3½–5 minutes. Serve immediately.

Hard-boiled: Boil for about 5 minutes (during this stage, you can use the back of a spoon to roll the eggs carefully around in the saucepan; this helps keep the yolk in the centre of the egg and makes cut eggs more attractive). Reduce heat, and simmer the eggs for 10 minutes. Plunge the cooked eggs into cold water, cracking the shells. When cool, peel the eggs under running water (this makes peeling easier).

Nutrition data per 50 g egg: 306 kJ (73 cal), Carbohydrate 0 g, Fat 5 g, Protein 6 g.

Preparation time: 7 mins (soft), 17 mins (hard). Cooking equipment: small saucepan.

Scrambled Eggs

Serves: 1

2 eggs
2 tbsp skimmed milk
pinch white pepper
1 tsp parsley, chopped
    (optional)
1 tsp butter or *margarine*
    or *use a good quality,*
    non-stick cooking spray

A good scrambled egg is firm but moist and creamy. To obtain perfect results, it is important to cook it slowly, over gentle heat. Egg toughens and becomes stringy or watery if you cook it over high heat.

Method:

1. Lightly beat together the eggs, milk, pepper and parsley, if liked.
2. In a small saucepan or heavy-bottomed frying pan, melt the butter or margarine over low to medium heat, or spray the pan well with non-stick cooking spray.
3. Add the egg mixture to the pan. Using a wooden spoon, stir gently over low to medium heat, until the egg begins to thicken.
4. Cook the egg, stirring constantly, until it is still very moist but does not run when the pan is tilted. Remove from the pan. Do not overcook the egg or it will toughen. Serve immediately.
5. Serve Scrambled Eggs on a slice of wholemeal toast.

To vary: Add 1 tsp of grated Parmesan cheese at Step 1. Instead of parsley, add 1 tsp of fresh finely chopped chives or a good pinch of dried, or ½ tsp fresh oregano.

Nutritional data per serving: 824 kJ (197 cal), Carbohydrate 2 g, Fat 15 g, Protein 14 g.

Preparation time: 10 minutes. Cooking equipment: small saucepan or frying pan.

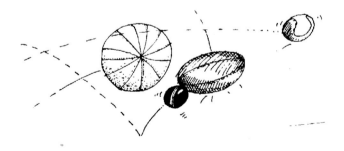

French-style Omelette

Serves: 1

2 eggs

4 tbsp water or skimmed milk

pinch white pepper

1 tsp butter or margarine
  or use a good quality
  non-stick cooking spray

Omelettes are quick to make, very tasty, versatile and nutritious and can be served for any meal. With a sweet filling they make a delicious dessert.

Method:

1. Lightly beat eggs with water or milk and the pepper.
2. Over low to medium heat, melt the butter or margarine in a small, heavy-based frying pan or omelette pan, or spray the pan well with non-stick cooking spray.
3. Add the egg mixture to the pan. Keep heat at low to medium. Tilt pan to distribute egg evenly.
4. Leave the egg to set for 1 minute. As the egg begins to set, tilt the pan and use an egg slice or spatula to lift the edge of the omelette carefully, allowing the uncooked egg on top to run underneath.
5. Leave the egg to set for a further 30 seconds. Lift the opposite edge of the omelette and let egg run underneath again. If you are making a filled omelette, add the filling at this point.
6. When the omelette is set underneath but is still moist on top, use an egg slice or spatula to fold it in half.
7. Cook the folded omelette until golden underneath.
8. Slide cooked omelette on to a plate. Serve immediately.

To vary: Serve omelettes plain, or with ham, tomato and onion, mushroom and spring onion, asparagus and cottage cheese, or create a filling of your own. You can make a single, family-sized omelette, but it is actually quicker to make individual ones, using 2 eggs per omelette. Different fillings add flavour and colour.

To store: Omelettes should be served and eaten immediately. Any leftovers can be kept, covered, in the refrigerator for a day and then chopped and used in sandwiches, salads, fried rice or Stir-fried Vegetables (page 88).

Nutritional data per serving: 882 kJ (211 cal), Carbohydrate 4 g, Fat 15 g, Protein 15 g.

Preparation time: 10 minutes. Cooking equipment: small, heavy-based frying pan or omelette pan.

QUICK TIP: To test the freshness of eggs, lower gently into cold water. Fresh eggs sink; stale eggs float to the surface.

Egg & Asparagus Mornay

Serves: 2

250 g (8 oz) cooked macaroni

4 hard-boiled eggs, sliced

315 g (10 oz) canned asparagus, drained and cut into 2.5 cm (1 in) pieces

½ tsp prepared English mustard

½ recipe Low-fat Cheese Sauce (page 179)

4 tbsp breadcrumbs

An ideal light meal, this dish is special enough to serve to guests for a brunch.

Method:

1. Spray a casserole dish with non-stick cooking spray. Spoon in the macaroni and spread out evenly.
2. Top the macaroni with the sliced hard-boiled eggs. Sprinkle the asparagus pieces over.
3. Mix the mustard with the Cheese Sauce. Pour over the egg and asparagus.
4. Sprinkle with the breadcrumbs. Bake in a pre-heated oven for 20–30 minutes, or until well browned on top.
5. Serve hot, accompanied by a fresh, green salad.

Nutritional data per serving: 2,258 kJ (540 cal), Carbohydrate 46 g, Fat 18 g, Protein 51 g.

Preparation time: Starting with pre-cooked eggs, macaroni and sauce – 45 minutes.

Cooking equipment: casserole dish. Oven temperature: 180°C/350°F/gas 4.

Eggs Florentine

Serves: 1

90 g (3 oz) cooked fresh spinach or frozen spinach, thawed and well drained

2 tbsp cottage cheese

pinch of nutmeg

2 eggs

Method:

1. In a saucepan, combine the spinach, cheese and nutmeg. Heat thoroughly but do not boil, or the cheese will toughen.
2. Meanwhile, poach the eggs until well set.
3. Spoon the heated spinach mixture in a neat round in the centre of a dinner plate. Arrange the poached eggs on top. Serve and eat immediately.

Nutritional data per serving: 1,023 kJ (244 cal), Carbohydrate 2 g, Fat 15 g, Protein 26 g.

Preparation time: 15 minutes. Cooking equipment: frying pan and saucepan.

NUTRITIOUS SNACKS, DIPS & SPREADS

Getting the kilojoules (calories) you need can be a problem when you have a heavy training schedule and still need to eat nutritious foods. You may find yourself being tempted to pick up a chocolate bar or doughnut to provide the extra energy you need. Unfortunately, convenience snack foods tend to contain a high proportion of fat and are generally low in essential vitamins and minerals.

Nevertheless, snacking is certainly important for athletes with busy schedules. You will need to choose snacks low in fat, but high in carbohydrates – these not only help boost your performance, but also help improve your nutritional status. The snack recipes in this chapter are not only delicious, but have been specially devised to fit in with a healthy eating plan.

Where Snacks Fit In

- When you work out your meal plans, you need to include snacks. We give the nutritional data per serve for each recipe in this book, so it is easy to work out where snacks fit in with your overall diet.

- Don't use snacks in addition to an eating plan which already has enough kilojoules (calories) – use snacks as part of your eating plan, to make up your daily energy needs.

We have created snack foods which are high in complex carbohydrate, easy to make, and contain nutritionally valuable ingredients. They range from wonderful wholemeal sandwiches packed with energy and much more, to home-made Energy Bars (page 67) and muffins. Add fresh fruit to this and you have all the alternatives you need – and all the inducement not to reach for a fat-laden 'quick fix'.

Makes your snacks in advance and take them with you.

SANDWICHES

One of the best-known 'fast foods' is sandwiches, which can be as simple as bread and cheese, or more complex gourmet feasts. Whatever the case, as an athlete you can turn the simple sandwich into an important source of nutrients in your daily diet.

Starting from a basis of bread, which provides the necessary carbohydrate and fibre (extra, if you use wholegrain breads), the filling you choose can supply the vitamins, minerals and protein that make up a balanced meal.

Sandwiches can be served closed or open, toasted (possibly in an electric or camp-style sandwich maker), or layered to make club sandwiches.

Sandwich Fillings

The choice of fillings for sandwiches and rolls is endless – only limited by what you are prepared to try.

Traditionally, the bread for sandwiches is spread with softened butter or margarine to add flavour and to prevent the bread becoming soggy. However, sandwiches are still tasty and certainly lower in fat if you leave out the butter or margarine.

Protein-plus Fillings

Use small amounts of one of these protein foods:

- cold, cooked meat or chicken, shredded or finely chopped
- grated or sliced low-fat cheese
- chopped hard-boiled egg
- salmon or tuna canned in brine.

Topped off with lashings of:

- shredded lettuce, sliced tomato and cucumber, grated carrot, coleslaw, sliced mushrooms, beetroot, alfalfa, finely chopped celery, Tabbouleh (page 170).

Combination Fillings

Cheese and ...

- cottage cheese ... with snipped chives or pickled dill cucumbers ... or with chopped pineapple and sultanas ... or with asparagus
- grated low-fat hard cheese ... with grated apple and carrot, chopped celery and pecan or walnuts; bind with Yoghurt Dressing (page 182) ... or with asparagus ... or with mustard and black olives ... or with fruit chutney and thinly sliced green apple
- ricotta cheese ... with sliced cucumber, tomato and chopped fresh basil, or with chopped celery and walnuts.

Meat or Chicken and ...

- chutney or mustard topped with thinly sliced cold meat of any variety
- chopped chicken, chives and parsley bound with Yoghurt Dressing (page 182)
- fruit chutney, chopped chicken and thinly sliced raw mushrooms
- chopped chicken, walnuts and celery or green pepper bound with commercial reduced calorie dressing
- wholegrain mustard, chopped lean ham and grated apple
- fruit chutney with slices of lean cooked lamb and apple
- Chicken Liver Pâté (page 70), sliced tomato and cucumber.

Fish and ... (no, *not* chips!)

- salmon or tuna (canned in brine) drained, mashed with curry powder, lemon juice and commercial reduced calorie dressing
- salmon or tuna (canned in brine) and sliced cucumber or celery, topped with Yoghurt Dressing (page 182)
- canned crab meat, thinly spread Tartare Sauce (page 180) with lemon juice and finely chopped parsley
- ricotta cheese, prawns and thinly sliced cucumber.

Egg and ...

- hard-boiled eggs mashed with: chopped chives *or* gherkin, shredded lettuce and commercial reduced calorie dressing ... or with curry powder, alfalfa or bean sprouts and Yoghurt Dressing (page 182)
- scrambled eggs with finely chopped lean ham.

Vegetables and ...

- thinly sliced tomatoes, seasoned with pepper, chopped mint and vinegar
- grated carrot and sultanas or crushed peanuts
- sliced cucumber and alfalfa sprouts
- canned baked beans, lightly mashed and seasoned with Tabasco if desired
- peanut butter and sliced cucumber or chopped celery.

Sweet Sandwich Fillings

- mashed banana, lemon juice and cinnamon
- chopped raisins and mint
- peanut butter and honey
- cottage or ricotta cheese and jam
- cottage or ricotta cheese with chopped dried figs
- chocolate and nut spread
- lemon curd
- honey
- jam.

Toasted Ham 'n' Egg

Serves: 1

2 slices wholemeal bread
1 egg
60 g (2 oz) grated low-fat
   hard cheese
1 tsp chopped chives
2 tbsp chopped ham
2 tbsp chopped tomato
   (optional)
ground black pepper

Method:

1. Lightly toast the bread on one side only. Place the bread toasted-side down.
2. Lightly beat the egg. Add all remaining ingredients and combine well.
3. Spread the egg mixture on the toast and place under grill until topping begins to brown. Serve immediately.

Nutritional data per serving: 1,153 kJ (275 cal), Carbohydrate 23 g, Fat 10 g, Protein 23 g.

Preparation time: 8 minutes.

Salmon & Spring Onion

Serves: 1

2 slices wholemeal bread
60 g (2 oz) canned salmon
1 tbsp tomato sauce
2 spring onions, finely
   chopped
2 tsp lemon juice
ground black pepper

Method:

1. Lightly toast the bread on one side only. Place the bread toasted-side down.
2. Combine remaining ingredients to make a coarse paste. Spread on toast.
3. Place under the grill until heated through, about 5 minutes. Serve immediately.

Nutrition data per serve: 1,395 kJ (333 cal), Carbohydrate 28 g, Fat 11 g, Protein 30 g.

Preparation time: 8 minutes.

Chicken Balls

Serves: 6

600 g (1 lb 3 oz) chicken
   breasts, skinned and
   minced
1 small clove garlic,
   crushed
1 egg
1 tsp mixed dried herbs or
   chopped fresh parsley
ground black pepper
1 tsp lemon juice
625 ml (1 pint) tomato
   juice

Great snack food and an excellent alternative to beef hamburgers. Chicken Balls keep well in the refrigerator and can be frozen.

Method:

1. In a bowl, combine the chicken, garlic, egg, herbs, pepper and lemon juice. Mix well. Leave to stand for 10 minutes.
2. With wet hands, form tablespoonfuls of the mixture into balls about the size of a walnut.
3. In a saucepan, bring the tomato juice to the boil. Reduce to a simmer. One by one, drop the chicken balls into the tomato juice and simmer for 20 minutes.
4. Use a slotted spoon to remove the chicken balls from the tomato juice.
5. By this stage, the juice should have reduced and thickened to the consistency of a sauce. If not, simmer the sauce for a little longer.

As a main course: Place the chicken balls in a serving dish and spoon over the sauce. Serve hot with baked or boiled jacket potatoes and steamed vegetables.

Alternatively, arrange the chicken balls on a bed of cooked spaghetti and spoon over the tomato sauce.

As an appetiser: Make the chicken balls a little smaller and serve on cocktail sticks. Arrange around a bowl of the sauce for dipping.

On the barbecue: Baste with the tomato juice during cooking.

To vary: You may substitute the chicken with lean minced veal, pork or beef.

To store: Store chicken balls in their sauce, covered, for up to 3 days in the refrigerator. Freeze chicken balls and sauce together.

Nutritional data per serving: 790 kJ (188 cal), Carbohydrate 4 g, Fat 6 g, Protein 30 g.

Preparation time: 45 minutes. Cooking equipment: large saucepan.

Frozen Fruit Yoghurt Sticks

Makes: 6–8

1 orange
125 g (4 oz) dried apricots
1 tsp apple juice
   concentrate
500 ml (16 fl oz) low-fat,
   natural yoghurt

Vary this recipe by using a purée of fresh or dried fruits, such as peaches or pears, or the pulp of fresh passion fruit. You can also freeze the mixture in an ice-cube tray. Try dropping a fruity ice-cube into one of the chilled beverages in 'High Protein Drinks' (pages 43–49).

Method:

1.   Finely grate the zest of the orange and measure off 1 tsp.
2.   Squeeze the orange to extract ½ cup of juice.
3.   In a small saucepan, combine the orange juice and zest, dried apricots and apple juice concentrate. Simmer gently for about 15 minutes, or until apricots are tender.
4.   Purée the apricots in a blender or food processor. Leave to cool.
5.   Pour the yoghurt into a jug. Fold in the apricot purée. Pour into icy-lolly moulds and insert sticks, or pour into an ice-cube tray.
6.   Freeze for several hours, or overnight.

To store: Yoghurt Sticks will keep indefinitely in the freezer or deep freeze.

Nutritional data per 50 g (2 oz) serving: 142 kJ (34 cal), Carbohydrate 6 g, Fat 0 g, Protein 2 g.
Preparation time: 20 minutes. Cooking equipment: small saucepan.

Piquant Truffles

Makes:
approximately 30

125 g (4 oz) dried apricots
250 ml (8 fl oz) water
45 g (1½ oz) desiccated
　coconut
2 tsp grated lemon rind
2 tsp apple juice
　concentrate
1 tbsp orange juice
good pinch of mixed spice

For coating:

45 g (1½ oz) desiccated
　coconut

Method:

1. In a small saucepan, simmer the apricots and water for about 15 minutes, or until completely softened.
2. Drain the apricots over a bowl and reserve the cooking liquid.
3. Place all the ingredients in a food processor, except the reserved cooking liquid and coconut for coating. Process ingredients very briefly, until the mixture clings together. If it is too dry and crumbly to hold together, add the reserved liquid, a little at a time, until you have the correct consistency; if too wet, add more coconut, a little at a time, until you can handle the mixture cleanly.
4. Spread the remaining coconut on a large sheet of greaseproof paper.
5. With wet hands, roll a heaped teaspoonful of the mixture between your palms until smooth and round.
6. Roll the rounded truffle in the coating coconut to cover. Place on a large plate. Use up the rest of the mixture in the same way.
7. Chill the truffles in the refrigerator for 1 hour, or until firm, before serving.

To store: Arrange the truffles in layers, with greaseproof paper between each layer, in an airtight container. Store in the refrigerator.

Nutritional data per 15 g (½ oz) truffle: 117 kJ (28 cal), Carbohydrate 2 g, Fat 2 g, Protein 0 g.

Preparation time: 45 minutes. Cooking equipment: small saucepan.

Chewy Fruit Fingers

Makes 8–10

90 g (3 oz) raisins or
    sultanas
90 g (3 oz) dried apricots,
    pears or peaches
90 g (3 oz) dates, stoned
45 g (1¹/₂ oz) ground
    almonds or hazelnuts
45–90 g (1¹/₂–3 oz)
    desiccated coconut

These are excellent snacks, packed with carbohydrates and very easy to prepare.

Method:

1. Using a food processor or the finest grinding attachment on your mincer (meat grinder), process all the dried fruits to a fine pulp.
2. In a bowl, combine fruit, ground nuts and half the shredded coconut. If the mixture is very sticky, add more coconut, a little at a time, until you can handle it cleanly.
3. Spoon the mixture on to a baking tray and press out, firmly and evenly, to form a large square, about 1 cm (¹/₂ in) thick.
4. Dip the blade of a small, sharp knife into very hot water and cut the flattened mixture into pieces about 1 x 5 cm (¹/₂ x 2 in). Do not separate the pieces.
5. Place the cut mixture in the refrigerator and leave to firm for about 1 hour.

To store: Wrap the pieces individually in cling film or greaseproof paper and place in a sealed airtight container. Keep in a cool place.

Nutritional data per 40 g (1 ¹/₂ oz) serving: 580 kJ (140 cal), Carbohydrate 16 g, Fat 8 g, Protein 2 g.
Preparation time: 10–15 minutes; chill for 1 hour before serving. Cooking equipment: food processor or mincer, baking tray.

Banana Truffles

Makes: approximately 30

1 ripe banana
150 g (5 oz) dates, stoned
150 g (5 oz) raisins
60 g (2 oz) shelled walnuts
90 g (3 oz) shredded coconut
(including 3–4 tbsp for
coating)

These are great, but keep an eye on how many you eat.

Method:

1. In a food processor or blender combine all the ingredients at once, except the coconut for coating. Process to the texture of fine breadcrumbs.
2. With wet hands, roll a tablespoonful of the mixture at a time to form smoothly rounded balls, then roll the balls in the coating coconut to cover.
3. Place completed shapes on a baking sheet and chill in the refrigerator until firm (about 2 hours).

To store: Arrange in layers (waxed paper between each), in an airtight container. Keep refrigerated.

Nutritional data per 30 g (1 oz) serving: 390 kJ (90 cal), Carbohydrate 12 g, Fat 5 g, Protein 1 g.

Preparation time: approximately 30 minutes; chill until firm, at least 2 hours before serving.

Energy Bars

Makes: 12–15

60 g (2 oz) dried apricots,
finely chopped
30 g (1 oz) unprocessed bran
45 g (1½ oz) desiccated coconut
3 tbsp slivered almonds
45 g (1½ oz) raw sugar
90 g (3 oz) rolled oats
90 g (3 oz) sultanas
60 g (2 oz) margarine
1 tbsp clear honey
2 eggs, lightly beaten

The fat content of these bars is fairly high so you should limit yourself – but they also carry a carbohydrate punch and are loaded with calories and dietary fibre.

Method:

1. In a large bowl, combine all the dry ingredients.
2. Melt the margarine and honey together, over a low heat. Add to the dry ingredients and mix well.
3. Add the lightly beaten eggs and stir well.
4. Spoon the mixture into a baking tray and press down firmly and evenly.
5. Bake in a pre-heated oven for about 25 minutes, or until golden-brown. Allow to cool completely before cutting into 12–15 even-sized rectangles.

To store: Keep Energy Bars in an airtight container, preferably lined with waxed paper.

Nutritional data per 30 g (1 oz) serving: 482 kJ (115 cal), Carbohydrate 13 g, Fat 6 g, Protein 2 g.

Preparation time: 30 minutes. Cooking equipment: small saucepan, baking tray, 28 x 18 cm (11 x 7 in). Oven temperature: 180°C/350°F/gas 4.

DIPS & SPREADS

The savoury mixtures in this chapter are excellent for cooks literally on the run. They are nutritious, simple to prepare and, if properly stored, can be made up to 2 days in advance.

Only serve as much of a dip as you need at that time. Any leftover dips should be discarded.

Versatile Dips

- Pre-dinner appetizer: surround by suitable foods for dipping.
- Entrée: spoon into individual pots; serve with triangles or fingers of wholemeal toast.
- At barbecues and picnics: pack in suitable containers, well sealed.
- For light meals, such as breakfasts and office lunches: use the dips and spreads as fillings for wholemeal sandwiches.

Foods to Serve with Dips & Spreads:

- cucumber wedges
- cauliflower and broccoli florets
- crusty wholemeal and dark rye bread
- green and red pepper
- sliced apple, tossed in lemon juice to prevent discoloration
- fresh pineapple pieces
- radish (try cutting in designs for effect)
- spring onion, neatly trimmed
- carrot wedges or sticks
- celery cut in narrow, 5 cm (2 in) long sticks
- cantaloupe or honeydew melon, cut into chunks
- kiwi fruit, cut in wedges
- mushrooms
- pitta (Lebanese) breads
- low-calorie biscuits
- toast

Curried Cottage Cheese

Serves: 6–8 as an appetizer

250 g (8 oz) cottage cheese

45 g (1½ oz) sultanas

60 g (2 oz) celery, finely chopped

1 tsp curry powder

ground black pepper

Serve chilled with sliced fresh vegetables, corn chips, biscuits or fingers of dry toast for dipping.

Method:
1. Combine all ingredients and blend well.
2. Spoon into a serving dish.

Nutritional data per serving: 178 kJ (43 cal), Carbohydrate 4 g, Fat 1 g, Protein 5 g.

Preparation time: 5–10 minutes; chill for 1 hour.

Equipment: blender or food processor.

Salmon Pâté

Serves: 4–8 as an
appetizer or entrée

1 medium can red salmon

2 tbsp tomato purée

1 small onion, finely
chopped

½ stick celery, finely
chopped

125 ml (4 fl oz) low-fat
natural yoghurt

2 tbsp lemon juice

½ tsp prepared English
mustard

white pepper, to taste

2 tsp gelatine

2 tbsp cold water

Method:

1. Remove any dark-coloured skin from the salmon. Use a fork to mash the salmon and crush the bones.

2. Add all remaining ingredients, except the gelatine and water.

3. In a small, heatproof bowl, sprinkle the gelatine over the cold water. Leave to stand for 5 minutes.

4. Stand the bowl of gelatine in a saucepan of hot water. Heat slowly and gently until the gelatine dissolves.

5. Add the gelatine to the salmon mixture. Combine thoroughly.

6. Pour mixture into a wetted mould, or suitable bowl. Cover and chill in refrigerator for at least 2 hours. Alternatively, spoon the mixture into individual moulds or little pots and chill as above.

As an appetizer or entrée: Carefully turn out the moulded pâté on to a serving platter, or scoop the set pâté into a serving bowl. If using individual moulds, turn on to entrée plates. Garnish with very thinly sliced cucumber. Serve with bite-sized bits of raw vegetable, triangles of dry toast, biscuits or crispbreads.

As a light meal: Use the pâté as a sandwich filling with crisp lettuce and sliced cucumber.

To vary: Add 2 tbsp of chopped capers, red or green pepper or dill cucumber.

To store: Best made the day before use. Keep covered in the refrigerator for up to 3 days. Not recommended for freezing.

Nutritional data per serving: 316 kJ (76 cal), Carbohydrate 3 g, Fat 3 g, Protein 9 g.

Preparation time: 20 minutes; chill to firm, at least 2 hours. Cooking equipment: mixing bowl, saucepan, shaped mould (optional).

Chicken Liver Pâté

**Serves: 6 as an appetizer;
4 as an entrée**

250 g (8 oz) chicken livers
   (hearts and blood vessels
   removed)
4 tbsp water
1 sprig fresh or good pinch
   of dried thyme
2 bay leaves
ground black pepper, to
   taste
125 ml (4 fl oz) port

Chicken Liver Pâté is traditionally made with lashings of butter and cream. This version avoids any additional fats, yet tastes delicious.

Method:

1. Wash, dry and roughly chop the livers, discarding any greenish portions (these are not a sign of deterioration, but may discolour the pâté).
2. In a heavy-based saucepan, bring the water to the boil. Add the liver and stir until lightly browned.
3. Add the thyme, bay leaves and black pepper. Cover, reduce heat and simmer gently for 10 minutes.
4. Add port and simmer, uncovered, a further 3 minutes.
5. If using fresh thyme, remove and discard the sprig. Remove and discard bay leaves.
6. Allow mixture to cool slightly. Purée liver and cooking liquids in a blender or food processor.

To store: Cover and keep refrigerated for up to 5 days. Do not freeze.

As an appetizer: Spoon the pâté into a serving bowl and chill for at least 1 hour before serving. Surround the dip with sliced fresh vegetables, biscuits or triangles of dry toast.

As an entrée: Spoon the pâté into small, individual pots or ramekins. Smooth over the surface and chill for at least 1 hour before serving. Place the pots on small plates and arrange a couple of dry toast triangles or crisp biscuits on each plate.

Pâté with Mushroom

Add 45 g (1½ oz) of chopped mushrooms at Step 3.

Pâté with Orange and Brandy

Instead of port, use 60 ml (2 fl oz) of fresh orange juice and 60 ml (2 fl oz) of brandy at Step 4.

Pâté with Pistachio or Pecan Nuts

Stir in 2 level tbsp of finely chopped nuts after the liver has been puréed.

Nutritional data per serving: 227 kJ (54 cal), Carbohydrate 2 g, Fat 2 g, Protein 5 g.

Preparation time: 30 minutes. Cooking equipment: saucepan, blender or food processor.

Hummus

Serves: 4–6 as an appetizer

---

90 g (3 oz) cooked and drained chick peas

1 clove garlic, crushed

pinch of cayenne pepper

1 tbsp lemon juice

1 tbsp low-fat natural yoghurt

1 tsp finely chopped fresh mint

As a snack or appetiser, serve Hummus with hot pita (Lebanese) bread, small pieces of sliced raw vegetables, triangles of dry toast, or biscuits.

Method:

1. Purée chick peas in a blender or food processor. Combine with all remaining ingredients.
2. To adjust consistency for dipping or spreading, add a little more lemon juice or yoghurt.
3. Spoon into a serving dish, cover and chill.

To vary: Stir in 2 tsp of toasted sesame seeds.

To store: Keep covered in the refrigerator for up to 3 days.

Nutritional data per serving: 80 kJ (19 cal), Carbohydrate 4 g, Fat 0 g, Protein 1 g.

Preparation time: using pre-cooked chick peas (page 144) or canned chick peas – 5 minutes. Equipment: blender or food processor.

Tzatziki Dip

Serves: 6 as an appetizer

---

100 g (3½ oz) cucumber, peeled and finely chopped

250 ml (8 fl oz) low-fat natural yoghurt

2 tsp olive oil

1½ tsp vinegar

1 small garlic clove, crushed

chopped parsley

Method:

1. Allow cucumber to stand for a while and drain off any juice.
2. In a bowl, combine all ingredients.
3. Cover and chill for 1 hour.

As an appetizer: This is a great accompaniment to Chicken Balls (page 63) and hot pitta bread.

For a light meal: Serve spooned over hot baked potatoes.

To store: Keep covered in the refrigerator for up to 3 days.

Nutritional data per serving: 189 kJ (45 cal), Carbohydrate 4 g, Fat 2 g, Protein 3 g.

Preparation time: 5 minutes; chill 1 hour before serving.

Ricotta Dip

**Serves: 6–8 as an
appetizer**

250 g (8 oz) ricotta or curd
  cheese
125 ml (4 fl oz) Vinaigrette
  Dressing (page 181)
ground black pepper
2 tbsp finely chopped
  parsley
2 tbsp finely chopped chives
  or spring onions
2 tbsp finely chopped
  gherkins

Serve the dip surrounded by sliced fresh vegetables, corn
chips, biscuits, or fingers of dry toast.

Method:
1. In a blender or food processor, blend cheese and
    dressing until smooth and creamy.
2. Stir in remaining ingredients. Spoon into a serving
    bowl and chill until required.

To store: Keep covered in the refrigerator for up to 3 days.

*Nutritional data per serving: 134 kJ (32 cal), Carbohydrate 1 g,
Fat 1 g, Protein 5 g.*

Preparation time: 5–10 minutes. Cooking equipment: blender or
food processor.

Spicy Dip

**Serves: 6–8 as an
appetizer**

250 g (8 oz) cottage cheese
125 ml (4 fl oz) low-fat
  natural yoghurt
1/2 red pepper, seeded
1/2 green pepper, seeded
1/4 cucumber, peeled
1 tsp prepared English
  mustard
dash of Tabasco
ground black pepper

Sprinkle with paprika and serve surrounded by sliced fresh
vegetables, corn chips, biscuits or fingers of dry toast.

Method:
1. Beat together the cottage cheese and yoghurt.
2. Add remaining ingredients and blend well.
3. Spoon into a serving dish and chill for at least 1 hour.

To store: Keep covered in the refrigerator for up to 3 days.

*Nutritional data per serving: 162 kJ (39 cal), Carbohydrate 2 g,
Fat 1 g, Protein 5 g.*

Preparation time: 5–10 minutes. Cooking equipment: blender or
food processor.

Salmon Cheesy Dip

Serves: 6–8 as an appetizer

125 g (4 oz) canned pink salmon, drained
250 g (8 oz) ricotta cheese
1 spring onion, finely chopped
1 tsp Worcestershire sauce
cayenne pepper, to taste

Using cottage or ricotta cheese, try a few finely chopped anchovies or capers instead of the salmon, or some cooked shrimps and a dash each of tomato and Tabasco.

Method:
1. Remove any dark skin from the salmon. Mash the salmon with a fork, crushing up the bones.
2. Add all remaining ingredients and blend well.
3. Chill well before serving. Serve the dip surrounded by sliced fresh vegetables, corn chips, biscuits or triangles of dry toast.

To store: Keep covered in the refrigerator for no more than 2 days.

Nutritional data per serving: 202 kJ (48 cal), Carbohydrate 1 g, Fat 2 g, Protein 7 g.
Preparation time: 5–10 minutes; chill for 1 hour.

Guacamole

Serves: 6–8 as an appetizer

2 ripe avocados
2 tbsp lemon juice
2 tomatoes, skinned, seeded and finely chopped
¼ green pepper, seeded and finely chopped
½ small onion, grated
1 clove garlic, crushed
½ tsp Worcestershire sauce
4 tbsp low-fat natural yoghurt

Method:
1. In a bowl, mash the avocado flesh and lemon juice.
2. Add remaining ingredients and beat together until smooth and creamy.
3. Spoon into a serving dish. Chill before serving with sliced fresh vegetables, corn chips, biscuits or fingers of dry toast for dipping.

To store: Keep covered in the refrigerator for 1 day.

Nutritional data per serving: 221 kJ (53 cal), Carbohydrate 1 g, Fat 1 g, Protein 1 g.
Preparation time: 5–10 minutes; chill for 1 hour. Cooking equipment: bowl, blender or food processor.

Baba Ghanoush

Serves: 6 as an appetizer

---

2 tbsp water

2 medium aubergines,
  peeled and diced

2 cloves garlic, finely
  chopped

4 tbsp tahina (sesame seed
  paste)

125 ml (4 fl oz) lemon juice
water

Garnish:

finely chopped parsley

Hot pitta bread, cut in wedges, makes a delicious and authentic accompaniment to this dip.

Method:

1. In a heavy-based saucepan, heat the 2 tbsp of water. Add the aubergine, cover and simmer gently for 20 minutes.
2. When the aubergine is completely soft, use a fork to mash until smooth.
3. Turn out into a bowl and set aside to cool.
4. Add the garlic, tahina and lemon juice to the mashed aubergine. Blend well.
5. Add water, a little at a time, beating well between each addition, until mixture is of spreading consistency.
6. Chill the Baba Ghanoush before serving. Garnish with a sprinkling of chopped parsley.

Microwave Method:

Cooking time: 8 minutes

Arrange the diced aubergine around the edge of a large, shallow dish. Add 2 tbsp of water and cover with cling film. Microwave on 'High' for 5–6 minutes, or until completely tender. Allow 2 minutes standing time. Proceed from Step 3 of the conventional method.

To store: Keep covered in the refrigerator for up to 3 days.

Nutritional data per serving: 203 kJ (48 cal), Carbohydrate 2 g, Fat 4 g, Protein 2 g.

Preparation time: 30 minutes. Cooking equipment: heavy-based saucepan.

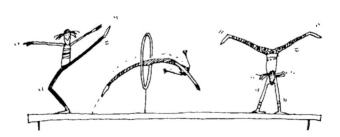

A well-balanced breakfast: Dried Fruit Compote (page 184), topped with plain, low-fat yoghurt or Starter's Muesli (page 52), yeast-free Quick Yoghurt Bread (page 204) and fresh fruit or fruit juice.

SOUPS

Soups are invaluable for athletes with intensive schedules and who need to maintain peak nutritional status. Starting with fresh ingredients, most soups take time to prepare; however, the investment in time is well worth the return.

Heartier soups, such as Lentil & Vegetable Soup (page 82), combine alternative protein sources such as lentils, with fresh vegetables which add to the fibre, vitamin and mineral content. Furthermore most soups can be prepared in large quantities, divided into single-meal portions and then frozen in well-sealed plastic bags or containers.

Most of us associate soups with winter weather, but a chilled soup is the ideal starter for a summer meal. There are some interesting chilled soups to be made from fresh fruits, cucumber and beetroot (borsch), as well as from gourds, such as pumpkin and butternut.

Store & Drink More – Soup by the Mug

A microwave is very handy for thawing and reheating individual servings of frozen soup.

- Place plastic bags in mugs suitable for the freezer *and* the microwave, and fill the bags with soup.

- Freeze soup in the mugs and then remove the mugs.

- To defrost and reheat, place a bag of frozen soup back into a mug and microwave on 'Medium' until the soup comes away from the bag.

- Place the still frozen soup-block into the mug, cover and microwave on 'High' for 1 minute. Break up the soup with a fork and then microwave on 'High' for a further 2–3 minutes, stirring once during cooking.

Meat/Chicken & Vegetable Soup *or* Basic Meat/Chicken Stock

***Makes: 1.4 litres
(2½ pints)***

2 lamb shanks or *500 g
(1 lb) chuck steak or a
1.5 kg (3 lb) chicken*
2 litres (3½ pints) water
2 medium onions
2 sticks of celery
1 large carrot
1 medium parsnip
pinch of dried mixed herbs
1 bay leaf
8 peppercorns or *coarsely
ground black pepper*

Method:

1. Place the meat/chicken and water in a large saucepan.
2. Peel and chop the onions. Wash and roughly chop the rest of the vegetables.
3. Add the vegetables, herbs and pepper to the saucepan.
4. Bring slowly to the boil. Reduce heat and simmer gently for 3 hours.
5. Strain the soup through sieve.

   Basic Meat/Chicken Stock: At this stage you have a Basic Meat/Chicken Stock. Chill in the refrigerator overnight and then skim off any congealed fat. Makes a good hot beverage, served in mugs.
6. To make a heartier soup, discard bones and trim any fat/skin off the meat/chicken. Cut the meat into small pieces and return it, along with the vegetables, to the stock.
7. Chill soup overnight in the refrigerator. Skim off any congealed fat.
8. Serve hot with meat/chicken and vegetables in each serving.

To store stock: Keep in a sealed container in the refrigerator; stock will keep for a week or two if re-boiled every few days. Freeze in an ice-cube tray. Then store cubes in a freezer bag for convenience.

To store soup: Keep covered in the refrigerator for up to 3 days. Freezes well in a suitable container.

To vary: Purée the vegetables in a food processor or blender. Scoop the purée into the stock, stir, reheat and serve.

Nutritional data per 250 ml (8 fl oz): 557 kJ (160 cal), Carbohydrate 5 g, Fat 5 g, Protein 17 g.

Preparation time: 15 minutes; to simmer about 3 hours. Leave to chill overnight. Cooking equipment: large, heavy saucepan, sieve.

Cream of Pumpkin Soup

Serves: 4

1 litre (1¾ pints) Basic Meat
  Stock (page 77) or 4 meat
  stock cubes dissolved in
  1 litre (1¾ pints) hot water
500 g (1 lb) pumpkin, peeled,
  seeded and chopped
30 g (1 oz) skimmed milk
  powder
125 ml (4 fl oz) cold water
Garnish:
finely chopped parsley

Method:

1. Pour stock into a large saucepan and add the pumpkin. Bring to the boil.
2. Reduce heat and simmer for 30 minutes, or until soft.
3. Purée mixture in a blender or food processor, or press through a wire sieve. Return purée to the saucepan and keep warm over low heat.
4. In a cup, blend the skimmed milk powder and cold water to a smooth paste. Gradually add the paste to the saucepan, stirring constantly.
5. Serve soup piping hot, sprinkled with chopped parsley. Accompany with crusty wholemeal bread.

Microwave Method:

Cooking time: 10 minutes.

Using the microwave, this soup has a very fresh flavour and vivid orange colouring.

Peel and seed the pumpkin and then grate it by hand or in a food processor. Place the grated pumpkin in a shallow dish. Add 4 tbsp of the stock, cover the dish with cling film and microwave on 'High' for 4–5 minutes. Leave to stand, covered, for 1½ minutes. Purée the cooked pumpkin as described in Step 3 of the conventional Method. In a microwave-proof soup tureen, mix the purée with the milk and cold water, to form a paste. Add the remaining stock, stir and cover with cling film. Microwave on 'High' for 3 minutes.

To vary: Add a good pinch of ground nutmeg to the puréed pumpkin and stock.

Rich Carrot Soup

Substitute the pumpkin with 500 g (1 lb) carrots, scrubbed and roughly chopped. Include 1 tsp curry powder and 30 g (1 oz) chopped parsley when returning purée to the saucepan. As a garnish, swirl a spoon of plain yoghurt into each bowl.

For a tangy, rather than a spicy, carrot soup – substitute the curry powder for the grated rind and juice of 1 orange. Add after stirring in the milk powder.

To store: Keep covered in the refrigerator for up to 3 days. Soup freezes well in a suitable container. Allow to thaw completely before reheating.

Nutritional data per serving: 169 kJ (40 cal), Carbohydrate 7 g, Fat 0 g, Protein 3 g.

Preparation time: 45 minutes. Cooking equipment: large saucepan, blender, food processor or sieve.

Pea & Ham Soup

Serves: 4

500 g (1 lb) ham or bacon
   bones
1 litre (1¾ pints) water
185 g (6 oz) split peas
1 large onion, chopped
2 sticks of celery, chopped
1 large carrot, chopped
1 small parsnip, chopped
ground black pepper
½ tsp mixed dried herbs

Method:

1. Place all the ingredients in a large saucepan.
2. Bring to the boil. Reduce heat and simmer until peas are soft – 1–2 hours. While simmering, skim away any scum that rises to the surface.
3. Remove and discard the bones. Serve soup hot with crusty wholemeal bread.

To vary: For a smooth soup, remove and discard bones and then process the soup in a blender. Reheat and serve.

To store: Keep covered in the refrigerator for up to 3 days.

Nutritional data per serving: 748 kJ (178 cal), Carbohydrate 18 g, Fat 3 g, Protein 21 g.

Preparation time: 1½–2 hours. Cooking equipment: large saucepan.

Onion Soup

Serves: 4

1 medium onion, sliced
1 litre (1¾ pints) Basic
   Meat Stock (page 77) or 2
   beef stock cubes dissolved
   in 1 litre (1¾ pints) water
2 tsp soy sauce

Method:

1. In a saucepan, bring the onion stock to the boil. Simmer for 30 minutes.
2. Stir in the soy sauce.
3. Serve hot, accompanied by wholemeal bread.

To store: Keep covered in the refrigerator for up to 3 days.

Nutritional data per serving: 50 kJ (13 cal), Carbohydrate 2 g, Fat 0 g, Protein 1 g.

Preparation time: 40 minutes. Cooking equipment: large saucepan.

French-style Onion Soup

Toast thick slices of French stick (baguette). Top toast with grated low-fat hard cheese. Serve the soup in individual, oven-proof bowls or ramekins. Float a slice of toast in each bowl. Place the bowls under a hot grill to melt and brown the cheese. Serve at once.

Creamy Corn Chowder

Serves: 4

1½ litres (2¾ pints) Basic
  Chicken Stock (page 77)
  or 2 chicken stock cubes
  dissolved in 1½ litres
  (2¾ pints) water

3 large potatoes, chopped

1 onion, chopped

1 stick of celery, chopped

1 medium red pepper,
  seeded and chopped

375 g (12 oz) sweetcorn
  kernels

30 g (1 oz) wholemeal flour

500 ml (16 fl oz) skimmed
  milk

1 tbsp chopped parsley

Garnish:

finely chopped parsley

Method:

1. In a large saucepan, place the stock, potatoes, onion, celery, red pepper and sweetcorn.
2. Bring to the boil. Reduce heat and simmer for 30 minutes. Leave to cool.
3. Purée mixture in a blender or food processor, or press through a wire sieve.
4. Clean the saucepan and return the purée to it. In a bowl, blend the flour and milk to a thin, smooth paste. Add to the soup.
5. Reheat soup, stirring constantly, until thickened.
6. Simmer for 2 minutes.
7. Serve the soup with triangles of dry toast or crusty wholemeal bread.

To vary: Add 90 g (3 oz) diced cooked chicken and 2 chopped spring onions at Step 5. Omit the parsley.

To Store: Keep covered in the refrigerator for up to 3 days. Bring to the boil before serving. To freeze the soup, prepare it as far as the end of Step 3. Freeze. Complete preparation just before serving.

Nutritional data per serving: 1,197 kJ (286 cal), Carbohydrate 56 g, Fat 2 g, Protein 13 g.

Preparation time: 45 minutes. Cooking equipment: large saucepan, blender, food processor or sieve.

QUICK TIP: An easy, high-carbohydrate soup can be made by puréeing cooked pumpkin, cauliflower and leeks together with stock and adding 185 g (6 oz) cooked brown rice.

Minestrone

Serves: 8

45 g (1½ oz) dried haricot
   beans

45 g (1½ oz) dried kidney
   beans

2 tbsp water

2 onions, chopped

2 cloves garlic, crushed

2.5 litres (4½ pints) water

2 potatoes, chopped

3 carrots, chopped

4 tomatoes, chopped

2 sticks of celery, chopped

3 courgettes, chopped

60 g (2 oz) green beans,
   sliced

60 g (2 oz) wholemeal
   macaroni

30 g (1 oz) parsley, chopped

This classic and very nutritious soup looks after itself with a good long simmering period – leaving you free to get on with other things.

Method:

1. Place haricot and kidney beans in a bowl and cover with cold water. Leave to soak overnight.
2. In a saucepan, heat 2 tbsp of water and sauté the onion and garlic.
3. Add water and soaked beans to the saucepan. Bring to the boil and boil rapidly for 10 minutes. Reduce heat, cover pan and simmer gently for 2 hours.
4. Add all the vegetables. Bring to the boil. Reduce heat, cover and simmer gently for another hour. Stir occasionally.
5. Add macaroni and bring soup to the boil 10–15 minutes before serving.
6. Stir in parsley and serve the soup piping hot.

To vary: Use 90 g (3 oz) of brown rice instead of macaroni. Add the rice with vegetables at Step 4.

To store: Cover and keep in refrigerator for up to 3 days. Freeze the soup in a suitable container. Bring to the boil before serving.

Nutritional data per serving: 284 kJ (68 cal), Carbohydrate 14 g, Fat 0 g, Protein 3 g.

Preparation time: soak beans overnight; make soup – about 3 hours. Cooking equipment: large saucepan.

Potato & Leek Soup

Serves: 4

750 ml (24 fl oz) Basic
  Chicken Stock (page 77)
  or 2 chicken stock cubes
  dissolved in 750 ml
  (24 fl oz) water
1 leek, chopped
3 large potatoes, chopped
1 onion, chopped
2 sticks of celery, chopped
500 ml (16 fl oz) skimmed
  milk
ground white pepper

Method:

1. To a large saucepan, add the stock or water and the prepared vegetables. Bring to the boil.
2. Reduce heat and simmer for 30 minutes, or until vegetables are tender.
3. Purée the mixture in a blender or food processor, or press through a wire sieve.
4. Return purée to the saucepan. Add the skimmed milk and white pepper to taste. Stir and re-heat.

To vary: Instead of leeks, add 2 chopped spring onions to the puréed soup.

To store: Keep covered in the refrigerator for up to 3 days. Not suitable for freezing.

Nutritional data per serving: 594 kJ (142 cal), Carbohydrate 27 g, Fat 0 g, Protein 8 g.

Preparation time: 45 minutes. Cooking equipment: large saucepan, blender, food processor or sieve.

Lentil & Vegetable Soup

Serves: 4

1 litre (1¾ pints) water
90 g (3 oz) onion, finely
  chopped
1 medium potato, scrubbed
  and diced
60 g (2 oz) celery, sliced
90 g (3 oz) brown lentils
1 small carrot, sliced
2 tbsp parsley, chopped
ground black pepper
2 small courgettes, sliced

Serve hot with chopped parsley sprinkled on top, accompanied by crusty wholemeal bread.

Method:

1. In a large saucepan, combine all the ingredients except the courgettes. Cover and bring to the boil.
2. Reduce heat and simmer for 30 minutes, or until vegetables and lentils are tender.
3. Add sliced courgettes and simmer a further 5 minutes.

To vary: Add ½ tsp of ground coriander at Step 3.

To store: Keep covered in the refrigerator for up to 3 days. Not suitable for freezing.

Nutritional data per serving: 218 kJ (52 cal), Carbohydrate 11 g, Fat 0 g, Protein 2 g.

Preparation time: 45 minutes. Cooking equipment: large saucepan.

Sweet & Sour Soup

Serves: 4

1 tbsp water

2 white onions, finely sliced

1 litre (1¾ pints) Vegetable
  or Basic Meat Stock
  (page 77), or 2 stock
  cubes dissolved in 1 litre
  (1¾ pints) water

1 large beetroot, peeled and
  grated

ground black pepper

1 tbsp vinegar (less if
  preferred)

2 tsp raw sugar

Garnish:

low-fat natural yoghurt

spring onions, sliced

Method:

1. In a large saucepan, heat the water, add the onion and sauté until transparent.

2. Add the stock, grated beetroot, black pepper, vinegar and sugar. Bring to the boil.

3. Reduce heat and gently simmer soup, uncovered, for 1–1½ hours or until beetroot is completely tender and the soup has thickened slightly.

As a first course: Ladle the hot soup into individual bowls. Add 1 tbsp of yoghurt to each bowl and sprinkle over a little sliced spring onion. Crusty wholemeal bread makes a good accompaniment.

As a light meal: Serve the soup hot, with baked jacket potatoes. In this case, you might like to leave out the yoghurt garnish and put 1 tbsp of cottage cheese into each potato.

To vary: Add the grated rind and juice of 1 orange, instead of the vinegar.

To store: Keep covered in the refrigerator for up to 3 days. Freezes well in a suitable container. Reheat thoroughly before serving.

Nutritional data per serving: 153 kJ (37 cal) , Carbohydrate 8 g, Fat 0 g, Protein 1 g.

Preparation time: 1³/₄ hours. Cooking equipment: large saucepan.

VEGETABLES

As everybody knows, vegetables are nutritionally valuable; they are a rich source of many vitamins and minerals, and therefore vital to top performance and good health. They also provide important dietary fibre. Vegetables are low in fat and some, for instance potatoes, are high in energy-giving carbohydrate, as well as in Vitamin C. For the athlete, vegetables are an essential part of your daily food intake.

For more wonderful ways to enjoy the good things vegetables offer, see the recipes in 'Salads' (pages 164–73) and 'Carbohydrate & Protein Alternatives' (pages 143–163).

Versatile Vegetables

- They can be eaten at every meal and as a part of every course, including dessert – try moist Carrot Cake with its creamy, tangy topping (page 205).

- Economical – buy in season for the best value. Frozen vegetables can also be economical; there is no waste – you use what you need and return the rest to the freezer.

- The colour and texture of properly cooked vegetables tempt both the eye and the palate.

- Vegetables are great meal 'extenders' when used in stews, pies and casseroles.

- Eat them raw or cooked. Some vegetables you may have thought should always be cooked may be just as good eaten raw – try using fresh spinach in salads.

- Fresh is best – but only if really fresh.

Note: Frozen vegetables are just as nutritious. Harvested at the peak of their freshness and nutrition, they are available all year round.

TIPS ON CHOICE, STORAGE & PREPARATION

General

- Vegetables are vulnerable to poor handling; vital nutrients, texture and appearance may be lost if poorly handled and/or prepared.

- Avoid buying vegetables that have been standing unshaded in the sun.

- When packed under cling film and displayed for hours under neon lighting, vegetables begin to sweat and lose valuable nutrients.

- Vegetables should be exposed to heat for the shortest possible time during and after cooking, as some vitamins can be destroyed by heat.

- Cook vegetables in the least possible amount of water. Some vitamins can be washed away.

Leafy Green Vegetables

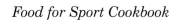

(e.g. cabbage, spinach and Brussels sprouts)

Look for: Crisp, green leaves – avoid those that are soft, bruised or wilted.

Storage: Unwashed, in the refrigerator until needed.

Preparation: Wash quickly and thoroughly in cold water. Do not leave vegetables standing in water – water-soluble vitamins are lost this way. Shake off excess water or use paper towels to pat dry.

- Add dressing just before serving a fresh salad or the vegetables will wilt.
- **Tip:** Freshening up lettuce or celery is easy if you place them in iced water for 1 hour.

Tubers & Root Vegetables

(e.g. carrot, potato, turnip and swede)

Look for: Firm, unblemished vegetables.

Storage: Cut off the leafy tops of carrots and parsnips and store the vegetables in the refrigerator. Store most other roots and tubers in a dry, dark, cool place.

Preparation: Scrub clean – avoid peeling. The peel contains important nutrients and fibre. Potatoes should be cooked until they are tender but still hold their shape.

BASIC COOKING METHODS FOR VEGETABLES

The wide range of options for cooking vegetables adds to their versatility. You can steam, boil, bake, roast, fry or cook them in a microwave.

Cooking Time

This varies according to the type, quality, texture, quantity and size of vegetable. Large quantities or big pieces and older vegetables will take longer to cook than smaller quantities or small pieces and younger vegetables.

Do not over-cook vegetables: Slightly under-cooked vegetables have better nutritional value than over-cooked ones: some vitamins and minerals are water-soluble or can be destroyed by prolonged exposure to heat. They also offer better colour, texture and flavour.

Baking

Cooking by dry, radiant heat in the oven or over barbecue coals. Best for firm vegetables, such as jacket potatoes, sweet potatoes, pumpkin and butternut.

Cooking equipment: Foil, if desired, otherwise bake whole, uncovered.

Basic method: Preheat oven to 180°C/350°F/gas 4. Scrub vegetables and remove any blemishes, but do not peel. If you like crispy baked potatoes, use a fork to pierce the skins once or twice. Place on a baking sheet and bake until tender.

Blanching

Using this method, vegetables are cooked for a few seconds in boiling water, or in a microwave. Blanching brightens the colour and very slightly tenderises fresh green vegetables while retaining their nutritional value and crisp texture (see Gado Gado, page 96).

Blanching is also used to make peeling easier for some vegetables and fruit, for instance tomatoes and peaches.

Tip: Vegetables such as cabbage and onion may be blanched to make them less pungent, before use in salads or cooked dishes.

Traditional Methods

Blanching vegetables for use in cooked dishes, salads or as a side dish: Fill a saucepan with water and bring to a rapid boil. Plunge in the prepared vegetables, one variety at a time, and leave for no more than 1 minute, or until colour intensifies. Immediately plunge the blanched vegetables into cold water and drain.

Blanching vegetables or fruit to be peeled: Pour over enough boiling water to just cover. Leave to stand for 1 minute. Pour off water. The skins slip off easily.

Microwave Methods

For firm vegetables (e.g. carrots, French beans, broccoli or cauliflower): Arrange the vegetables around the outer edge of a large, shallow dish. Add 1–3 tablespoons of water, depending on quantity. Loosely cover with cling film. Microwave for 1–2 minutes, depending on quantity. Remove from microwave and immediately refresh under cold, running water.

For tender vegetables (e.g. mangetout): Arrange vegetables in a dish, as described above. Add only 1 tablespoon of water. Microwave on 'High' for 30–60 seconds, depending on quantity. Immediately refresh under cold, running water.

Boiling

With this method, vegetables are cooked in a small quantity of rapidly boiling water. It is suitable for most vegetables.

Cooking equipment: Saucepan large enough to take the vegetables without having to pile them too deeply on top of each other.

Basic method: Pour a small amount of water (about 2.5 cm/1 in) in to the saucepan and bring to a rapid boil. Add the prepared vegetables and return to the boil. Boil until vegetables are tender but still crisp to bite. Drain and serve as soon as possible.

Note: Swiss chard and spinach need no added water. Wash leaves thoroughly under cold, running water. Shake off excess water, do not dry. Place wet leaves, whole or torn into bite-sized pieces, in a large saucepan over high heat. Cover and cook for 5–7 minutes.

Grilling

Quick cooking under dry radiant heat. An excellent method for softer vegetables such as tomatoes, green or red peppers and mushrooms.

Cooking equipment: Oven grill element, electric or gas grill or directly over barbecue coals.

Basic method: Preheat grill. Alternatively, allow barbecue flames to die down, leaving very hot, red coals. Place vegetables, whole or sliced, on a grill pan about 7 cm (3 in) below the element, or on a grid 10 cm (4 in) above the barbecue coals. Cook vegetables quickly.

Microwave Cooking

This is usually a great time-saver for cooking small quantities of vegetables. Because microwaved vegetables are usually cooked with very little added liquid, they lose only minimal amounts of vitamins and minerals.

The wattage of microwave ovens can vary and this can affect cooking times. Refer to your manual for appropriate instructions and cooking times.

Basic method: Wash and prepare the vegetables as described in your recipe. Place them in a single layer in a large, shallow dish. Add approximately 2 tbsp of water and cover with a lid or cling film. Cook the vegetables on 'High' for 2–5 minutes, depending on quantity and texture – if in doubt, refer to your microwave manual.

General Rules for Microwaving Vegetables

- For evenly cooked vegetables, try keeping cut pieces to a uniform size and thickness.
- When cooking whole vegetables – rotate once or twice while cooking.
- Arrange tender asparagus tips and broccoli florets towards the centre of the dish; these parts are less dense and need less cooking than the tougher stalks.
- Whole vegetables to be cooked in the skin (e.g. potatoes) should be pricked with a fork a few times. This allows steam to escape and prevents vegetables splitting or bursting.
- Microwaving saves much of the natural flavour of vegetables – salt isn't usually needed.
- Microwaved vegetables must be allowed to stand for a short while after cooking. This ensures they will be tender without losing their texture.

Steaming

Vegetables are cooked in the steam rising off boiling water – suitable for most vegetables.

Cooking equipment: Use a tiered metal or bamboo steamer or a colander with raised base, placed inside a saucepan with a tight-fitting lid. The water in the saucepan should not touch the contents of the colander. **Using a steamer:** Pour in enough water to quarter-fill the base of steamer or the saucepan over which you suspend your steamer. Bring water to the boil before placing vegetables in steamer. Add prepared vegetables and cover. Steam vegetables until tender but still crisp to bite. Serve immediately, or chill, covered, for a crisp salad.

Stir-frying & Sautéing

Vegetables are cooked over high heat on the cooker in a little oil, water, stock or tomato juice.

Cooking equipment: Large frying pan or wok.

Basic method: Scrub vegetables and cut them up as directed in your recipe. Place the pan or wok over high heat. Add the cooking liquid: oil should be too hot to hold your hand over for more than a few seconds; other liquids should be brought to a simmer. Add the vegetables and use a spatula to lift and turn constantly until just softened. If you have a fairly large amount of vegetables, they can be cooked as above and then covered so they complete cooking in their own steam.

Roasting & Deep-frying

Both these methods involve cooking food in fat or oil which adds significantly to your overall fat intake. These are not recommended cooking methods.

TIPS FOR VERSATILE VEGETABLES

- Add variety to your meals by trying different combinations such as:

  - courgette, onion and/or tomato

  - peas and sweetcorn

  - mashed carrot and parsnip (using skim milk to soften)

  - cabbage, apple and leek or onion

  - spinach and red or green pepper or spring onion

  - aubergine, tomato and onion.

- Onions, cabbage and lettuce can be sautéed in stock or low-salt soy or teriyaki sauce.

- Herbs, garlic, onion, tomato juice, wine or even fruit or vegetable juice add flavour.

- Lemon juice can be sprinkled over vegetables such as broccoli or asparagus.

- Sprinkle a few sesame seeds, poppy seeds or chopped nuts on top of vegetables such as carrots, cauliflower or beans.

Stir-fried Vegetables

Serves: 6

½ *Chinese cabbage or small green cabbage*
125 ml (4 fl oz) water
1 stock cube
1 medium white onion, quartered
1 tsp minced fresh ginger
150 g (5 oz) broccoli, broken into florets
1 medium carrot, sliced
90 g (3 oz) mangetout
90 g (3 oz) bean shoots
125 g (4 oz) mushrooms, sliced
1 tbsp soy sauce

Stir-fry is best served with rice or noodles.

Method:

1. *Using Chinese cabbage:* Cut off woody ends of stalks. Cut stalks off leaves and cut the stalks into lengths of about 2.5 cm (1 in). Cut cabbage leaves into shreds, about 5 cm (2 in) long and 1.5 cm (½ in) wide.
   Using green cabbage: Remove woody stem completely and shred leaves, as above.

2. Place wok or frying-pan over high heat. Add water and stock cube and stir to dissolve. Bring to a simmer.

3. Add onion and ginger. Cook for 1 minute. Add cabbage stalks, broccoli, carrots and mangetout. Use a spatula to lift and turn constantly for 2 minutes.

4. Add cabbage leaves, bean shoots and mushrooms. Lift and turn mixture to combine ingredients. Cover wok, lower heat and simmer for 3 minutes.

5. Add soy sauce. Lift and turn vegetables to mix through. Serve immediately.

Nutritional data per serving: 172 kJ (41 cal), Carbohydrate 6 g, Fat 0.1 g, Protein 4 g.

Preparation time: 20 minutes. Cooking equipment: wok or large frying pan.

Caponata

Serves: 4

1 medium aubergine,
   washed and cut into
   small cubes
1 tbsp cooking salt
2 tbsp water
1 medium onion, roughly
   chopped
2 medium red peppers,
   seeded and diced
1 stick of celery, sliced
440 g (14 oz) canned
   tomatoes, chopped
8 black olives, halved and
   pitted
1 clove garlic, crushed
1 tbsp capers
3 tbsp malt vinegar
1 tbsp sugar
ground black pepper

Try Caponata, served hot, as a sauce with pasta.

Method:

1. Sprinkle cubed aubergine with salt. Place in a colander, cover with a plate and weigh down (a pan of water makes a good weight) for 20–30 minutes. This helps remove excess moisture and acidity from the aubergine.

2. Meanwhile, in a large frying pan bring the 2 tbsp of water to a simmer. Add the onion, red pepper and celery, simmer, stirring constantly, for 10 minutes. Set aside.

3. Rinse aubergine under cold running water. Use paper towels to pat completely dry.

4. Add aubergine and tomato to the onion mixture. Return to a medium heat and cook for 8 minutes, stirring occasionally.

5. Add the olives, garlic, capers, vinegar and sugar. Season with black pepper to taste. Simmer gently over medium heat for 15–20 minutes, or until vegetables are tender.

As an accompaniment: This dish can be served hot or chilled. It is an excellent side dish for both meat and fish.

Nutritional data per serving: 59 kJ (14 cal), Carbohydrate 10 g, Fat 1.5 g, Protein 2.5 g.

Preparation time: 1¹/₄ hours. Cooking equipment: colander, large frying-pan and saucepan.

QUICK TIPS: Always keep some frozen, pre-chopped vegetables on hand. Add these to some cold, cooked brown rice, heat, and top with low-fat cheese for a simple but delicious meal.

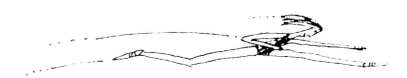

Crunchy Vegetable Loaf

Serves: 6

2 tbsp water

2 medium onions, chopped

2 sticks of celery, chopped

½ green pepper, chopped

2 tsp curry powder

100 g (3½ oz) cooked
  potato, mashed

100 g (3½ oz) cooked
  pumpkin, mashed

250 g (8 oz) ricotta cheese

125 g (4 oz) cashew nuts,
  coarsely ground

45 g (1½ oz) rolled oats

2 tbsp chopped parsley

1 tsp fresh chopped thyme
  or ¼ tsp dried

Topping:

sesame seeds

By cooking the potato and pumpkin in the microwave you can shorten the preparation time for this superb dish.

Method:

1. In a frying pan, heat the water. Add the onions, celery, green capsicum and curry powder. Sauté for 3 minutes.
2. In a bowl, combine the sautéed vegetables with the rest of the ingredients.
3. Line a loaf tin with foil and spray with non-stick baking spray. Sprinkle sesame seeds over base of tin, then shake tin so that seeds adhere to sides as well.
4. Spoon vegetable mixture into the tin and press down firmly. Bake in a preheated oven for 40 minutes.
5. Remove from oven and leave for 5 minutes. Turn on to serving dish and carefully remove foil.
6. Place under the hot grill for 3–5 minutes or until crisp and well browned.

As a main course: Cut the loaf into thick slices, spoon over hot simple curry sauce and serve.

As a light meal or lunch: Serve the loaf cold with a salad of sliced cucumbers in Vinaigrette Dressing (page 181).

Nutritional data per serving: 550 kJ (129 cal), Carbohydrate 14 g, Fat 5 g, Protein 9 g.

Preparation time: 55 minutes. Cooking equipment: frying pan, loaf tin, approximately 20 x 10 cm (8 x 4 in).

Oven temperature: 180°C/350°F/gas 4. Grill temperature: high.

Microwave Method:

Cooking time: pumpkin and potato pre-cooked – 25 minutes.

Prepare all the vegetables as described in Ingredients. Place the onions, celery, green capsicum and curry powder in a shallow dish. Cook on 'High' for 1½ minutes, stir and cook a further 1½ minutes. In a bowl, combine all the ingredients. Spray a microwave-safe ring mould or loaf tin with non-stick baking spray and sprinkle base with sesame seeds. Spoon the loaf mixture into the tin and press down firmly. Microwave on 'High' for 15 minutes. Remove from microwave and allow 5 minutes standing-time before turning out on to a heatproof platter. Place under a hot grill for 3–5 minutes, or until well-browned.

Jacket Potatoes

Serves: 4 as an accompaniment; 2 as a light meal

4 medium-sized potatoes

Surely the best meal-in-one around, baked jacket potatoes with a savoury filling pack a delicious carbohydrate punch.

Method:

1. Wash potatoes well, but do not peel. Prick several times with a fork or skewer. For crispy skin, do not cover. For softer skin, wrap potatoes in foil.

2. Bake the potatoes in a pre-heated oven for 45–60 minutes or until soft when tested with a skewer.

Nutritional data per serving: 301 kJ (72 cal), Carbohydrate 17 g, Fat 0 g, Protein 1 g.

Preparation time: 1 hour 10 minutes. Oven temperature: 180°C/350°F/gas 4.

Fillings for Jacket Potatoes

Sultana & Pecan Nut Filling

Serves: 2

2 tbsp ricotta cheese
2 tsp sultanas
2 spring onions, finely chopped
2 tsp coarsely chopped pecan nuts
ground black pepper
Garnish:
fresh parsley, chopped

Method:

1. Slice off the tops of the baked potatoes. Using a teaspoon, carefully scoop out enough of the potato flesh to leave a firm shell.

2. Combine the potato flesh with the other ingredients. Spoon back into the potato shells.

3. Reheat in a preheated oven for about 5–10 minutes. Serve immediately, garnished with chopped fresh parsley.

Nutritional data per serving: 118 kJ (28 cal), Carbohydrate 8 g, Fat 3 g, Protein 6 g.

Preparation time: 15 minutes. Oven temperature: 180°C/350°F/gas 4.

Tomato & Onion Filling

Serves: 2

1 small onion, finely
    chopped
2 tbsp water
1 medium tomato, chopped
½ tsp fresh chopped basil
    or oregano, or good pinch
    of dried
ground black pepper

Method:

1. Heat the water in a frying pan, add the onion and sauté gently until transparent.
2. Add tomato, fresh or dried herbs and black pepper. Simmer till tender. Set aside.
3. Slice off the tops of the baked potatoes. Using a teaspoon, carefully scoop out enough of the potato flesh to leave a firm shell.
4. Combine the potato flesh with the tomato mixture. Spoon back into the potato shells.
5. Reheat in moderate oven for about 5–10 minutes. Serve immediately.

Nutritional data per serving: 181 kJ (43 cal), Carbohydrate 9 g, Fat 0 g, Protein 2 g.

Cottage Cheese & Chive Filling

Serves: 2

2 tbsp cottage cheese
4 chives, finely snipped

Method:

1. Cut a small, deep cross in the top of each potato. Gently press the sides of the potato to force the cross open.
2. Place 1 tbsp cottage cheese in the opening of each potato. Sprinkle over chives. Serve immediately.

Nutritional data per serving: 130 kJ (31 cal), Carbohydrate 1 g, Fat 1 g, Protein 5 g.

Salmon Filling

Serves: 2

4 tbsp canned salmon
4 chives, finely chopped
2 tbsp low-fat cottage
    cheese

Method:

1. Slice off the tops of the baked potatoes. Using a teaspoon, carefully scoop out enough of the potato flesh to leave a firm shell.
2. Combine the potato flesh with the other ingredients. Spoon back into the potato shells.
3. Reheat in a moderate oven for about 5–10 minutes. Serve immediately.

Nutritional data per serving: 910 kJ (217 cal), Carbohydrate 1 g, Fat 11 g, Protein 29 g.

A small handful of dried fruit and nuts, and two open sandwiches with tasty toppings of ricotta cheese, herbs, tomato and pine nuts. A winning plate of Cream of Pumpkin Soup (page 78), with a dollop of plain, low-fat yoghurt.

Cheesy Mashed Potatoes

Serves: 2

2 medium potatoes

4 tbsp skimmed milk

2 tbsp grated low-fat hard
   cheese

chopped parsley

Method:

1. Boil the potatoes in water until tender. Drain and peel.
2. In a bowl, mash the potatoes and skimmed milk until smooth. Add the grated cheese and parsley and combine well.
3. Serve warm.

Microwave Method:

Cooking time: 6–7 minutes.

Peel and thinly slice the potatoes. Arrange around the edge of a large, shallow dish. Cover with cling film and microwave on 'High' for 6 minutes. Drain the potatoes, add the milk and mash. Return to microwave and reheat on 'High' for 30 seconds–1 minute. Stir in the grated cheese and parsley and serve.

Nutritional data per serving: 546 kJ (130 cal), Carbohydrate 20 g, Fat 4 g, Protein 6 g.

Preparation time: 25 minutes. Cooking equipment: medium-sized saucepan.

Beans Parisienne

Serves: 4

3 tbsp blanched almonds,
   slivered

200 g (7 oz) fresh French
   beans

2 tsp lemon juice

½ clove garlic, crushed

pinch of ground black
   pepper

Method:

1. Dry-fry almonds in a small frying pan over medium heat until golden brown.
2. Top and tail the beans. Add a little water to a large saucepan and bring to a rapid boil. Add the beans and cover saucepan. Return to the boil and cook for 3–5 minutes until tender but still crisp to bite.
3. Drain the beans and return to the saucepan. Reduce heat. Quickly add almonds, lemon juice, garlic and pepper, toss gently with beans to combine well.

As an appetizer: Chill the beans and serve with a tangy dip such as Tzatziki (page 71).

As an entrée: Serve hot or chilled with Vinaigrette Dressing (page 181).

Nutritional data per serving: 213 kJ (51 cal), Carbohydrate 2 g, Fat 4 g, Protein 2 g.

Preparation time: 15 minutes. Cooking equipment: small frying pan, large saucepan.

Mushroom Stroganoff

Serves: 4

2 tbsp water

2 medium onions, sliced

1 red or green pepper,
  seeded and diced

16–20 medium button
  mushrooms, sliced

3 spring onions, chopped

2 tsp paprika

250 ml (8 fl oz) low-fat
  natural yoghurt

Garnish:

parsley, chopped

Method:

1. In a frying pan, bring the water to a simmer and add the onion, red or green capsicum and the mushrooms. Simmer gently for 5 minutes.

2. Add spring onion and paprika and simmer gently, stirring occasionally, for a further 5 minutes.

3. Combine the mushroom mixture and yoghurt. Garnish with parsley. Do not re-heat.

As a light meal: Sprinkle over the garnish of chopped parsley. Serve Mushroom Stroganoff with brown rice or noodles, or use as a topping for jacket potatoes.

As an accompaniment: This is an excellent sauce for grilled meats or fillets of chicken and fish.

To vary: Purée in a blender or food processor and use as a smooth sauce with any of the serving suggestions above.

To store: Keep covered in the refrigerator for up to 3 days.

Nutritional data per serving: 281 kJ (67 cal), Carbohydrate 9 g, Fat 1 g, Protein 6 g.

Preparation time: 15 minutes. Cooking equipment: frying pan.

QUICK TIP: When you cook your evening meal, always cook a bit extra and incorporate this into the next day's eating plan (extra chicken can be used in sandwiches; stir-fry can be reheated, and so on).

Gado Gado

Serves: 6

90 g (3 oz) bean shoots

90 g (3 oz) French beans

315 g (10 oz) broccoli
florets

100 g (3½ oz) carrots, sliced

90 g (3 oz) cabbage, diced

1 medium green pepper,
seeded and sliced

90 g (3 oz) mangetout

2 medium onions, cut into
8 wedges

3 tomatoes, cut into wedges

1 medium-sized cucumber,
peeled and diced

3 hard-boiled eggs, cut into
quarters

Serve Gado Gado as an appetiser or entrée, accompanied by warm Satay (Peanut) Sauce with Chilli (page 177).

Method:

1. Fill a medium-sized saucepan with water and bring to a rapid boil. Plunge the vegetables, dealing with each variety separately, into the boiling water, except the tomatoes and cucumber.

2. Blanch each kind of vegetable in the boiling water for no more than 1 minute, or until the colour intensifies. Quickly place the blanched vegetables in the colander and immediately refresh under cold, running water – this preserves the colour and crispness.

3. Bring the water back to the boil before blanching the next type of vegetable.

4. Arrange all the ingredients on a platter.

Microwave Method:

Cooking time: 3 minutes.

The microwave is a real time-saver for this famous recipe: you can blanch several varieties of vegetable at once and you don't waste time waiting for water to return to the boil.

Prepare the vegetables as described above. Arrange the beans, broccoli (florets facing centre), carrot and green capsicum around the outer edge of a large, shallow dish. Add 1 tbsp of water, cover with cling film and microwave on 'High' for 1–2 minutes, or until vegetables are tender but still crisp and bright. Remove from oven and immediately refresh under cold water. Arrange the bean shoots, cabbage and mangetout in the same way and microwave on 'High' for 30–60 seconds. Refresh. Proceed as from Step 2 of the conventional method above.

To vary: Omit or add vegetables to suit your taste.

To store: Keep covered in the refrigerator and use on the same or next day.

Nutritional data per serving: 571 kJ (136 cal), Carbohydrate 17 g, Fat 3 g, Protein 11 g.

Preparation time: 30 minutes. Cooking equipment: large saucepan and colander.

Cheesy Peppers

Serves: 6

---

6 large, well-shaped red or
   green peppers

5 medium tomatoes or
   440 g (14 oz) canned
   tomatoes

125 g (4 oz) ricotta cheese

125 g (4 oz) low-fat cottage
   cheese

185 g (6 oz) cooked brown
   rice

3 spring onions, chopped

4 tsp fresh chopped basil
   or 1 tsp dried

2 tbsp chopped parsley

ground black pepper

2 egg whites

Serve the capsicum hot, with a grilled fish, meat or poultry.

Method:

1. Cut a shallow slice off the stalk end of each pepper to make 'caps' and set aside. Using a sharp knife, scrape out the seeds and white membrane from the pepper.

2. Two-thirds fill a large saucepan with water and bring to the boil. Add the capsicum and boil for 2 minutes. Remove and drain well. Set aside.

3. *Using fresh tomatoes:* peel and finely chop.
   Using canned tomatoes: drain well and retain juice.

4. Combine the two cheeses, stir in the tomatoes, rice, spring onions, basil, parsley and black pepper.

5. In a clean, dry bowl, whisk the egg whites until stiff. Carefully and lightly, fold into the cheese mixture.

6. Carefully spoon the cheese mixture into the capsicum shells. Cover each filled capsicum with a 'cap'. Stand the capsicum, upright, in a shallow baking tray. Pour 125 ml (4 fl oz) of water into the base of the tray or, if using canned tomatoes, use the reserved juice.

7. Bake in a preheated oven for 35 minutes. Arrange the capsicum on a plate and spoon over the cooking liquids. Serve hot.

Microwave Method:

Cooking time: 8 minutes.

Prepare the green pepper as described in Step 1 of the conventional method. Place the pepper in a 2 litre (3½ pint) casserole and microwave on 'High' for 2–3 minutes. Follow Steps 3–5 of the conventional method. Carefully spoon the filling mixture into the pepper shells and cover each one with its 'cap'. Stand the filled pepper upright in a wide, shallow dish. Pour 125 ml (4 fl oz) of water into the dish. Microwave on 'High' for 3–5 minutes.

To vary: Replace 125 g (4 oz) of the tomatoes with fresh mushrooms and/or courgettes, roughly chopped. Alternatively, add 2 tbsp of pine nuts.

To store: Keep covered in the refrigerator for up to 3 days.

Nutritional data per serving: 445 kJ (106 cal), Carbohydrate 14 g, Fat 2 g, Protein 9 g.

Preparation time: with rice pre-cooked – 60 minutes. Cooking equipment: large saucepan, shallow baking tray.

Oven temperature: 180°C/350°F/gas 4.

Madras Potatoes & Cauliflower

Serves: 6–8

125 ml (4 fl oz) water

3 medium potatoes,
  scrubbed and diced

1 medium cauliflower,
  broken into florets

1 tsp curry powder

2 bay leaves

pinch black pepper

2.5 cm (1 in) fresh ginger,
  peeled and grated

1/2 tsp paprika or chilli
  powder

1/2 tsp turmeric

1 tsp ground coriander

1 tsp ground cumin

250 ml (8 fl oz) boiling
  water

Garnish:

chopped parsley

The flavour of curried food improves with standing; this dish can be prepared 24 hours in advance. Cover and leave in a cool place (not the refrigerator), then reheat before serving.

Method:

1. Add the water to a large saucepan and bring to a simmer. Add the potato and cauliflower and sauté for 5 minutes.

2. Add all the other ingredients, except the 250 ml (8 fl oz) of boiling water. Toss together, over medium heat, for 5 minutes.

3. Add the boiling water, stir. Cover saucepan and bring to the boil. Reduce heat and simmer gently for 15 minutes or until vegetables are tender and have absorbed all liquid.

4. Serve hot, garnished with parsley. Accompany with boiled brown rice.

Nutritional data per serving: 168 kJ (40 cal), Carbohydrate 8 g, Fat 0 g, Protein 2 g.

Preparation time: 30 minutes. Cooking equipment: large saucepan.

QUICK TIP: Use low-fat yoghurt instead of soured cream on jacket potatoes, and with tacos and curries.

Curried Brussels Sprouts

Serves: 4

315 g (10 oz) Brussels
   sprouts, trimmed
1 tsp butter or margarine
4 spring onions, chopped
1 stick of celery, finely
   chopped
1 level tsp curry powder

Garnish:
   toasted almond slivers or
   sesame seeds

Leftovers from this dish, combined with other vegetables, make great Bubble & Squeak (page 151).

Method:

1. Add 2.5 cm (1 in) water to a large saucepan and bring to the boil. Add the Brussels sprouts, cover saucepan and boil rapidly for 5–7 minutes, or until cooked, but still crunchy. Drain and set aside.
2. Dry the saucepan, return to medium-high heat. Add butter or margarine and melt.
3. Add spring onions and celery and sauté for 2 minutes.
4. Add curry powder and cook and sauté for 2 minutes.
5. Add Brussels sprouts to the saucepan and toss while reheating to combine all ingredients.

Microwave Method:

Cooking time: 5 minutes.

The microwave enhances the colour of Brussels sprouts, while retaining their shape, texture and nutritional value.

Prepare the sprouts as described above and arrange them around the edge of a shallow dish. Add 1 tbsp of water, cover with cling film and microwave on 'High' for 3 minutes. Remove from oven, drain in a colander and set aside. Put the butter or margarine in the dish and melt in the microwave on 'High' for 30 seconds. Add remaining ingredients, except the sprouts, stir and microwave on 'High' for 1–2 minutes. Add Brussels sprouts and stir. Reheat in the microwave on 'Medium' for 30–60 seconds.

To store: Best freshly prepared, but leftovers will keep, covered in the refrigerator, for up to 3 days.

Nutritional data per serving: 101 kJ (24 cal), Carbohydrate 1.5 g, Fat 1 g, Protein 2 g.

Preparation time: 15 minutes. Cooking equipment: large saucepan.

Cabbage Medley

Serves: 6

125 ml (4 fl oz) water

1 chicken stock cube, crumbled

1 level tsp curry powder

1 large onion, finely chopped

90 g (3 oz) French beans, topped and tailed

juice of 1 lemon

250 g (8 oz) cabbage, finely shredded

Method:

1. Add the water to a large frying pan and heat. Add crumbled stock cube, curry powder and onion. Simmer gently until onion softens.
2. Add beans, cover pan, simmer gently for 5 minutes.
3. Add lemon juice and cabbage. Cover pan and simmer gently, over medium heat, for a further 10 minutes, stirring frequently.
4. Serve hot, as a main dish or accompaniment.

Microwave Method:

Cooking time: 13 minutes.

Place the water, crumbled stock cube, curry powder and chopped onion in a large, shallow dish. Stir and microwave on 'High' for 2 minutes. Add the beans, stir and microwave on 'High' for 3–4 minutes. Add the lemon juice and cabbage and microwave on 'High' for 5–7 minutes, stirring once during cooking.

Nutritional data per serving: 282 kJ (67 cal), Carbohydrate 11 g, Fat 0.3 g, Protein 6 g.

Preparation time: 25 minutes. Cooking equipment: large frying-pan with lid.

QUICK TIPS: Try these quick vegetable-based meal ideas.

- Steam or bake whole potatoes in their jackets. Serve topped or filled with low-fat ricotta cheese mixed with chopped parsley, chopped onion and a sprinkle of pepper and parmesan cheese.
- Cut up a butternut squash and bake in a moderate oven until tender with 1 tbsp of clear honey and 1 tbsp of sesame seeds.
- Corn-on-the-cob takes only minutes to cook in the microwave or on the stove. Sprinkle with lemon juice and black pepper for a delicious high-carbohydrate snack.
- Mix together a small can of red kidney beans, some sliced spring onion and red pepper, low-fat plain yoghurt and a touch of garlic.

Sweet & Sour Cabbage

Serves: 6

½ small red cabbage

1 green apple, peeled and
 finely sliced

1 medium onion, finely
 chopped

90 g (3 oz) canned
 unsweetened pineapple
 pieces, drained and juice
 reserved

2 tbsp pineapple juice
 (from reserved quantity)

2 tbsp white vinegar

ground black pepper

This is an ideal dish to serve hot with grilled pork cutlets or other pork dishes. Try replacing the vinegar with finely grated rind and juice of an orange.

Method:

1. Remove and discard central stalk of cabbage. Finely slice the leaves.
2. Add 1 cm (½ in) of water to a large frying-pan and bring to a gentle simmer. Add cabbage, apple and onion and sauté for 3 minutes.
3. Add pineapple pieces, the 2 tbsp reserved pineapple juice, vinegar and pepper. Lift and turn mixture to combine well. Simmer a further 12 minutes, stirring occasionally.

To store: Best used freshly prepared. Can be kept, covered, in the refrigerator for up to 3 days.

Nutritional data per serving: 141 kJ (51 cal), Carbohydrate 12 g, Fat 0 g, Protein 1.25 g.

Preparation time: 25 minutes. Cooking equipment: large frying pan.

Classic Potato Bake

Serves: 4

---

4 medium potatoes,
  scrubbed clean
1 small onion, finely sliced
500 ml (16 fl oz) skimmed
  milk
2 tbsp low-fat yoghurt
good pinch of dry mustard
ground black pepper
2 hard-boiled eggs
1 tbsp parsley, chopped

You can serve this dish hot or cold.

Method:

1. Slice potatoes, without peeling, into 1 cm (½ in) slices. In a casserole, arrange the slices in overlapping layers. Scatter over the sliced onion.
2. Combine the milk, yoghurt, mustard and black pepper. Pour over the potato.
3. Cover and bake in a preheated oven for 30 minutes, or until the potato is tender.
4. Slice the hard-boiled eggs and arrange on top of the potato. Sprinkle with parsley before serving.

To vary: Sprinkle ½ tsp caraway seeds over the potato at Step 2.

Nutritional data per serving: 688 kJ (164 cal), Carbohydrate 25 g, Fat 0.3 g, Protein 9 g.

Preparation time: 40 minutes. Cooking equipment: casserole with lid 1.75 litre (3 pint) capacity.
Oven temperature: 180°C/350°F/gas 4.

Tomato & Onion Bake

Serves: 4

---

2 large tomatoes, sliced
1 large white onion, finely
  sliced
pinch of mixed dried herbs
ground black pepper
2 tbsp water
4 tbsp fresh breadcrumbs

Serve hot with grilled fish, meat or chicken.

Method:

1. Arrange tomatoes and onions in layers in a small casserole. Sprinkle herbs and pepper between each layer. Finish with a layer of tomato.
2. Sprinkle the water over the vegetables, then sprinkle over the breadcrumbs and bake in a preheated oven for 30 minutes.

As an entrée or light meal: Serve hot with fresh brown bread or Jacket Potatoes (page 91).

Nutritional data per serving: 255 kJ (61 cal), Carbohydrate 13 g, Fat 0 g, Protein 3 g.

Preparation time: 35 minutes. Cooking equipment: small casserole.
Oven temperature: 190°C/375°F/gas 5.

FISH & SEAFOOD

All fish and seafood are excellent sources of protein, vitamins and minerals. Although fish has a lower fat content than meat, and therefore has lower energy value, the type of fat found in fish is thought to protect you against heart disease.

You should include fish and seafood in your diet and it's worth learning how to prepare it properly. The most important hint to cooking fish well is to remember that a fillet of fish is not a lamb chop! It cooks far more quickly than meat and becomes dry and coarse-tasting when over-cooked. Fish is perfectly cooked the moment a fork will easily flake the flesh. Don't give fish 'just a moment more' or you could ruin it.

As for seafood, as soon as the flesh whitens and becomes opaque, it is ready.

Many people have a resistance to handling whole fish, so it is a good idea to get the fishmonger to scale and gut it for you. However, many of the popular varieties of fish can be bought filleted (without bones) and ready for you to transform into a delectable meal.

HOW TO CHOOSE & COOK FISH

Baking

Baked fish is easy to cook and lends itself to a variety of flavourings. As fish is more delicate than meat, take special care not to over-cook baked fish or it will become hard and dry.

Choose: Medium-sized, whole fish with firm flesh (e.g. mullet, trout or herring). Fillets or cutlets of cod, halibut, haddock and similar-textured fish, are also good for baking.

Basic method: Season the fish with herbs, garlic, lemon juice or black pepper, according to your taste. Place in a lightly greased shallow casserole. If you like, add finely sliced onion, a bay leaf and herbs. Pour in about 125–250 ml (4–8 fl oz) of liquid (depending on the amount of fish); low-fat milk or a mixture of low-fat milk and water is ideal. Bake, covered, in the oven at 180°C/350°F/gas 4 for 15–20 minutes, depending on the size of the fish. Baste the fish a few times with the cooking liquid while it is cooking. The fish is done if it flakes easily when separated with a fork.

Note: A good way to keep baked fish moist is to wrap it in foil. Try Fish in Foil (pages 106–7).

Shallow-frying & Deep-frying

This means cooking in hot oil or fat. Most foods will absorb a significant amount of oil when fried, so we do not recommend this cooking method for the serious athlete.

Grilling or Barbecuing

This is a dry-heat cooking method. Take special care not to over-cook grilled fish as it will become hard and dry. Frequent basting with marinade helps prevent this.

Choose: Small whole fish, such as sardine, whiting, or mackerel. Also excellent are fillets, cutlets or steaks of tuna, cod, plaice or sole.

Basic method: Using whole fish, score the skin diagonally across the sides in a few places. Season fish to taste – lemon juice, ginger, soy sauce, herbs and black pepper are good flavourings. If you like, brush with a marinade. Arrange fish 10–12 cm (4–5 in) below the preheated grill or, if barbecuing, 30 cm (12 in) above glowing coals. Grill fish slowly, turning once during cooking. Baste frequently with marinade or lemon juice.

Allow: 8–10 minutes for fish fillets, cutlets or kebabs; 10–15 minutes for small, whole fish; 30–35 minutes for whole large fish.

Poaching

The fish is gently simmered in a little liquid in the oven or on the hob.

Choose: For a special event, poach a whole, medium-sized fish, such as sea trout or a small salmon. Fillets or cutlets, such as haddock, plaice or cod are also good choices.

Basic method: Place the fish in a shallow saucepan or casserole. Add sufficient cold liquid – water, tomato juice, fish stock or a mixture of milk and stock – to barely cover the fish. Season with black pepper and herbs such as thyme or oregano. If desired, add a bay leaf and sliced onion or celery to the poaching liquid. Cover and bring to a gentle simmer – do not boil.

Allow: 5–8 minutes for thin fillets, such as whiting; 10 minutes for thicker pieces; 30–35 minutes for whole fish. Remove cooked fish from the saucepan and use the cooking liquids as the basis for a sauce.

Steaming

Fish cooked in the steam rising off boiling water.

Look for: Small, whole fish, such as trout. For fillets or cutlets, try plaice or sole.

Basic method: Season fish with lemon juice, herbs and black pepper. Fill the bottom half of a steamer with boiling water. Place the fish on a steamer tier. If you like, you can arrange thin rings of onion or finely chopped celery or carrot on top of the fish. Cover with a tight-fitting lid. Steam over rapidly boiling water for 10–15 minutes or until a fork easily flakes the fish – do not over-cook.

QUICK TIP: Buy fresh fish fillets in bulk from the market and freeze individual portions.

Whole Fish in Ginger

Serves: 4

1 kg (2 lb) whole fish,
   scaled and gutted
2 tsp finely chopped or
   grated, fresh ginger
1 clove garlic, crushed
4 tbsp soy sauce
juice of 1 lemon
185 ml (6 fl oz) dry white
   wine
2 tsp raw sugar
Garnish:
thin slices of lemon

Method:

1. Using a very sharp knife, score the skin of the fish, 3 or 4 times, at equal intervals, on each side, at an angle to the backbone. Place fish in a baking dish.
2. Combine remaining ingredients to make a marinade, and pour over the fish.
3. Bake the fish, uncovered, in a preheated oven for 30 minutes, or until fish is tender. Baste frequently with the marinade during cooking.
4. Serve the fish whole, with brown rice and a green salad, garnished with lemon slices.

Nutritional data per serving: 1,184 kJ (283 cal), Carbohydrate 5 g, Fat 6 g, Protein 46 g.

Preparation time: 40 minutes. Cooking equipment: baking dish.
Oven temperature: 180°C/350°/gas 4.

Sweetcorn & Salmon Rissoles

Makes: 8

4 tbsp dry wholemeal
   breadcrumbs
185 g (6 oz) cooked brown
   rice
125 g (4 oz) canned salmon
220 g (7 oz) canned
   sweetcorn kernels
1 egg, lightly beaten
ground black pepper
1 tbsp finely chopped
   parsley

Serve the rissoles hot or cold with rice and Classic Tomato Sauce (page 176) or Sweet & Sour Sauce (page 175).

Method:

1. Spread out the breadcrumbs on a plate or board.
2. In a bowl, combine the rice, salmon, sweetcorn, egg, pepper and parsley. With wet hands, shape mixture into 8 rissoles.
3. Roll the rissoles in the breadcrumbs, pressing them in firmly, so the crumbs stick.
4. Lightly grease a baking tray. Place the rissoles on the tray. Bake in a pre-heated oven for 15 minutes. Turn rissoles over and bake a further 15 minutes.

To store: Store, covered, in the refrigerator for up to 2 days.

Nutritional data per rissole: 381 kJ (91 cal), Carbohydrate 11 g, Fat 3 g, Protein 4 g.
Preparation time: with rice pre-cooked – 40 minutes. Cooking equipment: baking tray.
Oven temperature: 180°C/350°F/gas 4.

FISH IN FOIL

Fish wrapped in foil before cooking will keep beautifully moist and absorb the taste of any herbs and flavourings cooked with it. This is an excellent way to prepare fish for the barbecue but is just as good when baked in the oven. The following are two methods for Fish in Foil; both recipes are worth the small effort to prepare them.

Piquant Fish in Foil

Serves: 2

2 large fillets of fish (e.g. cod or haddock)

1 tsp finely chopped, fresh tarragon or a good pinch of dried

2 tsp very finely chopped parsley (optional)

ground black pepper

1 small onion, thinly sliced

1 lemon, thinly sliced

juice of 1 lemon

1 tbsp dry white wine (optional)

Method:

1. Cut 2 pieces of foil big enough to enclose the fish fillets comfortably. Spray foil well with non-stick cooking spray.

2. Place the fish fillets on the pieces of foil. Sprinkle each fillet with the herbs and black pepper. Arrange several onion rings and 1 or 2 slices of lemon on each fillet.

3. Mix lemon juice and white wine, if using, pour over the fish.

4. Wrap each fillet securely in foil, sealing along the tops, so that the juices aren't lost during cooking or when the foil parcels are opened.

5. Place the foil parcels, sealed side up, on a baking tray. Bake in a preheated oven *or* over glowing barbecue coals, for 30 minutes.

6. Open foil along the sealing edge and serve immediately. Baked jacket potatoes and a crisp salad

Microwave method:

Cooking time: 6–10 minutes.

Using the microwave you cannot, of course, cook the fish in foil – however, you can achieve results very quickly. Place the fish fillets in a shallow dish. Sprinkle over herbs and black pepper. Arrange onion rings on top of the fish. Top each fillet with 1 or 2 slices of lemon. Mix the lemon juice and white wine and pour over fish. Cover the dish with cling film or a lid. Microwave on 'High' for 6–8 minutes, or until a fork easily flakes the fish.

Nutritional data per serving: 535 kJ (128 cal), Carbohydrate 1 g, Fat 3 g, Protein 23 g.

Preparation time: 30–40 minutes. Cooking equipment: baking tray, foil.

Oven temperature: 180°C/350°F/gas 4.

Leaf-wrapped Fish in Foil

Serves: 4

4 large or 8 smaller leaves
  of spinach or lettuce
4 fillets of white fish
  (e.g. plaice or cod) or 4
  small, whole fish (e.g.
  trout), scaled and
  cleaned, but left whole
ground black pepper
1 lemon, thinly sliced

This impressive-looking dish is simple to prepare and excellent to cook on the barbecue. Wrapping fish in leaves keeps it moist, adds to the flavour and looks very attractive.

Method:

1. Place the washed leaves in a bowl. Pour over boiling water to cover and leave to soften for 3 minutes. Drain leaves and allow to cool.
2. Place each piece of fish on a large leaf, or on 2 smaller leaves placed side by side.
3. Sprinkle over black pepper. Arrange 2–3 slices of lemon on top of each piece of fish.
4. Wrap each piece of fish in leaves; if necessary, use small wooden skewers to hold in place.
5. Wrap each fillet securely in foil, sealing along the top so juices are not lost during cooking, or when the foil parcels arc opened.
6. Place the fish on a baking sheet and bake in a preheated oven, or barbecue over glowing coals. For fish fillets, 20 minutes; for whole fish, 30 minutes.
7. Open foil along the sealing edge and serve immediately. Fresh, wholemeal bread and a salad of steamed fresh vegetables make fine accompaniments.

Microwave Method:

Cooking time: Using 3 large fillets – 6–8 minutes.

Using the microwave you cannot, of course, cook the fish in an outer wrapping of foil. However, this dish is attractive when wrapped only in the leaves and cooked in a casserole; the microwave enhances the green of the leaves. Prepare the leaves as in Step 2 of the Method above. Place each fish fillet on a single leaf large enough to enclose it completely. Sprinkle the fish with black pepper and arrange 2–3 slices of lemon on top of each fillet. Wrap leaves securely around the fish. Cover each parcel with cling film. Place on a plate, microwave on 'High' for 6 minutes if fillets are fairly thin, or 8 minutes if thick.

Nutritional data per serving: 631 kJ (151 cal), Carbohydrate 0.75 g, Fat 4 g, Protein 29 g.

Preparation time: 40 minutes. Cooking equipment: baking sheet, foil.

Oven temperature: 180°C/350°F/gas 4.

SWEET & SOUR FISH

These three, simple but delicious, fish recipes all gain character from the Sweet & Sour Sauce (page 175).

Grilled Fish in Sweet & Sour Sauce

Serves: 4

750 g (1 lb 8 oz) fish fillets
1 recipe Sweet & Sour
* Sauce (page 175)*

Method:

1. Grill fish fillets as described in Grilling (page 104).
2. Meanwhile, heat the Sweet & Sour Sauce.
3. Place fish on a serving platter and pour over the heated sauce. Serve with boiled brown rice.

Nutritional data per serving: 855 kJ (204 cal), Carbohydrate 4 g, Fat 4 g, Protein 36 g.

Preparation time: 15 minutes. Cooking equipment: barbecue or grill.

Simmered Sweet & Sour Fish

Serves: 4

750 g (1 lb 8 oz) fish fillets
1 recipe Sweet & Sour
* Sauce (page 175)*

Method:

1. Cut the fish fillets into neat strips or bite-sized pieces.
2. Pour the Sweet & Sour Sauce into a deep frying pan or saucepan.
3. Bring mixture to a gentle simmer. Add the fish and continue simmering gently, spooning over sauce occasionally, until a fork easily flakes the fish (a further 5 minutes). Try not to move the fish around too much or it may fall apart.
4. Serve hot on a bed of boiled brown rice.

Nutritional data per serving: 855 kJ (204 cal), Carbohydrate 4 g, Fat 4 g, Protein 36 g.

Preparation time: 10 minutes. Cooking equipment: deep frying pan or saucepan.

Sweet & Sour Tuna

Serves: 4

440 g (14 oz) canned tuna,
   well drained
1 recipe Sweet & Sour
   Sauce (page 175)

Method:

1.   Pour the Sweet & Sour Sauce into a saucepan. Add the drained tuna.
2.   Over medium heat, gently stir mixture to break fish into bite-sized pieces – take care not to let it disintegrate.
3.   Serve hot with an accompaniment of boiled brown rice or, as a snack, heaped on to wholemeal toast.

Nutritional data per serving: 617 kJ (148 cal), Carbohydrate 4 g, Fat 3 g, Protein 26 g.

Preparation time: 5 minutes. Cooking equipment: saucepan.

Baked Fish Somerset

Serves: 4

3 slices wholemeal bread
2 large fish fillets
   (500 g/1 lb total weight,
   e.g. haddock or cod)
2 spring onions, chopped
large pinch dried mixed
   herbs
ground black pepper
rind of ½ lemon, finely
   grated
2 eggs
500 ml (16 fl oz) skimmed
   milk
juice of 1 lemon

Method:

1.   Arrange the slices of bread on the bottom of a casserole.
2.   Arrange the fish fillets on top of the bread.
3.   Sprinkle over the chopped spring onions, mixed herbs, pepper and lemon rind.
4.   Beat the eggs and milk together. Add the lemon juice and stir. Pour over the fish.
5.   Place the casserole dish in a large, ovenproof dish. Carefully pour water into the larger dish, to reach two-thirds up the outside of the casserole.
6.   Bake in a preheated oven for 45 minutes, or until the egg mixture has set and a fork easily flakes the fish.
7.   Serve hot, accompanied by a crisp green salad with a tangy dressing.

To store: Cover and store in the refrigerator for not more than a day.

Nutritional data per serving: 912 kJ (218 cal), Carbohydrate 11 g, Fat 6 g, Protein 30 g.

Preparation time: 55 minutes. Cooking equipment: casserole, ovenproof dish.

Oven temperature: 160°C/325°F/gas 3.

Fish & Rice Ratatouille

Serves: 2

280 g (9 oz) cooked rice

2 large fish fillets or cutlets
    (e.g. cod or halibut)

1 small green pepper,
    seeded and diced

2 small courgettes, diced

2 medium tomatoes, diced

6 large mushrooms, diced

1 small aubergine, diced

1 clove garlic, finely
    chopped

½ tsp dried mixed herbs

ground black pepper

juice of 1 lemon

This delicious dish can be served hot or cold.

Method:

1. Spread the cooked rice over the bottom of a casserole.
2. Arrange fish on top of the rice.
3. Combine all remaining ingredients, spoon over fish.
4. Cover casserole dish with a lid or foil. Bake in a preheated oven for 30 minutes.

Microwave Method:

Cooking time: with rice pre-cooked – 10 minutes.

Prepare foods as described in Ingredients. Pre-cook the diced eggplant: place in a shallow dish, add 1 tbsp of water and cover dish with cling film. Microwave on 'High' for 2 minutes. Remove from oven and set aside.

Spoon the cooked rice into a casserole forming an even layer. Arrange the fish fillets or cutlets on top. Mix the remaining ingredients, including the eggplant, and spoon over the fish. Cover casserole with a lid or cling film and microwave on 'High' for 6–8 minutes, or until fish flakes easily. Leave dish covered and allow 2 minutes standing time before serving.

To cook rice in the microwave. Place 150 g (5 oz) rice in a shallow dish. Add 440 ml (14 fl oz) boiling water and ½ tsp oil. Cover dish with cling film and microwave on 'Medium' for 6 minutes, and then on 'High' for 3 minutes. Stand for 2 minutes, then drain and rinse.

To vary: Instead of the fish, use 2 chicken breasts or veal cutlets. Omit the rice, but prepare and cook the dish as above. Two jacket potatoes can be baked while the fish is cooking.

Nutritional data per serving: 1,862 kJ (445 cal), Carbohydrate 46 g, Fat 7 g, Protein 52 g.

Preparation time: with rice pre-cooked – 30–40 minutes. Cooking equipment: casserole with lid or foil to cover.

Oven temperature: 180°C/350°F/gas 4.

High-octane carbohydrate: Classic Tomato Sauce (page 176) (front left), superb colour and texture in Spinach Fettuccine (page 148) (back left) and in Silver & Jade Salad (page 164) (back right). Vegetable Lasagne (page 149) (front right).

Salmon, Potato & Rice Bake

Serves: 4

440 g (14 oz) canned
    salmon, drained

375 g (12 oz) cooked brown
    rice

3 large potatoes, peeled and
    thinly sliced

440 g (14 oz) canned
    tomatoes, chopped (juice
    retained)

2 sticks of celery, chopped

1 large green pepper, seeded
    and chopped

2 Granny Smith apples,
    grated

15 g (½ oz) parsley, finely
    chopped

1 carrot, grated

This is a carbohydrate-rich recipe that is delicious hot, and then served as a cold leftover for the next day's lunch or supper. The vegetables and salmon make it a nutritious meal-in-one.

Method:

1. In a bowl, combine the salmon and rice.
2. Arrange the sliced potato in the bottom of the casserole. Spoon over the rice and salmon mixture.
3. Cover with layers of the remaining ingredients.
4. Bake in a preheated oven for 30–40 minutes.
5. Serve hot or cold.

Microwave Method:

Cooking time: with rice pre-cooked – 15 minutes.

Peel and thinly slice the potatoes. Arrange the slices in a shallow casserole. Pour over 125 ml (4 fl oz) of water. Cover with cling film and microwave on 'High' for 2½ minutes. Move outer slices to the centre of the dish and microwave a further 2½ minutes. Remove from oven. Drain tomatoes and discard juice. Mix cooked rice and salmon and spoon over potatoes. Cover with layers of the remaining ingredients. Cover with cling film and microwave on 'High' for 9–10 minutes. Allow 3 minutes standing-time before serving.

Note: You could par-boil the uncooked rice, using the conventional method, while the potatoes are in the microwave. The rice will then complete cooking once it is incorporated into the dish, as above.

Nutritional data per serving: 1,568 kJ (375 cal), Carbohydrate 48 g, Fat 10 g, Protein 27 g.

Preparation time: with rice pre-cooked – 40 minutes. Cooking equipment: casserole.

Oven temperature: 180°C/350°F/gas 4.

Scallops Capricorn

Serves: 4

750 g (1 lb 8 oz) scallops

220 g (7 oz) canned
   pineapple pieces (juice
   reserved)

125 g (4 oz) mushrooms,
   chopped

2.5 cm (1 in) knob of fresh
   ginger, thinly sliced

2 tbsp soy sauce

½ green pepper, seeded and
   chopped

Take care not to over-cook the scallops or they will be dry and tasteless.

Method:

1. Spray frying pan with non-stick cooking spray.
2. Heat the pan till very hot but not smoking. Stir-fry the scallops quickly, in two batches, about 3 minutes for each batch. Set aside on a plate.
3. Add the pineapple and its juice, mushrooms, ginger and soy sauce. Simmer gently until cooking liquids have almost evaporated.
4. Add the capsicum and simmer a further 5 minutes.
5. Add scallops, stir to combine and heat through. Serve immediately, accompanied by boiled brown rice.

Nutritional data per serving: 1,041 kJ (249 cal), Carbohydrate 5 g, Fat 5 g, Protein 45 g.

Preparation time: 20 minutes. Cooking equipment: large frying pan.

Baked Whiting

Serves: 4

4 fillets (approximately
   750 g/1 lb 8 oz) whiting
   (or other firm-fleshed,
   white fish)

1 tbsp lemon juice

250 ml (8 fl oz) skimmed
   milk

ground black pepper

good pinch of dried
   oregano

6 spring onions, finely
   chopped

The delicate taste of whiting is best appreciated when there are few strong competing flavours.

Method:

1. Rub fish with lemon juice. Place in a shallow casserole. Pour over skimmed milk.
2. Season with black pepper and oregano. Sprinkle over the spring onion. Cover with a lid, or foil. Bake in a preheated oven for 20 minutes.

Nutritional data per serving: 833 kJ (199 cal), Carbohydrate 4 g, Fat 4 g, Protein 36 g.

Preparation time: 20 minutes. Cooking equipment: casserole with lid. Oven temperature: 180°/350°F/gas 4.

Tuna & Mushrooms

Serves: 4

2 tbsp water

1 large onion, chopped

470 g (15 oz) canned tuna
   in brine, drained

8 large mushrooms, sliced

½ tsp chopped fresh
   oregano or good pinch of
   dried

200 ml (7 fl oz) low-fat
   natural yoghurt

2 tbsp tomato paste

1 tbsp finely chopped
   parsley

Substitute pieces of cooked chicken for the tuna.

Method:

1. Heat the oil in a frying pan. Add the onion and sauté gently until transparent.
2. Add tuna and stir until heated through. Add mushrooms and oregano and stir for 1 minute.
3. Add yoghurt and tomato paste. Stir over gentle heat – do not boil. Remove from the heat. Stir in chopped parsley. Spoon hot on to a bed of cooked pasta, such as fettuccine or spaghetti.

Nutritional data per serving: 733 kJ (175 cal), Carbohydrate 7 g, Fat 3 g, Protein 30 g.

Preparation time: 10 minutes. Cooking equipment: large frying pan.

Mixed Seafood Crêpes

Serves: 4
(allow 2 crêpes/
pancakes per serving)

250 g (8 oz) mixed seafood,
   cooked

1 recipe Low-fat Cheese
   Sauce (page 179)

juice and rind of 1 lemon

8 crêpes or pancakes
   (pages 159–60)

Garnish:

lemon wedges

parsley

A ready-made combination of cooked seafood is often available from fishmongers and supermarkets. Mixed seafood also comes ready to use in cans.

Method:

1. Combine all filling ingredients.
2. Fill and roll up the crêpes or pancakes. Place filled crêpes/pancakes, side-by-side, in the baking dish.
3. Bake in a preheated oven for 20 minutes.
4. Serve immediately, garnished with lemon wedges and parsley, if liked.

Nutritional data per serving: 835 kJ (200 cal), Carbohydrate 5 g, Fat 8 g, Protein 28 g.

Preparation time: with seafood, crêpes/pancakes and cheese sauce pre-prepared – 25 minutes.

Cooking equipment: baking dish. Oven temperature: 180°C/350°F/gas 4.

MEAT, POULTRY & GAME

MEAT

Meat is a major source of vital nutrients for athletes, especially protein, Vitamin B, iron and zinc. It can also be high in fat, which is why red meat has been less popular in the last few years. Today, however, meat is bred to be leaner. Through wise shopping and careful cooking you can, in fact, enjoy the many nutritional benefits of meat without adding significantly to your fat intake.

Fat content varies greatly between the different cuts and types of red meat; it can be as little as 7% or as much as 80% of the energy value of meat. The fat on meat is usually easy to see as a solid band around the edge (think of a rump steak), or as threads of fat spread throughout the muscle, called marbling.

- As a general rule, choose the leaner cuts and trim away all visible fat from meat, rather than omitting this important food from your diet.

- Avoid cooking methods that require adding fat to meat, such as frying or roasting with extra oil.

POULTRY

All poultry is an excellent protein food for athletes. In our recipes we have limited the choice of poultry to chicken and turkey as these tend to carry less fat than birds such as duck or goose. Most poultry is very versatile and lends itself to just about any cooking method, from barbecuing to mincing, or baking in the oven.

In general, choose the white meat of poultry, especially breast, as this tends to be less fatty than darker cuts. But remember that the darker meat contains useful iron, so use your discretion. Also, avoid eating the skin of poultry as there is a layer of fat directly beneath it. Suppliers, aware of people's need for a low-fat diet, now sell ready-skinned chicken breasts.

GAME

Because of the animals' diet, game meats tend to be low in fat and to have a distinctive flavour, making them an excellent source of protein for athletes and adding variety to your diet.

Commonly eaten varieties of game are rabbit, hare, venison (deer), pheasant and partridge. Some types of game are not available all year round, but it is usually easy to find rabbit at a reasonable price. Rabbit is very lean, containing less than 2% fat, so is ideal for athletes.

Because of their low fat content, rabbit and other game can become dry while cooking. As a result, it is usually best to use a slow, moist cooking method, such as stewing. Game should be prepared using the minimum amount of added fat (butter, oil or cream).

Note about rabbit: When preparing rabbit, cut it into pieces and soak for about half an hour in cold water to which a teaspoon of vinegar or lemon juice has been added. This whitens the flesh, making it more attractive, and softens the 'gamey' flavour of this delicious meat. After soaking, drain the meat well and pat dry.

STORING MEAT

Short-term

Cover fresh meat with cling film and store in the refrigerator for a maximum of 2 days.

Long-term

Meat, including game and poultry, keeps well when frozen. As soon as possible after purchase, place the meat in freezer bags and remove air before sealing; this prevents freezer burn. Pack the meat flat in the freezer and freeze at –18°C (0°F) or below. In this way, meat will keep for 6–12 months, depending on the temperature of your freezer.

Thaw frozen meat slowly. You should place it in the refrigerator for at least 24 hours before it is needed. Larger cuts may need more time. **Never re-freeze meat once it has been thawed.**

HOW TO CHOOSE & COOK MEAT

The parts of the beast that have had the least exercise are usually best in flavour and texture, such as the loin and rump, which are taken from the area around the backbone. Even though these cuts tend to be more expensive, they take less time to cook, so you save on energy costs.

Cuts taken from the limbs and neck tend to be tougher and require a longer cooking period. For this reason, these cuts are usually cooked in liquid, as stews or casseroles. They are usually less expensive to buy and can be very tasty if properly prepared.

Boiling

There are several classic meat dishes which are boiled, for instance corned beef and bollito misto (Italian mixed boiled meats). Corned meats tend to contain a lot of salt, so you need to watch your consumption of these.

Meats boiled with water and vegetables will give you stock (see Basic Meat Stock, page 77) which has many uses in cooking and can even be drunk by itself as a hot beverage.

Grilling or Barbecuing

Quick cooking with dry (radiant) heat. Use an electric or gas grill, hot barbecue coals or a charcoal grill.

You would usually reserve grilling for small cuts of tender, best-quality meat. Meat is often marinated before grilling and then basted with marinade to keep it moist while cooking.

Choose

Beef: Good cuts would include fillet, rump, porterhouse, entrecote, sirloin and T-bone steaks.

Lamb: For grilling, try lean chops or fillets.

Pork: Today, many cuts of pork are trimmed of fat and make an ideal choice for grilling and baking. Try butterfly steaks or fillets of pork. You can also use cuts from the rib and loin.

Grilling times

Steak (2.5 cm/1 in thick)

Rare: Sear (seal) the meat and grill 3–4 minutes on each side.
Well-done: Sear (seal) the meat and grill 5 minutes each side.

Chop (approximately 2.5 cm/1 in thick)

Rare: Sear (seal) the meat and grill 3–4 minutes on each side.
Well-done: Sear (seal) the meat and grill 4–5 minutes each side.

Roasting (Baking)

Meat may be roasted in the oven under dry (radiant) heat. You may roast in a roasting pan, or in a cooking bag or wrapped in foil, which helps keep the meat moist as it cooks.

Usually only the best and most tender cuts of meat are roasted. As a cooking method, roasting develops the flavour and softens the inside of meats, while browning the outside.

Choose

Beef: Many people prefer roasts cut from the hindquarter of the beast, where the meat is fine in texture, but also tends to be expensive. Whole fillet, rump or sirloin are all excellent for roasting. The forequarter of the beast does provide some good cuts for roasting, although the meat is usually less fine. Try blade or rib.

Lamb: Leg of lamb is probably the best known cut for roasting, but you can also roast shoulder or neck. A de-boned shoulder of lamb, stuffed and then rolled, also makes a delicious family roast. For a special occasion, try using a whole 'rack' of rib loin chops (where the chops have not been separated) to make a 'crown roast'.

Pork: Cuts most often used for roasting include those from the loin, rump and leg.

Basic Roasting Method (Slow Roasting)

1. Clean meat with a damp cloth and trim away all visible fat. Weigh meat to estimate cooking time (see 'Roasting Times').

2. If needed, tie or skewer meat into shape. De-boned cuts can be filled, rolled and trussed.

3. Season meat as desired. Grease the base of a deep, heavy, oven-proof dish or roasting-pan.

4. For every 2 kg (4 lb) of meat, add 4–5 tbsp of stock, fruit juice or tomato juice to the pan.

5. Cover roasting pan with a lid or foil. Roast in a preheated oven at 190°C/375°F/gas 5.

6. For a well-browned roast, remove lid or foil for the last 15 minutes of roasting time.

7. Allow roasted meats to 'rest' for 10 minutes before carving.

Fast Roasting

This method requires a moderately hot oven (190–200°C/375–400°F/gas 5–6). It is recommended for only the best cuts of meat, such as fillet or rump. Prepare and cook the meat as for 'Basic Roasting Method'. Baste the meat as it cooks and brown it only briefly before serving.

Roasting in Cooking Bags

This is an excellent roasting method as the meat retains its moisture. Prepare the meat as for Steps 1 and 2 of 'Basic Roasting Method'. Place the meat in a roasting bag and secure with a tag. Roast in a preheated oven at 190°C/375°F/gas 5 for the first 30 minutes, then reduce heat to 160°C/325°F/gas 3 for the rest of the roasting time. To brown the meat, open the bag for the last 15 minutes.

Foil-wrapped Roasting

This method is particularly good for very lean cuts, keeping them juicy and tender – and your oven clean.

Prepare the meat as for Steps 1 and 2 of 'Basic Roasting Method'. Use heavy-duty foil to completely enclose the meat. Seal the foil along the top and fold the ends upwards to keep in the juices.

Cooking time: Allow an extra 15–20 minutes to the overall cooking time, to account for heat penetrating the foil. Try Fillet of Beef with Blueberries (page 121).

Roasting Times

Beef

Rare to Medium: 20–30 minutes/kg (2 lb), plus 15 minutes extra.
Well done: 40 minutes/kg (2 lb), plus 20 minutes extra.

Lamb

Rare to Medium: 30–40 minutes/kg (2 lb), plus 10–15 minutes extra.
Well done: 40–60 minutes/kg (2 lb), plus 15 minutes extra.

Pork

Roasted pork is not usually served rare, so you should allow 70–80 minutes per kg (2 lb), plus 30 minutes extra.

Stir-fry

Here meat is tossed or fried in a very small amount of butter or other fat. However, because you need to keep your fat content low, we recommend that you stir-fry very small pieces of meat, a few at a time, in a small quantity of rapidly boiling water, stock or tomato juice.

Steaming

This involves the cooking of meats in the steam rising from boiling water. You would usually steam only small cuts of meat, suitable for domestic steamers. The steamer should be the pot-with-funnel variety, rather than made of bamboo which allows nutritious juices to drip away.

Steamed meats can be bland, but if you use suitable herbs or interesting sauces during cooking, the results will be tasty. Whole chicken thighs, for instance, are delicious if placed in the steamer tiers, covered with rings of raw onion and a crumbled stock cube, plenty of herbs and black pepper, and then steamed for 15–20 minutes.

Stews, Braised Dishes & Casseroles

Stewed meat involves slow, moist cooking on the stove. The meat is cooked in its own juices with the addition of a liquid, herbs and vegetables. Use a heavy-bottomed saucepan with a tight-fitting lid.

A casserole is not a cooking method but the container in which a stew is cooked in the oven. However, today many people call any stew that is cooked, covered, in the oven a 'casserole'.

Braising means browning a piece of meat quickly in hot fat or oil before adding liquid for the rest of the cooking process.

Stews and casseroles are economical. They often use the less expensive, tougher, coarser cuts of meat, which become tender in the slow cooking process. Meat is stewed in liquid in a covered pot. This keeps the meat moist and provides a gravy.

Choose

Veal: All veal cuts are suitable for stews. Knuckle is a favourite cut; neck is also delicious.

Beef: Choose cuts such as topside and rump, or stewing steak. Before serving, you must cool the cooked stew or casserole and remove any fat that settles on top.

Mutton or Lamb: Chops are good cooked in this way, and you can use the less expensive cuts as stewing will tenderise them. Also try neck or shin.

Pork: Buy lean pork. Belly pork and chops from any part of the beast are good for using in stews and casseroles.

Basic Method for Stews & Casseroles

1. Trim meat of all visible fat and cut into neat, even-sized pieces, about 2.5 cm (1 in). If meat is very tough, cut pieces even smaller.

2. Place meat in a heavy-based saucepan or casserole which has a tight-fitting lid.

3. Prepare vegetables and add to meat.

4. Add water or meat/vegetable stock. Use approximately 1 litre (1¾ pints) liquid to 1 kg (2 lb) meat.

5. Add herbs and flavourings as desired.

6. *For stews:* Bring to the boil. Reduce heat immediately and simmer for 1½–2 hours, or until meat is completely tender. Stir the stew occasionally to prevent sticking and burning.

   For casseroles: Bake, covered, in the oven at 160–180°C/325–350°F/gas 3–4, for 2–3 hours, or until meat is completely tender.

7. Thicken (as below, or according to your recipe) and serve.

Note: Stews and casseroles improve in flavour if left to stand. This means you can store the cooked dish in the refrigerator overnight. The following day, skim away any fat that has settled on top, reheat the dish and serve.

Thickening & Reducing Stews and Casseroles

If you like a thicker gravy for a stew or casserole you can do this in one of three ways.

Thickening with flour/cornflour (cornstarch): Use this method at the beginning or end of the cooking process. To keep fat content down, the stews and casseroles in this book have

---

been thickened with a blend of liquid (stock, water or milk) and flour or cornflour. The mixture is stirred in and cooked briefly just before serving. Cornflour is less likely to cause lumps, so we use this in preference to flour.

If flour is to be used as thickening at the start of the cooking, meat can be tossed in flour before being seared (sealed) in hot fat, or dropped into boiling water or stock.

Thickening with a beurre manié: At the end of the cooking period you can add a beurre manié (a stiff blend of fat and flour) to thicken a stew or casserole. However, we do not recommend this as it adds fat to the dish.

Reducing: Remove the lid from the saucepan or casserole during the last 30 minutes of cooking-time. This allows the cooking liquid to evaporate, leaving a thicker gravy. Reducing is most successful in dishes containing plenty of vegetables which break down during cooking and help thicken the gravy.

Notes on Meat

Meat is often the most expensive ingredient in a meal, but it is such a valuable source of protein, vitamin and minerals for athletes that it deserves a place in your diet. The following hints may help you get the best for your money:

- **Bacon** is a luxury – try bacon pieces and ham bones for flavouring, cut off any fat.

- **Bones, scraps and cheap cuts** are a good base for soups and home-made stock, but …

- **Calculate cost per serve.** Cheaper cuts often include a lot of waste in fat, bone and gristle, and …

- **Cheap cuts** can be tough and require long, slow cooking. What you save at the till you may spend on electricity or gas.

- **Fresh meat** keeps well when frozen, so it's worth bulk-buying when you see specials.

- **Imagination** keeps costs down; use 'meal extenders' such as rice, breadcrumbs and vegetables (included in casseroles and stews) and pasta. Dried beans, lentils and peas also work well.

- **Marinate** less tender steaks for several hours before cooking.

- **Minced meat** is not only one of the cheapest meats, it is also one of the most versatile. Choose lean, topside mince.

- **Price and nutrition** do not always relate when buying meat. For example, liver is often cheaper than most other meats – but it is especially rich in iron and Vitamin B12.

Important: In all cases, cool the cooked dish and remove any fat that settles on top before reheating and serving.

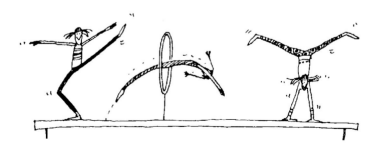

Fillet of Beef with Blueberries

Serves: 4

1 kg (2 lb) fillet of beef,
* trimmed of visible fat*
2 tsp chopped fresh oregano
* or 1 tsp dried*
3 small sprigs fresh
* rosemary or 1 tsp dried*
250 ml (8 fl oz) port
1 tbsp plum jam
350 g (11 oz) blueberries
Garnish:
whole chives

A delicious, impressive-looking dish, for special occasions, yet so simple to prepare. Leftovers make excellent gourmet sandwiches. If you can't buy fresh blueberries, use canned or frozen.

Method:

1. Place the beef on a large piece of foil. Sprinkle with all the herbs. Wrap the beef in foil, sealing along the top. Place in a baking dish and bake in a preheated oven for 30 minutes.
2. Carefully unwrap and remove the foil, letting the juices run into the baking dish. Add the port to the juices. Leave the fillet to stand in the juices, then return to the oven, uncovered, for a further 15 minutes.
3. Remove from oven. Set the fillet aside, loosely covered with foil, in a warm place.
4. Strain the juices into a saucepan. Add the jam. Place over medium heat and stir until the jam has melted.
5. Add the blueberries and simmer for 8–10 minutes.

To serve: Cut the beef into thick slices and arrange on individual dinner plates. Spoon about 2 tbsp of sauce over each portion. Garnish with whole chives. Alternatively, place the beef on a serving platter and cut into thick slices but keep the shape. Spoon the sauce down the length of the fillet, heaping the berries along the centre. Garnish with whole chives.

To vary: Use black grapes instead of blueberries.

To store: Cover with cling film and store in the refrigerator for up to 2 days.

Nutritional data per serving: 2,113 kJ (505 cal), Carbohydrate 26 g, Fat 19 g, Protein 59 g.

Preparation time: approximately 1 hour. Cooking equipment: baking dish, foil, saucepan.

Oven temperature: 200°C/400°F/gas 6.

Steak & Onion Filled Crêpes or Pancakes

Serves: 4
(allow 2 crêpes/
pancakes per serving)

500 g (1 lb) beef fillet
2 tbsp Worcestershire sauce
1 clove garlic, crushed
2 tsp oil
1 large onion, sliced
6 medium mushrooms,
    sliced
60 ml (2 fl oz) dry red wine
1 tbsp cornflour
    (cornstarch)
2 tbsp water
To serve:
8 crêpes or pancakes
    (pages 159–60)
plain yoghurt
chopped parsley

Method:

1. Slice beef into very thin strips. Place in a bowl with Worcestershire sauce and garlic. Leave to stand for 10 minutes.
2. In a frying pan, heat the oil until smoking hot. Add the beef and stir-fry, lifting and turning continually, for 3 minutes.
3. Add the onion and mushrooms and stir-fry, lifting and turning continually, for a further 2 minutes.
4. Add the wine and stir mixture for 1–2 minutes.
5. In a cup, stir the cornflour and water together to make a smooth paste. Add to the pan.
6. Bring to the boil, stirring continually, until the mixture thickens.
7. Reduce heat and simmer, uncovered, for 2 minutes.
8. Fill and roll up the crêpes or pancakes. Place the filled crêpes/pancakes, side-by-side, in the baking dish. Bake in a preheated oven for 10 minutes.
9. Serve hot with a topping of plain yoghurt and a sprinkling of chopped parsley.

Nutritional data per serving: 1,335 kJ (319 cal), Carbohydrate 6 g, Fat 15 g, Protein 38 g.
Preparation time: with pancakes pre-prepared – 40 minutes. Cooking equipment: frying-pan, rectangular baking dish.
Oven temperature: 180°C/350°F/gas 4.

Balinese Spiced Liver & Rice

Serves: 4

Coconut milk:

45 g (1½ oz) desiccated coconut
345 ml (11 fl oz) boiling water

Spice paste:

2 small onions, grated
1 clove garlic, crushed
¼ tsp turmeric
½ tsp brown sugar
pinch of black pepper
pinch of salt
1 tbsp soy sauce
1 bay leaf
1 tsp minced chilli
1 tbsp peanut butter
juice of ½ lemon

500 g (1 lb) chicken livers, sliced
750 g (1½ lb) cooked brown rice

Garnish:

tomato and cucumber wedges

Method:

1. *Make the coconut milk:* Combine coconut with boiling water. Leave to stand for 5 minutes. Strain, reserving liquid; then press the coconut to extract any remaining moisture. Reserve.

2. *Make the spice paste:* Mix all the paste ingredients together. If the paste is too thick, add a little water.

3. In a saucepan, bring the paste to a gentle simmer and cook, stirring frequently, for 5 minutes.

4. Add the chicken livers and cook, stirring gently, until the livers change colour.

5. Add the reserved coconut milk. Slowly bring the mixture to the boil, stirring constantly. Reduce heat, simmer until the mixture thickens, about 5 minutes.

6. Serve hot on a bed of boiled brown rice. Garnish with wedges of tomato and cucumber.

To store: This dish should be prepared and eaten on the same day.

Nutritional data per serving: 2,423 kJ (579 cal), Carbohydrate 63 g, Fat 20 g, Protein 35 g.

Preparation time: 30 minutes. Cooking equipment: medium-sized saucepan.

Pork with Mango

Serves: 4

Sauce:

2 small mangoes

250 ml (8 fl oz) dry white wine

3 tbsp mango chutney

4 tbsp spring onions, chopped

Pork:

1 tsp oil

4 lean pork schnitzels (approximately 150 g/5 oz each)

2 tbsp water

Garnish:

4 spring onions

This is one of those wonderful recipes that is very easy to prepare and yet looks and tastes good enough for a special event. Simple boiled rice and a crisp green salad round out the meal.

Method:

1. *To make the sauce:* Peel the mangoes. Cut away and roughly slice the flesh.

2. Place the mango flesh in a saucepan. Add white wine and chutney. Bring to the boil, reduce heat and simmer until the sauce has reduced by half, about 15 minutes.

3. If you want a smooth sauce, purée the hot fruit mixture in a food processor or blender, or press through a sieve. Return to the saucepan and reheat.

4. Add the chopped spring onions. Return to the boil, reduce heat and simmer for a further 2–3 minutes.

5. *To prepare the pork schnitzels:* While the sauce is simmering, at Step 2, wipe a large frying pan with the oil and heat over medium–high heat.

6. Fry the schnitzels, turning occasionally, until browned on both sides, about 10 minutes.

7. Remove the cooked schnitzels from the pan. Add 2 tbsp water to the pan, as well as the sauce. Heat, stirring constantly, for about 3 minutes.

8. Arrange the schnitzels on individual dinner plates. Spoon over the sauce and garnish with the whole spring onions.

Nutritional data per serving: 1,666 kJ (398 cal), Carbohydrate 16 g, Fat 14 g, Protein 43 g.

Preparation time: 40 minutes. Cooking equipment: saucepan, frying pan.

Skewered Lamb & Vegetables

Serves: 4

500 g (1 lb) lean lamb
 fillets
4 medium tomatoes
4 medium white onions
2 small green peppers
12 small button
 mushrooms
1 tbsp soy sauce
2 tbsp lemon juice
750 g (1½ lb) cooked rice or
 couscous

An excellent recipe for the barbecue that works equally well when cooked under the grill.

Method:

1. If using bamboo skewers, leave them in water to soak for a couple of hours beforehand.
2. Dice the lamb into 2.5 cm (1 in) cubes.
3. Cut the tomatoes and onions into segments, to make 12 pieces in all. Cut the seeded flesh of the peppers into strips and then into 12 squares. Trim off any woody ends of the mushroom stalks.
4. Thread lamb, tomato, onion, pepper and mushroom on to the skewers, leaving 2.5 cm (1 in) free at each end.
5. In a bowl, mix soy sauce and lemon juice. Brush the marinade liberally over the skewered ingredients. Reserve the rest of the soy mixture for basting.
6. Place skewers under the grill or on the barbecue. Grill, turning once, for about 7 minutes each side. While cooking, baste the skewers frequently, to prevent drying out.
7. Serve on a bed of rice or couscous.

To vary: Use chicken, fish or pork instead of diced lamb. You can use other vegetables, such as sliced courgette, or fruit, such as pineapple. Try serving this dish souvlaki-style – wrapped in hot pitta (Lebanese) bread with Tabbouleh (page 170).

Nutritional data per serving: 2,054 kJ (491 cal), Carbohydrate 67 g, Fat 7 g, Protein 39 g.

Preparation time: 20 minutes. Cooking equipment: 12 short metal or bamboo skewers (if bamboo, soak to prevent catching on fire).

Grill or barbecue temperature: high.

Liver in a Sherry & Yoghurt Sauce

Serves: 4

2 tbsp water

1 large onion, sliced

500 g (1 lb) lamb's or calf's
  liver, thinly sliced

2 bacon-flavoured stock
  cubes or a ham bone

375 ml (12 fl oz) boiling
  water

2 tbsp dry sherry

ground black pepper

2 tsp soy sauce

1 tbsp cornflour
  (cornstarch)

2 tbsp water

2 tbsp low-fat plain
  yoghurt

Method:

1. In a frying pan, heat 2 tbsp water. Add the onion and sauté until transparent.
2. Add the liver and cook, turning frequently, over medium heat, until the liver changes colour.
3. *Using stock cubes:* Dissolve the cubes in the boiling water before adding to the pan.
   Using a ham bone: Add to the pan with the water.
4. Add sherry, pepper and soy sauce to the pan. Stir.
5. Simmer gently, uncovered, stirring occasionally, for 20 minutes.
6. Meanwhile, blend the last 2 tbsp water with the cornflour to make a smooth paste. Add to the pan and stir constantly until mixture thickens.
7. Remove from the heat. Stir in the yoghurt.
8. Serve hot, accompanied by noodles or rice.

Nutritional data per serving: 1,147 kJ (274 cal), Carbohydrate 7 g, Fat 10 g, Protein 36 g.

Preparation time: 40 minutes. Cooking equipment: large frying pan.

Pork & Apple Baked Schnitzels

Serves: 4

4 pork schnitzels

1 large onion, sliced

100 g (3½ oz) rice

250 ml (8 fl oz) boiling
   water

1 large carrot, peeled and
   sliced

2 large apples, peeled and
   sliced

4 large mushrooms, sliced

ground black pepper

½ tsp Chinese five-spice
   powder

This is the sort of dish you can assemble quickly and then put in the oven and leave it to cook while you attend to other things.

Method:

1. Spray frying pan with non-stick cooking spray *or* wipe out pan with oil. Heat until very hot but not smoking.

2. Add schnitzels to the pan. Brown both sides, about 5 minutes a side, turning once. Remove the meat, set aside. Add the onion to the pan and sauté in the juices left by the meat.

3. Spread out the rice in the bottom of a casserole. Pour over the boiling water.

4. Place schnitzels, side-by-side, on top of the rice. Arrange layers of the cooked onion, carrot, apples and mushrooms. Sprinkle over the pepper and five-spice powder.

5. Cover and bake in a preheated oven for about 1¼ hours or until vegetables are tender.

6. Serve immediately, accompanied by a Mixed Green Salad (page 166).

Nutritional data per serving: 1,535 kJ (367 cal), Carbohydrate 19 g, Fat 13 g, Protein 45 g.

Preparation time: 1 3/4 hours. Cooking equipment: frying pan, casserole.

Oven temperature: 180°C/350°F/gas 4.

Savoury Minced Beef (Meat Sauce)

Serves: 4

250 ml (8 fl oz) stock or 1
  beef cube dissolved in
  250 ml (8 fl oz) hot water
500 g (1 lb) lean minced
  beef
1 tbsp tomato paste
1 medium carrot, grated
1 medium courgette, grated
1 clove garlic, crushed
1 medium onion, finely
  chopped
good pinch of dried mixed
  herbs
ground black pepper

Mince is economical and, if you buy top-quality lean mince (as we have for this recipe), the fat content is acceptable. This recipe makes a wonderful meat sauce for pasta, and can be transformed into a host of variations. Double or treble this recipe and store the surplus in your freezer.

Method:

1. In a large saucepan, bring the stock to the boil.
2. Add meat and stir into boiling stock, to seal the meat, about 5 minutes.
3. Add all the remaining ingredients and combine well. Return to the boil.
4. Reduce heat and simmer gently for 30 minutes.

As a simple, light meal: Serve on toast or with hot pita (Lebanese) bread. Alternatively, serve Meat Sauce with cooked pasta.

To vary: A dash of Worcestershire or Tabasco will make a more piquant sauce.

To store: Keep covered in the refrigerator for up to 3 days.

Nutritional data per serving: 1,034 kJ (247 cal), Carbohydrate 6 g, Fat 14 g, Protein 26 g.

Preparation time: 40 minutes. Cooking equipment: large saucepan.

Mexican Chilli Beans

Add a can of kidney beans, an extra tablespoon of tomato paste, a few drops of Tabasco and ½ tsp each of ground cumin and coriander. Serve in warmed taco shells with grated low-fat hard cheese, lettuce, tomato, mushroom and onion.

Iron-enriched Meat Sauce

Replace 100 g (3½ oz) of the beef with 2 minced lamb kidneys or 100 g (3½ oz) minced liver.

Protein-power: Fillet of Beef with Blueberries (page 121), served on a bed of brown rice accompanied by lightly steamed squash.
This photograph kindly sponsored by the Australian Meat and Livestock Corporation.

Beef Stroganoff

Serves: 6

750 g (1 lb 8 oz) lean rump
   or *fillet of beef*
ground black pepper
125 ml (4 fl oz) water
2 tbsp tomato paste
2 tbsp brandy
250 g (8 oz) button
   mushrooms
8 spring onions, chopped
2 tsp cornflour (cornstarch)
1 tbsp water
60 ml (2 fl oz) low-fat
   natural yoghurt

Method:

1. Cut the meat into 1 cm (½ in) slices, cutting across the grain.
2. Sprinkle the slices with pepper. Use a meat mallet to flatten each slice.
3. In a frying-pan, combine 125 ml (4 fl oz) water and tomato paste. Bring to the boil.
4. Add half the meat. Cook quickly for 3–5 minutes, then remove with a slotted spoon. Return to the boil and repeat for remaining meat.
5. Drain the meat, reserving the cooking liquid.
6. Return all the meat to the frying-pan, pour over the brandy, heat and ignite.
7. When flame dies, pour over the reserved juices. Add the mushrooms and simmer, stirring occasionally, for 4 minutes.
8. Stir in the spring onions.
9. In a cup, stir the cornflour and water to a smooth paste. Add to the frying-pan and bring to the boil, stirring constantly until the sauce thickens. Reduce to a simmer and cook a further 2 minutes.
10. Drain off sauce into a bowl. Turn heat off completely, but leave meat in the frying-pan. Stirring constantly, gradually add the yoghurt to the sauce. Do not reheat.

To serve: Pour the yoghurt sauce over the meat. Do not re-heat or the yoghurt will separate. Serve with an accompaniment of boiled brown rice or, even better, hot, cooked noodles, sprinkled with poppy seeds.

To vary: Substitute sliced veal, pork or chicken for the beef.

To store: Keep covered in the refrigerator for up to 3 days. Reheat slowly over very gentle heat. Do not allow to boil. Prepare as far as Step 7 before freezing. Complete preparation on the day of use.

Nutritional data per serving: 1,225 kJ (293 cal), Carbohydrate 3 g, Fat 17 g, Protein 39 g.

Preparation time: 25 minutes. Cooking equipment: large frying pan.

Creamy Veal Paprika

Serves: 4

4 veal cutlets

1 small green pepper

1 small red pepper

125 ml (4 fl oz) low-fat
  natural yoghurt

1 tbsp tomato paste

2 tbsp water

1 beef cube, crumbled

1 tsp paprika

Try this recipe with chicken breasts instead of veal.

Method:

1. Slice veal into long, thin strips, 1 x 5 cm (½ x 2 in).

2. Wash and seed the green and red peppers. Cut the flesh into strips, also about 1 x 5 cm (½ x 2 in).

3. In a saucepan, combine yoghurt, tomato paste, water, beef cube and paprika. Mix well and bring to the boil.

4. Add the veal and peppers. Return to the boil and then reduce heat to simmer.

5. Simmer gently, uncovered, for 10 minutes, or until meat is tender and cooked through.

6. Spoon veal over a bed of boiled brown rice, or over cooked noodles that have been sprinkled with poppy seeds. Serve immediately.

Microwave Method:

Cooking time: 9 minutes.

As above for Steps 1 and 2. Prepare yoghurt mixture as at Step 3, and microwave in a suitable, non-metal container for 1 minutes on 'High'. Add veal and peppers and microwave on 'High' for 5 minutes. Stir veal mixture and microwave on 'High' for a further 3 minutes.

To store: Keep covered in the refrigerator for up to 3 days. Not suitable for freezing.

Nutritional data per serving: 969 kJ (231 cal), Carbohydrate 4 g, Fat 7 g, Protein 39 g.

Preparation time: 20 minutes. Cooking equipment: medium-sized saucepan.

QUICK TIP: Microwaving foods is an excellent way to prepare low-fat meals. It is quick and easy, and vitamin and mineral losses are minimal. Almost all foods can be cooked successfully in a microwave – you will need to refer to your microwave manual for specific cooking instructions.

Beef à la Pizzaiola

Serves: 4

4 litres (7 pints) water
440 g (14 oz) brown rice
500 g (1 lb) lean beef fillet
2 tsp water
1 small clove garlic,
    crushed
2 large tomatoes, peeled
    and chopped
4 leaves fresh basil,
    roughly chopped
2 spring onions, chopped
45 g (1½ oz) mushrooms,
    sliced

Although beef fillet is a relatively expensive cut of meat, in this recipe you use only 500 g (1 lb) and it feeds 4 people. The meat cooks quickly, so there is little shrinkage and, as fillet is lean, there is no waste.

Method:

1. In a large saucepan, bring the water to a rapid boil. Add the rice. Return water to the boil while stirring the rice with a fork. Boil rice, uncovered, for 30–40 minutes or until tender. While the rice is boiling, move on to Steps 2–5.
2. Cut the beef into thin strips – 1 x 5 cm (½ x 2 in).
3. In a large frying pan, heat 2 tsp of water, add the garlic and sauté until softened, about 3 minutes.
4. Add the chopped tomato, basil and spring onion to the pan. Cook for 2–3 minutes, stirring constantly.
5. Add the strips of beef and the mushrooms. Simmer for 5–8 minutes, or until meat is cooked through.
6. Drain the cooked rice in a colander.
7. Spoon the beef and sauce on to a bed of the cooked rice.

To vary: Use veal, pork or chicken instead of beef. For a more piquant sauce, add a few drops of Tabasco.

To store: Keep covered in the refrigerator for up to 3 days.

Nutritional data per serving: 1,713 kJ (409 cal), Carbohydrate 26 g, Fat 17 g, Protein 39 g.

Preparation time: 40 minutes. Cooking equipment: large saucepan, large frying pan.

Hearty Beef & Vegetable Casserole

Serves: 4

2 tbsp flour

pinch of salt

pinch of pepper

500 g (1 lb) lean stewing
  beef, trimmed of all
  visible fat

1 medium onion, diced

2 medium carrots,
  scrubbed and diced

2 medium potatoes,
  scrubbed and diced

1 medium leek, sliced

315 ml (10 fl oz) Basic
  Meat Stock (page 77) or 1
  beef stock cube dissolved
  in 315 ml (10 fl oz) water

2 level tbsp tomato paste

dash of Tabasco

1 tbsp chopped parsley

This is an ideal dish for the athlete with a busy lifestyle –
it can be prepared the day before and kept, covered in the
refrigerator, for up to 2 days before reheating and serving.

Method:

1. In a plastic bag, combine the flour, salt and pepper.
    Add the beef to the bag and shake well to coat with the
    flour mixture.
2. Arrange the meat in the base of a casserole. Cover with
    the diced vegetables. Combine the stock, tomato paste,
    Tabasco and parsley and pour over the vegetables.
3. Cover casserole and leave to bake at 180°C (350°F) for
    2 hours.
4. Serve hot with wholemeal bread and salad.

To store: Keep covered in the refrigerator for up to 2 days.
Reheat thoroughly before serving.

Nutritional data per serving: 1,538 kJ (368 cal), Carbohydrate 22 g, Fat 10 g, Protein 48 g.

Preparation time: 2 hours. Cooking equipment: casserole with lid.

Oven temperature: 180°C/350°F/gas 4.

QUICK TIP: Mix lean meat for casseroles, stews or mince dishes, with low-fat, high-
carbohydrate foods such as rice and legumes.

Shepherd's Pie

Serves: 6

6 medium potatoes
750 g (1 lb 8 oz) lean lamb
    or beef, minced
1 large onion, diced
2 tbsp tomato paste
500 ml (16 fl oz) Basic
    Meat Stock (page 77) or 2
    beef stock cubes dissolved
    in 500 ml (16 fl oz) hot
    water
ground black pepper
½ tsp mixed dried herbs
2 tbsp skimmed milk

The traditional recipe for Shepherd's Pie uses leftover cold lamb which is minced and flavoured. The 'pie' is topped with mashed potato and then baked. Nowadays, we start off with fresh minced meat, preferably lamb, but beef is also suitable.

Method:

1. Peel and halve the potatoes. Place in a saucepan and cover with water. Bring to the boil, reduce heat and simmer for 20 minutes, or until tender.

2. Meanwhile, in a second saucepan, dry-fry the meat and onion over medium heat, until the meat is browned and crumbly.

3. Add the tomato paste, stock, black pepper and herbs and stir. Bring to the boil. Then reduce heat and simmer, uncovered, until the cooking liquids have reduced and thickened to a sauce, about 20 minutes.

4. Drain the cooked potatoes and add the skim milk. Use a fork or vegetable masher to mash until smooth and fluffy.

5. Spoon the cooked meat into a casserole or pie dish and spread evenly. Spoon over the mashed potato, and use the back of a fork to spread evenly over the meat.

6. Bake Shepherd's Pie in a preheated oven for 20 minutes, or until the potato has browned on top.

7. Serve the pie hot, accompanied by cooked vegetables, such as steamed green peas and carrots or a green salad.

Nutritional data per serving: 1,288 kJ (308 cal), Carbohydrate 20 g, Fat 14 g, Protein 28 g.

Preparation time: 1 hour. Cooking equipment: 2 large saucepans, casserole or pie dish.
Oven temperature: 200°C/400°F/gas 6.

Spicy Liver with Rice

Serves: 2

60 ml (2 fl oz) water

150 g (5 oz) chicken or
    lamb's liver, cut in strips

4 spring onions, chopped

30 g (1 oz) mushrooms,
    chopped

½ clove garlic, crushed

2 tomatoes, peeled and
    chopped

4 tbsp cooked peas

1 beef stock cube, crumbled

pinch of ground cloves

pinch of ground cinnamon

pinch of black pepper

375 g (12 oz) cooked brown
    rice

Method:

1. In a frying pan, heat the water and sauté the liver, spring onions, mushrooms and garlic for 5 minutes.
2. Add the tomatoes, cooked peas, stock cube and spices. Simmer, stirring, over medium heat, for 3 minutes.
3. Add the cooked rice and stir constantly until heated through.
4. Serve at once.

Nutritional data per serving: 2,007 kJ (480 cal), Carbohydrate 54 g, Fat 12 g, Protein 42 g.

Preparation time: starting with cooked rice – 15 minutes.

Cooking equipment: frying pan.

Chicken Soy

Serves: 6

6 spring onions, chopped

2 cloves garlic, crushed

2 tsp green ginger, grated

125 ml (4 fl oz) soy sauce

4 tbsp dry sherry

6 chicken breasts, skinned

Garnish:

finely chopped parsley

Method:

1. Prepare the marinade. In a bowl, combine all the ingredients except the chicken.
2. Place chicken in a baking dish. Pour over marinade. Refrigerate for 2 hours, turning occasionally.
3. Pour off the marinade and reserve. Arrange the chicken breasts in the baking dish again. Strain the marinade and pour over the chicken breasts.
4. Bake in a preheated oven for 40 minutes, basting occasionally.
5. Remove chicken from baking dish and arrange on a serving platter. Brush with pan juices.

To vary: Before baking, sprinkle with 3 tbsp sesame seeds. **To store:** Keep covered in the refrigerator for up 3 days. Not recommended for freezing as the chicken dries out.

Nutritional data per serving: 1,136 kJ (271 cal), Carbohydrate 4 g, Fat 7 g, Protein 44 g.

Preparation time: including marinating time – 3 hours. Cooking equipment: baking dish.

Oven temperature: 180°C/350°F/gas 4.

Hawaiian Chicken & Rice

Serves: 6

315 g (10 oz) brown rice

750 ml (24 fl oz) water

4 chicken breasts

1 tbsp soy sauce

250 ml (8 fl oz) water

1 medium green pepper,
*   seeded and diced*

1 medium red pepper,
*   seeded and diced*

10 rings unsweetened,
*   canned pineapple,*
*   drained (juice reserved)*
*   and chopped*

6 tbsp of the reserved
*   pineapple juice*

ground black pepper

Method:

1. Rinse the rice under cold, running water. Place the rice in a large saucepan, cover with 750 ml (24 fl oz) water. Bring to the boil – boil for 30–35 minutes.

2. Meanwhile, in a saucepan, combine the chicken breasts, soy sauce and the 250 ml (8 fl oz) of water. Bring to the boil, reduce heat and simmer for 7–10 minutes.

3. Remove chicken. Leave cooking juices in the saucepan and set aside.

4. Cut the chicken breasts across into narrow strips.

5. Return the chicken to its cooking juices in the saucepan. Add all remaining ingredients. Stir mixture over low heat for about 10 minutes, or until completely heated through.

6. Drain the cooked rice, rinse under hot, running water.

7. Stir the rice into the other ingredients or arrange the chicken on a bed of the cooked rice.

Nutritional data per serving: 932 kJ (223 cal), Carbohydrate 22 g, Fat 4 g, Protein 25 g.

Preparation time: 35 minutes. Cooking equipment: 2 saucepans.

QUICK TIP: When you do have time, prepare meals in bulk, divide into portions and freeze. Casseroles, soups, and low-fat sauces can be frozen easily and will reheat in the microwave quickly.

Chicken with Currant & Orange Sauce

Serves: 4

4 chicken breasts, skinned
grated rind and juice of
  3 oranges
4 tbsp redcurrant jelly
1 tbsp brandy
150 g (5 oz) redcurrants,
  stalks removed
150 g (5 oz) blackcurrants,
  stalks removed

Garnish:

4 orange segments
sprigs of red- and
  blackcurrants

If fresh red- or blackcurrants are not available, make this flavoursome dish with 315 g (10 oz) of grapes or 125 g (4 oz) of sultanas. Boiled rice and a fresh, green salad make good accompaniments to this special dish.

Method:

1. Lightly grease a frying pan or spray it with non-stick cooking spray. Heat pan over medium-high heat; add 1 or 2 chicken breasts at a time to the pan and brown quickly on both sides.

2. Place the browned chicken breasts, side-by-side, in a baking dish. Cover with a lid or with foil. Bake in a preheated oven for 10 minutes.

3. While the chicken bakes, prepare the sauce. In a saucepan, combine the orange juice and redcurrant jelly and stir, over medium heat, until the jelly melts.

4. Add the brandy, red- and blackcurrants and grated orange rind. Bring to the boil, stirring gently. Reduce heat to very low, keeping sauce warm.

5. Remove chicken breasts from oven and place on a chopping board.

6. Using a very sharp knife, slice the breast, to make very thin slices or, for a more attractive finish, slice each breast into 4 very thin slices – but only three-quarters the way along.

7. Place a chicken breast on each plate. Carefully fan out the slices of each chicken breast. Spoon over the warm sauce. Arrange an orange segment and a sprig each of fresh red- and blackcurrants beside each chicken breast.

Nutritional data per serving: 1,612 kJ (385 cal), Carbohydrate 19 g, Fat 9 g, Protein 54.5 g.

Preparation time: 30 minutes. Cooking equipment: large frying pan, baking dish, saucepan.

Oven temperature: 220°C/425°F/gas 7.

Chicken Satay

Serves: 4
(2 small skewers each)

500 g (1 lb) chicken fillets
2 tbsp lemon juice
2 tbsp soy sauce
1 small onion, grated
1 clove garlic, crushed
1 tsp oil

An Indonesian recipe that makes a great alternative for the barbecue.

Method:

1. Cut chicken into small cubes.
2. Thread the chicken on to skewers. Arrange the skewers in a flat dish.
3. Combine remaining ingredients to make a marinade. Brush over the chicken. Leave chicken to marinate for at least 1 hour, turning occasionally.
4. Grill or barbecue the Chicken Satay, turning frequently and basting occasionally with marinade.
5. Serve hot accompanied by Satay (Peanut) Sauce with Chilli (page 177).

To vary: Use pork, beef or lamb fillet in place of chicken.

To store: Use on day of preparation, but it can be marinated for some hours, covered, in the refrigerator.

Nutritional data per serving: 907 kJ (217 cal), Carbohydrate 2 g, Fat 7 g, Protein 36 g.

Preparation time: 1 hour. Cooking equipment: 8 metal or wooden skewers (if wooden, soak to prevent scorching), grill or charcoal barbecue.

Chicken & Vegetable Curry

Serves: 2

2 chicken breasts, skinned

1 small onion, roughly chopped

2 tsp mild curry powder

½ tsp minced fresh or ground ginger

2 tbsp water

250 ml (8 fl oz) chicken stock

½ medium carrot, thinly sliced

½ green pepper, seeded and roughly chopped

90 g (3 oz) French beans, sliced

1 tbsp cornflour (cornstarch)

2 tbsp water

1 tbsp cashew nuts or slivered almonds

Method:

1. Preheat the grill to medium. Cut chicken breasts into cubes. Grill the chicken until tender but cooked through – about 7 minutes.

2. Set chicken aside, loosely covered, and keep warm.

3. In a saucepan over medium heat, combine the onion, curry powder, ginger and 2 tbsp of water. Cook, stirring constantly, for 3 minutes.

4. Add the chicken stock and vegetables.

5. Bring to the boil, reduce heat and simmer for 15 minutes, or until the vegetables are just tender. Remove from heat.

6. Mix the cornflour and 2 tbsp of water to a smooth paste. Add to the saucepan and stir in. Return to the heat and bring to the boil, stirring constantly, until the mixture thickens. Reduce heat and simmer for 2 minutes.

7. Add chicken and nuts, mix well and heat through.

8. Serve immediately on a bed of boiled brown rice or wholemeal macaroni.

Nutritional data per serving: 2,157 kJ (515 cal), Carbohydrate 30 g, Fat 15 g, protein 67 g.

Preparation time: 1 hour. Cooking equipment: large saucepan.

Grill temperature: medium.

Golden Chicken Risotto

Serves: 4

2 tbsp water

1 large onion, chopped

1 clove garlic, crushed

315 g (10 oz) brown rice

1.5 litres (2¾ pints) Basic
    Chicken Stock (page 77)
    or 4 chicken stock cubes
    dissolved in 1.5 litres
    (2¾ pints) water

4 chicken breasts, diced
    finely

1 tsp turmeric

20 almonds, blanched and
    halved

3 tbsp raisins

Method 1 – Stove top:

1. In a large saucepan, heat the water. Add the onion and sauté till softened.
2. Add the garlic and sauté for 2 minutes.
3. Add the rice and 360 ml (12 fl oz) Basic Chicken Stock. Bring to the boil. Reduce heat and simmer for 20 minutes, stirring occasionally and adding more stock, as necessary, to prevent sticking.
4. Add the diced chicken breasts, turmeric, almonds and raisins.
5. Continue simmering a further 20–25 minutes, adding remaining stock as necessary, until the rice is tender. There should be no liquid in the finished risotto.
6. Serve hot, accompanied by a green salad.

Method 2 – Oven (Casserole):

1. Place all ingredients in a casserole.
2. Cover and cook in a preheated oven for 1 hour, or until rice has absorbed the stock.
3. Serve hot, accompanied by a green salad.

Nutritional data per serving: 1,902 kJ (454 cal), Carbohydrate 26 g, Fat 14 g, Protein 58 g.

Preparation time: approximately 1 hour. Cooking equipment: saucepan, large saucepan or casserole with lid.
Oven temperature: 180°C/350°F/gas 4.

Food for Sport Cookbook

Chicken in Filo Pastry

Serves: 4

2 cooked chicken breasts,
    finely chopped
1 egg, lightly beaten
1 chicken stock cube,
    crumbled
1 small onion, finely
    chopped
30 g (1 oz) bean sprouts
30 g (1 oz) mushrooms,
    finely chopped
30 g (1 oz) soft wholemeal
    breadcrumbs
½ fresh marjoram or a
    good pinch of dried
½ tsp fresh rosemary or a
    good pinch of dried
12 sheets filo pastry
2 tbsp skimmed milk, for
    glazing

For a delicious change, make this recipe with a can of tuna in place of the chicken.

Method:

1. In a bowl, combine all ingredients, except the pastry and milk.
2. Fold a sheet of filo pastry in half, widthwise. Brush lightly with milk.
3. Repeat with another 2 sheets of pastry, placing them on top of the first, to give a total of 6 layers.
4. Place a quarter of the filling mixture along the edge of the pastry. Roll up the pastry, tucking in the ends just before making the final roll to give a neat parcel.
5. Place the completed roll, sealed-side down, on a lightly greased baking sheet.
6. Repeat filling and rolling, as above, for the remaining pastry and filling.
7. Brush each roll with milk. Bake in a preheated oven for 15 minutes, or until pastry is crisp and golden brown.
8. Serve hot, accompanied by Classic Tomato Sauce

To store: Keep covered in the refrigerator for up to 3 days. Reheat at 180°C/350°F/gas 4 for 10 minutes. To freeze the Chicken in Filo Pastries, bake them for only 10 minutes at Step 7, or until pastry is palest gold. Before use, thaw completely and then reheat thoroughly at 180°C/350°F/gas 4 for 10 minutes.

Notes: One 375 g (12 oz) packet of filo pastry yields 35 sheets. One slice of wholemeal bread yields 30 g (1 oz) fresh breadcrumbs. A food processor or blender makes this easy; a hand grater is slower but still works.

Nutritional data per serving: 1,185 kJ (283 cal), Carbohydrate 30 g, Fat 6 g, Protein 29 g.

Preparation time: 45 minutes. Cooking equipment: baking sheet.

Oven temperature: 220°C/425°F/gas 7.

Coq au Vin

Serves: 4

4 chicken breasts
3 tbsp brandy
2 medium white onions
2 cloves garlic
2 large sprigs parsley
2 large sprigs thyme
2 bay leaves
ground black pepper
250 ml (8 fl oz) dry red
   wine
60 g (2 oz) small button
   mushrooms

Garnish:

finely chopped parsley

This classic French dish has been modified to suit sportsmen and women everywhere.

Method:

1. Lightly wipe saucepan with oil or spray saucepan with non-stick cooking spray. Heat until very hot but not smoking. One at a time, quickly brown each chicken breast on both sides, about 2 minutes a side.
2. Place all the browned chicken breasts in a frying pan. Pour over the brandy. Ignite and then let the flame burn out. Remove from heat. Set chicken aside. Do not wash out the frying pan.
3. Chop each onion into 8 large pieces.
4. In a saucepan, place the chicken, onion, garlic, parsley, thyme, bay leaves and black pepper.
5. In the frying pan used to brown the chicken breasts, add the wine and heat gently. Stir to dissolve the chicken brownings. Pour over the chicken in the saucepan.
6. Stir to combine. Cover saucepan and bring to the boil.
7. Reduce heat and add the mushrooms. Simmer gently for 30 minutes.
8. Remove the herbs. If desired, transfer chicken to a warmed serving dish. Sprinkle with chopped parsley.
9. Serve with an accompaniment of baby potatoes boiled in their jackets and steamed or boiled green beans and small whole onions.

To vary: Instead of brandy and red wine, use 1 tbsp redcurrant jelly dissolved in 250 ml (8 fl oz) hot water.

To store: This dish can be prepared up to 3 days in advance. Re-heat thoroughly before serving. Do not freeze.

Nutritional data per serving: 1,632 kJ (390 cal), Carbohydrate 4 g, Fat 9 g, Protein 55 g.

Preparation time: 45 minutes. Cooking equipment: frying pan, large saucepan.

CARBOHYDRATE & PROTEIN ALTERNATIVES

As an athlete, there are some advantages in replacing meat, poultry and fish from time to time as your principal sources of protein, particularly to replenish glycogen stores. If you choose to use protein alternatives, you need a good nutritional understanding of these foods so you can select and balance your meals.

If you are a vegetarian athlete, or if you are thinking about becoming a vegetarian, your diet will need special attention. To ensure you receive adequate nutrients, read 'Special Groups, Special Needs' (page 31–7) for more detailed information.

Properly Planned Non-meat Meals

- They are high in fibre, unrefined carbohydrates and protein.
- Non-meat meals tend to be low in fat.
- Non-meat meals can be cheaper than meat- and fish-based meals.

A note of warning: Adding cheese, cream, butter, margarine or oil increases the fat content of meals, even if they are based on alternative protein foods.

The following are particularly valuable if your diet does not contain meat.

PULSES (LEGUMES)

This group of foods is an excellent sources of protein, iron, fibre and unrefined carbohydrates. Most pulses are a useful source of calcium, potassium and B Group vitamin. They all have a low fat content.

Most pulses need long, slow cooking to make them easily digestible. Plan ahead for pulse-based meals. Once cooked, dishes using pulses usually freeze well. You can cook large quantities and divide them into portions to be frozen for future use. Look also for canned beans and chick peas — these are good alternatives and save time.

Mung Beans, Split Peas & Lentils

These don't need to be soaked before you cook them, although they do need long, slow cooking. Pick over to remove any extra bits and pieces. Wash them well in cold water; throw away any that float to the top.

Place pulses in a saucepan, cover with cold water and bring to the boil. Boil for 25–35 minutes, or until soft, but not mushy.

- Allow 750 ml (24 fl oz) of water to 220 g (7 oz) of mung beans, split peas or lentils.
- Yield when cooked: approximately 625 g (1¼ lb).

Whole Dried Beans & Chick Peas

Soak for 12 hours, or overnight, before cooking. Discard any discoloured ones or any that float to the surface. A quicker alternative is to place the clean, picked-over pulses in a saucepan. Cover with cold water and bring to the boil for 3 minutes. Remove from heat, cover and leave for 1–2 hours before cooking.

- Allow 750 ml–1 litre (1¼–1¾ pints) of water to 185 g (6 oz) of beans, whole dried peas and lentils.
- Yield when cooked: 375–440 g (12–14 oz).

You can cook beans in their soaking water; but if you find them too strongly flavoured cooked this way, discard the water and use fresh. Bring the beans and water to a boil. Boil rapidly for 10 minutes, then reduce heat and simmer gently until tender.

Pressure Cooking

Using this method, pulses cook in about one third of the time and require about half the normal quantity of water.

Approximate Cooking Time for Pulses

Red (orange) lentils	½ hour
Black and mung beans	½–1 hour
Adzuki, borlotti, butter, cannellini and haricot beans	1–1½ hours
Split peas, chick peas and green lentils	1–1½ hours
Black-eyed, lima and red kidney beans	1–1½ hours
Broad beans	2½ hours
Soya beans	3½–4 hours

Substituting Beans

Borlotti beans and red kidney beans can be interchanged. Cannellini can be used instead of haricot beans. Butter and lima beans can be interchanged. Soya beans can be used to replace haricot, cannellini or red kidney beans in recipes. However, soya beans will need a longer cooking time than the others.

CEREALS

This term includes the edible grains and the products made from them. The most commonly used cereals are: wheat, rice, corn, barley, millet, oats and rye. Tapioca, semolina, cassava meal and sago are also counted as cereals, and these are rich in starch.

Cereals – Plus Factors

- All cereals are rich in carbohydrate.
- Most unrefined or whole cereals are high in fibre.
- All have a low fat content.

RICE

Rice is the staple crop of many nations of the world, and is often the main source of food. Rice is an excellent food for athletes as it is high in complex carbohydrate and low in fat. Brown rice, in particular, is high in fibre and B-group vitamins.

Not only is rice a nutritious food, it tastes great and is extremely versatile. There are many varieties of rice now available, ranging from the familiar white or brown long-grain rice to speciality ones such as basmati and the so-called glutinous rice used by the Japanese to make sushi. Rice is also marketed in a variety of convenience packs; follow the instructions for using.

White Long-grain Rice
Long-grain rice is the separating grain which is delicious in the many international dishes of Asia, India and Spain.

Brown Long-grain Rice
This rice retains the natural bran layer which is rich in many vitamins and minerals, including rice bran oil. This long-grain rice is firm in texture, with a slightly nutty flavour.

White Medium-grain Rice
Better known as risotto or arborio rice, this is the softer cooking medium-grain rice which has the advantage of being able to carry flavours and colours well. Its soft, creamy texture makes it ideal for desserts such as Creamy Rice (page 196). It absorbs as much as five times its weight in liquid.

Easy-cook Long-grain White or Brown Rice
Sometimes called parboiled or pre-fluffed rice, this variety is a good choice for the novice cook. It is steamed under pressure before milling which hardens the grain, reducing the possibility of over-cooking. This process also helps to retain much of the natural vitamin and mineral content.

Jasmine or Thai Fragrant Rice
This long-grain white rice has a delicate jasmine fragrance which makes it perfect for inclusion in Asian dishes and with curries and seafood.

Cooking Methods:

The rapid boil and absorption methods are the most common ways of cooking rice. If liked, stock may be used instead of water. Because each type of rice has a different cooking time, it is best to refer to the instructions on the individual packs. For example, brown rice generally takes about double the cooking time of white rice. The quickest way to cook rice, however, is in the microwave.

PASTA

Pasta contains a high percentage of unrefined carbohydrate and has a low fat content which make it a valuable food for athletes. With its gentle flavour and substantial bulk, it is a versatile and economical base for many dishes.

Although pasta is usually served hot, it works very well in cold dishes and you will find several recipes using cold cooked pasta in this book.

Good quality pasta is always made from hard or durum wheat. When cooked, this type of pasta has a better texture and flavour than other varieties. Check the ingredients listed on the packet to be sure the pasta is made from hard wheat. Wholemeal pasta is even higher in energy-rich carbohydrates than the normal variety.

Basic Pasta Cooking Method:

- Allow 4 litres (7 pints) of water to 500 g (1 lb) of pasta. Bring the water to a rapid boil, add the pasta and return to the boil. *Note:* On average, 250 g (8 oz) of dried pasta will provide 4 servings.

- Cooking time varies according to the type and shape of pasta. In general, pasta should be boiled until *al dente*, which means tender but still firm to the bite.

- Drain cooked pasta immediately, as it will continue cooking in its own heat for a short while after it is removed from the saucepan. For salads, turn the hot pasta out into a colander and cool it immediately under cold, running water.

Pasta Marinara

Serves: 4

315 g (10 oz) pasta
  (e.g. spaghetti, tagliatelle
  or macaroni)
2 tbsp water
½ medium onion, peeled
  and chopped
1 clove garlic, crushed
250 ml (8 fl oz) skimmed
  milk
2 tsp cornflour (cornstarch)
170 g (6 oz) mixed cooked
  seafood (e.g. calamari,
  oysters, prawns, clams)
1 tbsp chopped parsley
ground black pepper

Method:

1. Two-thirds fill a large saucepan with water and bring to a rapid boil. Add pasta and boil rapidly until *al dente* (tender, but still firm to the bite) – 10–12 minutes.

2. While the pasta cooks, prepare the sauce. In a medium-sized saucepan, heat the 2 tbsp water. Add the onion and garlic and sauté till softened.

3. In a cup, blend 1 tbsp of the milk with the cornflour, to make a smooth paste. Then stir in the remainder of the milk. Add to the onion and garlic. Bring to the boil, stirring constantly, until sauce thickens. Reduce heat to a simmer and cook a further minute.

4. Over medium heat, add all the remaining ingredients and stir to combine and heat through.

5. Drain the pasta and add to the sauce. Gently toss to combine. Serve at once.

Nutritional data per serving: 745 kJ (178 cal), Carbohydrate 24 g, Fat 2 g, Protein 17 g.

Preparation time: 15 minutes. Cooking equipment: medium-sized saucepan, large saucepan.

Pancakes (page 159) made with half-and-half white and wholemeal flours and rolled around freshly cooked mixed seafood and Low-fat Cheese Sauce (page 179). Try other fillings, such as mushroom & spring onion.

Spinach Fettuccine

Serves: 2

500 g (1 lb) fresh spinach
  or 500 g (1 lb) frozen,
  chopped spinach
150 g (5 oz) spinach
  fettuccine (green)
1 tbsp pine nuts
1 tbsp water
½ small onion, finely
  chopped
½ clove garlic, crushed
½ tsp chopped fresh basil
  or a good pinch of dried
ground black pepper
250 g (8 oz) ricotta cheese

Method:

1. *Using fresh spinach:* Trim away any roots and woody ends of stems. Rinse spinach thoroughly under cold, running water – do not dry the spinach. Heat a large saucepan. Put the wet spinach into the saucepan, cover and cook over high heat for 5–8 minutes, or until tender. Remove from heat and drain in a colander. Set aside.

    Using frozen spinach: Place in a saucepan and thaw over low to medium heat. Remove from heat, drain well and squeeze to remove excess liquid. Set aside.

2. Two-thirds fill a large saucepan with water and bring to a rapid boil. Add the fettuccine and boil for 10–12 minutes, or until it is *al dente* (tender, but firm to bite).

3. Meanwhile, in a dry frying pan, brown the pine nuts over medium heat, stirring constantly to ensure even colouring and prevent burning. Remove from pan and set aside.

4. Return pan to the heat. Add the tablespoon of water, onion, garlic, basil and pepper. Sauté over low heat until the onion is transparent.

5. Drain the cooked fettuccine.

6. In a large saucepan, combine the cooked spinach, pine nuts, ricotta cheese and the onion. Add the fettuccine. Use two forks to gently lift and turn mixture to combine well. Serve hot.

Nutritional data per serving: 1,352 kJ (323 cal), Carbohydrate 26 g, Fat 9 g, Protein 35 g.

Preparation time: 30 minutes. Cooking equipment: 2 large saucepans, frying pan.

Vegetable Lasagne

Serves: 6–8

Vegetable Sauce:

2 courgettes, grated

2 cooking apples, peeled and grated

2 carrots, grated

3 sticks of celery, finely chopped

1 green pepper, seeded and finely chopped

6 mushrooms, sliced

4 tomatoes, chopped

2 cloves garlic, crushed

4 tbsp tomato paste

60 g (2 oz) parsley, finely chopped

2 sprigs each of fresh oregano, thyme and rosemary, finely chopped or ¹/₂ tsp dried mixed herbs

4 large sage leaves, finely chopped

ground black pepper

500 g (1 lb) instant wholemeal lasagne noodles

Cheese Sauce:

250 g (8 oz) ricotta cheese

500 g (1 lb) cottage cheese

125 ml (4 fl oz) skimmed milk

Topping:

2 tbsp low-fat hard cheese, grated

This dish is great for the busy cook as it can be prepared when you have the time and then frozen for later use.

Method:

1. In a bowl, combine all the Vegetable Sauce ingredients.
2. In a separate bowl, beat cottage and ricotta cheeses with the skimmed milk until smooth.
3. In a deep baking dish, make alternate layers of vegetable sauce, cheese sauce and lasagne noodles. Repeat layering until all the ingredients have been used. Your last layer should be of Cheese Sauce.
4. Top with grated cheese. Bake in a preheated oven for 1 hour. Serve hot, accompanied by a salad.

To vary: Different ingredients may be added, according to taste and availability. For example: flaked, oil-free canned tuna; black olives, pitted and sliced; cooked breast of chicken, shredded. By adding tuna or chicken, you can build up the protein content.

To store: Keep covered in the refrigerator for up to 2 days. Reheat or serve cold. This dish freezes very well. Prepare up to Step 3 and freeze in a dish that is suitable for freezing as well as for baking. Defrost the lasagne completely before baking as directed in Step 4.

Nutritional data per serving: 2,003 kJ (479 cal), Carbohydrate 61 g, Fat 9 g, Protein 35 g.

Preparation time: 1 ¹/₂ hours. Cooking equipment: deep baking dish. Oven temperature: 180°C/350°F/gas 4.

Savoury Potato Pie in a Rice Shell

Serves: 4

1 recipe Rice Pie Shell
(page 204)

4 medium potatoes, peeled
and grated

4 eggs, lightly beaten

125 ml (4 fl oz) skimmed
milk

4 tbsp grated low-fat hard
cheese

2 tbsp chopped parsley

1 tbsp chopped chives

1 onion, finely chopped

1 clove garlic, crushed

1 chicken stock cube,
crumbled

You can also use this mixture to make up individual pies.

Method:

1. Lightly grease a pie dish and line with Rice Pie Shell.
2. In a bowl, combine all the remaining ingredients. Spoon into the pie shell.
3. Bake in a preheated oven for 1 hour, or until well set and browned on top.
4. Serve hot or at room temperature, with a green salad if desired.

To vary: Add 4 tbsp of cooked shredded chicken.

To store: Keep covered, in the refrigerator, for up to 3 days.

Nutritional data per serving: 1,270 kJ (304 cal), Carbohydrate 25 g, Fat 10 g, Protein 29 g.
Preparation time: 1 1/4 hours. Cooking equipment: pie dish.
Oven temperature: 180°C/350°F/gas 4.

QUICK TIP: Always use minimum quantities of oil in cooking. Brush your pan with oil rather than pouring it in, or use a cooking spray.

Bubble & Squeak

Serves: 4

2 tsp oil

1 medium onion, finely sliced

approx. 500 g (1 lb) cooked, cubed, mixed vegetables (e.g. potato, cabbage – two classic ingredients – pumpkin, carrot, broccoli, peas, spinach and courgette)

ground black pepper

Method:

1. In a frying pan, heat the oil. Add the onion and gently sauté until lightly browned. Add mixed vegetables and pepper. Use a metal spatula to lift and turn mixture until well combined.

2. Press down the vegetables to make a flat cake in the frying pan.

3. Cook over medium heat for 5 minutes, or until the bottom of the 'cake' is well browned. Cut the hot Bubble & Squeak into wedges in the pan. Serve brown-side up.

To vary: For a heartier dish, add 60 g (2 oz) finely diced cold meat, chicken or ham with vegetables in Step 1.

Nutritional data per serving: 393 kJ (95 cal), Carbohydrate 13 g, Fat 3 g, Protein 5 g.

Preparation time: With pre-cooked vegetables – 10 minutes. Cooking equipment: frying pan.

Wholemeal Corn Fritters

Makes: 12

125 g (4 oz) wholemeal self-raising flour

1 egg, slightly beaten

4 tbsp skimmed milk

185 g (6 oz) canned sweetcorn kernels, drained

Serve corn fritters with soup, as a vegetable accompaniment to a main course, or on their own.

Method:

1. Make a well in the flour. Add the egg and milk to the well. With a wooden spoon gradually draw in the flour to make a smooth dough. Add corn and stir well.

2. Heat the pan over medium heat and grease lightly with a paper towel or brush dipped in oil.

3. When the pan is very hot, drop in tablespoonsful of corn mixture. Allow to cook for 2–3 minutes, or until golden-brown underneath. Flip over to cook the other side.

4. Repeat until all the mixture has been used.

To vary: Add 1 tbsp chopped lean ham at Step 1. **To store:** Prepared mixture should be used immediately. Cooked fritters are not as delicious when reheated.

Nutritional data per serving: 169 kJ (40 cal), Carbohydrate 7 g, Fat 1 g, Protein 2 g.

Preparation time: 15 minutes. Cooking equipment: frying pan.

Jumping Bean Bake

***Serves: 2 as a main
course; 4 as a side dish***

---

185 g (6 oz) lima beans
*250 ml (8 fl oz) tomato
    paste*
*good pinch of cayenne
    pepper*
½ tsp dried oregano
Topping:
2 tbsp dry breadcrumbs
*2 tbsp grated, low-fat hard
    cheese*

Method:

1. Place beans in a bowl and add sufficient water to cover.
   Leave to soak overnight.

2. The following day, drain the beans and rinse
   thoroughly under cold, running water. Place in a
   saucepan, add fresh water to cover. Bring to the boil,
   then reduce heat to simmer for 1 hour, or until tender.
   Drain beans, discard water. Set aside.

3. In a bowl, combine the tomato purée, cayenne pepper
   and oregano.

4. Lightly grease a pie dish or small casserole. Arrange a
   layer of beans on the base, cover with a layer of
   tomato; repeat layering.

5. Top with grated cheese and breadcrumbs.

6. Bake in a preheated oven for 15–20 minutes, or until
   topping has browned.

As an accompaniment: Serve hot, garnished with chopped parsley.

As a main course: Serve hot, accompanied by a crisp, green salad.

Nutritional data per serving: 1,081 kJ (259 cal), Carbohydrate 42 g, Fat 1 g, Protein 20 g.

Preparation time: soak beans – overnight; simmered on the stove – 1 hour; baked in the oven – 20 minutes.

Cooking equipment: medium-sized saucepan, pie dish or casserole.

Oven temperature: 180°C/350°F/gas 4.

Tortilla (Spanish Omelette)

**Serves: 4 as a main dish;
8 as an entrée**

---

*375 g (12 oz) sliced, cooked
     vegetables*

or

2 medium potatoes, sliced

*250 g (8 oz) pumpkin,
     peeled and sliced*

*125 g (4 oz) sweet potato,
     sliced*

1 medium courgette, sliced

1 tsp oil

1 tsp margarine or *butter*

1 large onion, sliced

4 large eggs

1 tbsp chopped parsley

ground black pepper

Method:

1. *Starting with uncooked vegetables:* Steam, boil or microwave the potatoes, pumpkin, sweet potato and courgette until tender.

2. In a large frying pan, heat the oil and margarine/butter. Add the onion and sauté until golden brown, about 5 minutes.

3. Add cooked vegetables to the pan, combine well and leave to heat through.

4. Meanwhile, beat together the eggs, parsley and pepper.

5. When the vegetables are hot, spread out evenly in the pan; keep heat at low to medium. Pour over egg mixture.

6. Tilt pan so the egg spreads evenly over the vegetables. Continue cooking over low to medium heat. As the edges of the omelette begin to set, use a spatula or egg slice to lift edges carefully and allow raw egg mixture to run underneath. When the omelette has set, use the spatula or egg slice to loosen the edges carefully all the way round.

7. Wipe a dinner plate, larger than the frying pan, with oil. Place the plate over the pan, like a lid. Using a cloth to hold the 'lid' on, turn the pan over so that the omelette falls onto the plate, bottom-side up. Set aside.

8. If necessary, scrape the frying pan of any scraps stuck to it. Lightly re-grease the pan. Now carefully slide the omelette back into the pan; it will be upside-down. Leave to fry gently for 5–7 minutes, or until golden-brown underneath. Slide cooked Tortilla on to a serving plate. Cut into wedges and serve hot or cold for

Nutritional data per serving: 920 kJ (220 cal), Carbohydrate 30 g, Fat 8 g, Protein 9 g.

Preparation time: using cooked, leftover vegetables – 15–18 minutes. Using fresh vegetables (depending on cooking method) – 20 minutes, plus 15–18 minutes frying time. Cooking equipment: saucepan, steamer or microwave oven, large frying pan.

Divine Lentil & Pumpkin Loaf

Serves: 8

250 g (8 oz) brown lentils,
  cooked (page 143)
500 g (1 lb) pumpkin,
  cooked
2 medium onions, finely
  chopped
185 g (6 oz) fresh
  breadcrumbs
ground black pepper
2 tbsp chopped parsley
4 tsp chopped fresh thyme
  or good pinch of dried
skimmed milk to bind

Serve with Classic Tomato Sauce (page 176) and a green salad.

Method:

1. Mash the lentils. Add all remaining ingredients, except the skimmed milk. Combine well. Add milk, a little at a time, until the mixture is moist and holds together.
2. Grease a loaf tin. Spoon in the lentil mixture and press down firmly. Bake in a preheated oven for 30 minutes.
3. Leave the loaf to cool in the tin for 10 minutes before turning out and cutting into thick slices. Serve hot.

To vary: Sprinkle 1 tbsp of toasted sesame seeds over the bottom of the greased loaf tin; gently shake seeds around so they cover sides and bottom of tin. **To store:** Keep covered in the refrigerator for up to 3 days. Do not freeze.

Nutritional data per serving: 917 kJ (219 cal), Carbohydrate 46 g, Fat 1 g, Protein 9 g.
Preparation time: using pre-cooked lentils and pumpkin – 40 minutes. Cooking equipment: loaf tin.
Oven temperature: 190°C/375°F/gas 5.

Adzuki Bean Simmer

Serves: 4

250 g (8 oz) raw adzuki
  beans
90 g (3 oz) carrot, diced
1 cup onion, diced
2 cloves garlic, crushed
6 mushrooms, sliced
½ tsp dried basil
600 ml (1 pt) vegetable stock
ground black pepper
1 tbsp soy sauce

Serve with wholemeal Pancakes (page 160) folded in four, or with chunks of crusty wholemeal bread.

Method:

1. Soak beans in water overnight. Drain beans in a colander and rinse well under cold water, then place in a saucepan, cover with fresh water and bring to the boil. Boil rapidly for 10 minutes, then reduce heat and simmer gently for 1½ hours, or until softened.
2. Drain beans. Return to the saucepan and add all other ingredients, except soy sauce. Bring to the boil, reduce heat and simmer gently for 45 minutes.
3. Add soy sauce and stir. Serve hot.

Nutritional data per serving: 459 kJ (110 cal), Carbohydrate 18 g, Fat 1 g, Protein 8 g.
Preparation time: Soak beans – overnight; cooking time – 1½ hours. Starting with cooked beans – 1 hour.
Cooking equipment: medium-sized saucepan.

Kitchri (Savoury Rice & Lentils)

Serves: 2 as a light meal;
4 as an accompaniment

---

250 g (8 oz) red lentils

2 large onions, finely sliced

220 g (7 oz) brown rice

1.15 litres (2 pints)
  vegetable stock

1½ tsp garam marsala

Garnish:

spring onions, finely
  chopped

A glance at the nutritional data for this recipe shows what a valuable dish this is in an athlete's meal plan.

Method:

1. Place lentils in a bowl of cold water; discard any that float to the surface. Rinse well under cold water.
2. In a large frying pan, combine the onions, rice and lentils. Add the stock and garam marsala; bring mixture to the boil over a high heat.
3. Reduce heat, cover and simmer for 45 minutes, or until rice and lentils are completely soft.
4. Garnish Kitchri with chopped spring onions; serve hot.

To store: Keep covered in the refrigerator for up to 3 days.

Nutritional data per serving: 574 kJ (137 cal), Carbohydrate 26 g, Fat 1 g, Protein 8 g.

Preparation time: 1 hour. Cooking equipment: frying pan with lid.

Wholemeal Pastry

You can use all wholemeal flour if you like, but the pastry will be heavier. A food processor is a great help; it turns pastry-making into a quick and easy process.

---

125 g (4 oz) plain
  wholemeal flour

125 g (4 oz) plain white
  flour

125 g (4 oz) butter or
  margarine

water

Method:

1. In a large bowl, combine the flours.
2. Use your fingers to rub the butter or margarine into the flour until the mixture resembles coarse breadcrumbs.
3. Add water, a little at a time, working in after each addition, until you have a soft dough.
4. Turn dough on to a lightly floured board and knead lightly until smooth. Use dough as required in recipe.

To store: Wrap the pastry in cling film and keep refrigerated for up to 3 days. To freeze, seal completely. Allow to thaw slowly before use.

Nutritional data per quantity: 7,294 kJ (1743 cal), Carbohydrate 191 g, Fat 101 g, Protein 30 g.

Preparation time: 15 minutes.

Macaroni Cheese

Serves: 2

90 g (3 oz) uncooked
  macaroni
350 ml (12 fl oz) Savoury
  White Sauce (page 177)
½ tsp dry mustard
ground black pepper
4 tbsp grated low-fat hard
  cheese

Topping:
2 tbsp grated low-fat hard
  cheese
4 tbsp dry breadcrumbs
  (optional)

Provided you use low-fat hard cheese, this is an ideal dish for athletes – low in fat, high in carbohydrate and with protein to boot. Pack a slice of Macaroni Cheese in your lunch box as a snack or work lunch.

Method:

1. Two-thirds fill a medium-sized saucepan with water. Bring to a rapid boil, add macaroni and cook until *al dente* (firm, but tender to bite) – 10–12 minutes. Drain.
2. While the pasta is cooking, prepare the Savoury White Sauce.
3. Add the cooked macaroni, mustard, pepper and grated cheese to the white sauce and stir gently to combine.
4. Lightly grease a shallow casserole and spoon in the macaroni mixture. Top with grated cheese and breadcrumbs.
5. Place under the grill or on the top shelf of the oven and heat until the topping has melted and turned golden-brown.
6. Serve hot, accompanied by a plain green salad.

To vary: Arrange thinly sliced fresh tomato over the macaroni. Sprinkle with oregano. Top with the grated cheese and breadcrumbs.

Nutritional data per serving: 841 kJ (101 cal), Carbohydrate 16 g, Fat 1 g, Protein 7 g.

Preparation time: 30 minutes. Cooking equipment: 2 medium-sized saucepans, small casserole.

Oven temperature: 220°C/425°F/gas 7 or grill on high.

Zoom Burgers

Serves: 4

220 g (7 oz) cooked brown
  lentils, lightly mashed
  (page 143)
185 g (6 oz) cooked and
  mashed potato
60 g (2 oz) carrot, grated
45 g (1½ oz) rolled oats
30 g (1 oz) fresh wholemeal
  breadcrumbs
1 medium onion, grated
1 egg, lightly beaten
½ tsp ground cumin
½ tsp turmeric
½ tsp ground coriander
2 tbsp chopped parsley
3–4 tbsp bran or
  wheatgerm, to coat

Place these on a bun with salad and you have a wonderful meal; slip Zoom Burgers into wholemeal pitta (Lebanese) bread, add salad and Yoghurt Dressing (page 182) and you have a winning meal.

Method:

1. Combine all the ingredients except bran or wheatgerm and mix well.
2. With wet hands, firmly mould the mixture into patty shapes. Coat each patty in the bran or wheatgerm; press in coating so it sticks to the patty.
3. Spray a baking tray with non-stick cooking spray *or* lightly grease the tray with oil. Place the patties on the tray.
4. Bake in a preheated oven for 20 minutes; use a metal spatula to turn the patties carefully over once during cooking.
5. Split open 4 wholemeal buns, fill each with a Zoom Burger. Add thin slices of apple, onion rings, crisp lettuce leaves and grated carrot, if liked.

To vary: Serve the burgers hot, accompanied by brown rice and one of these sauces: Classic Tomato Sauce (page 176), or Satay (Peanut) Sauce with Chilli (page 177).

To store: Keep covered in the refrigerator for up to 3 days. The burgers freeze well once cooked. Stack the burgers with a piece of wax paper between each, then wrap the stack securely with cling film and freeze. Defrost completely and then grill briefly before use.

Zoom Souvlaki

Split open 4 wholemeal pitta (Lebanese) breads to form pockets. Slide a Zoom Burger in each. Top up with finely chopped cucumber and tomato and a spoon of Yoghurt Dressing (page 182) or Hummus (page 71).

Nutritional data per serving: 780 kJ (180 cal), Carbohydrate 34 g, Fat 3 g, Protein 8 g.

Preparation time: starting with cooked lentils and potato – 30 minutes. Cooking equipment: baking tray.
Oven temperature: 220°C/425°F/gas 7.

Pitta Pizza

Serves: 2

2 large wholemeal pitta
(Lebanese) breads

1 recipe Pizza Sauce
(below)

2 large tomatoes, sliced

½ green pepper, seeded and
sliced

½ cup mushrooms, sliced

1 small onion, sliced

4 tbsp low-fat hard cheese,
finely grated

Method:

1. Spread pitta breads with Pizza Sauce, then sprinkle over all the other ingredients, finishing with the cheese.

2. Put on baking sheet and bake in a preheated oven for 20 minutes.

3. Serve pizzas hot from the oven, or fold in half to make a pizza sandwich and serve cold as a packed lunch.

Optional extras: black olives, pitted and chopped; peeled prawns; lean ham, finely chopped; sliced courgette.

To store: Prepare pizzas in advance up to Step 2. Wrap in cling film or slide into big freezer bags, and freeze until needed. When required, place frozen pizzas on a baking tray and bake in a preheated oven for 25 minutes.

Nutritional data per serving: 1,520 kJ (363 cal), Carbohydrate 68 g, Fat 3 g, Protein 19 g.

Preparation time: 1 hour. Cooking equipment: large saucepan, baking tray.

Oven temperature: 180°C/350°F/gas 4.

Pizza Sauce

Makes: enough for
2 large pizzas

2 large, ripe tomatoes

2 tbsp tomato paste

1 clove garlic, crushed

1 medium onion, sliced

½ tsp dried oregano

½ tsp dried basil

ground black pepper

60 ml (2 fl oz) water

This sauce can also be served hot with cooked pasta or grilled fish, meat or chicken.

Method:

1. Place tomatoes in a bowl and cover with boiling water. Leave to stand for 1 minute. Peel off skin which should come away easily. Chop the tomatoes.

2. In a medium saucepan, combine all the ingredients. Cover and simmer gently for 10 minutes.

3. Uncover saucepan and continue simmering gently for 10–15 minutes, or until reduced to a thick sauce.

To store: This sauce keeps well in a covered container in the refrigerator for up to three days.

Nutritional data per serving: 231 kJ (55 cal), Carbohydrate 11 g, Fat 0 g, Protein 4 g.

Preparation time: 20–30 minutes. Cooking equipment: medium-sized saucepan.

CREPES & PANCAKES

Crêpes are small, very thin pancakes; the raw batter is thinner than for pancakes. Pancakes make a hearty wrapping for a variety of fillings. The cooked pancake should be about 2 mm (⅛ in) thick. With either savoury (page 160) or sweet (pages 191–2) fillings, both crêpes and pancakes can be used for entrées, main courses, desserts or snacks.

Crêpes

Makes: 12 large or 24 small crêpes

125 g (4 oz) flour (use plain, wholemeal, or half-and-half)
3 eggs, lightly beaten
2 tsp oil or melted butter
375 ml (12 fl oz) skimmed milk

Method:

1. *Using a food processor:* Add all ingredients at once and process till smooth.
   Working by hand: Sift flour into a bowl (if using wholemeal flour, add any wheat husks left in sieve to the sifted flour). Make a well in the flour. Slowly add the beaten eggs, stirring continually to draw the ingredients together and prevent lumps forming. Mix oil or melted butter with the milk. Slowly add to the flour mixture, stirring continually, to form a thin, smooth batter. Batter should have the consistency of thin pouring cream. If too thick, add more milk, a little at a time, until you have it right.

2. Pour batter into a jug; leave to stand in a cool place for a minimum of 1 hour. If mixture has thickened, add more milk, a little at a time, to the consistency of thin pouring cream.

3. Lightly grease your pan and heat until very hot but not smoking. Pour in 2–4 tbsp batter, depending on size of pan; tilt pan to spread batter evenly. When fine bubbles appear on the surface of the crêpe and it appears dry, use an egg slice or spatula to flip and cook the other side until pale golden brown – about 5 seconds.

4. Repeat these steps for the remainder of the batter, re-greasing the pan between crêpes.

Use any of the filling mixtures (pages 160, 191–2), or make up your own. Crêpes can be filled and then served rolled up, or folded in halves or quarters.

To store: You can prepare crêpes and pancakes ahead of time, stacked up with waxed paper in between. They can then be stored in the refrigerator for up to 2 days, or packed in freezer bags and frozen until needed.

Nutritional data per large crêpe: 306 kJ (73 cal), Carbohydrate 10 g, Fat 2 g, Protein 4 g.
Preparation time: to make batter – 10 minutes; standing time for raw batter – 1 hour; cooking time –
20 minutes. Cooking equipment: crêpe pan or small, heavy-bottomed frying pan.

Pancakes

Makes: 8–10 large pancakes

---

90 g (3 oz) flour (use plain, wholemeal or half-and-half)
1 egg
315 ml (10 fl oz) milk

This is a traditional recipe and has a larger, heavier-textured result than crêpes. The pancakes should be about the size of a dinner plate, and about 2 mm (⅛ in) thick.

Method/Fillings/Storage:

Exactly as for crêpes.

Nutritional data per serving (2 pancakes): 188 kJ (45 cal), Carbohydrate 8 g, Fat 1 g, Protein 2 g.
Preparation time: to make batter – 10 minutes; standing time for raw batter – 1 hour; cooking time – 20 minutes. Cooking equipment: frying pan.

Savoury Crêpe & Pancake Fillings

The following three mixtures are excellent as fillings for crêpes and pancakes, but they can also be used as toppings for cooked pasta and jacket potatoes.

Mushroom

Sliced mushrooms and chopped onion sautéed in a little water, and tossed in Low-fat Cheese Sauce (page 179). Garnish with a sprinkling of chopped parsley.

Red Kidney Bean & Corn

Chopped green and red pepper and onion sautéed in a little water. Add red kidney beans, sweetcorn kernels, tomato paste, oregano, chilli powder and port. Use cornflour (cornstarch) to thicken if necessary. Top with grated low-fat hard cheese.

Spinach & Cheese

Sauté chopped onion in a little water. Combine with cooked, chopped spinach and Low-fat Cheese Sauce (page 179). Top with Parmesan cheese.

Rice, Cheese & Spinach in Filo Pastry

Serves: 4

250 g (8 oz) fresh spinach or 250 g (8 oz) frozen, chopped spinach

2 tbsp water

4 spring onions, chopped

125 g (4 oz) ricotta cheese

185 g (6 oz) cooked brown rice

2 tbsp lemon juice

pinch of grated nutmeg

12 sheets filo pastry

2 tbsp skimmed milk

Spoon over hot Neapolitan Sauce (page 176) or Low-fat Cheese Sauce (page 179) to make a delightful meal.

Method:

1. *Using fresh spinach:* Wash very thoroughly under cold, running water – do not dry. Chop roughly. Place wet, chopped spinach in a large saucepan. Cover and cook over high heat until tender, about 10 minutes. Remove spinach from saucepan and drain well.

   Using frozen spinach: Place frozen spinach in a saucepan. Cover and thaw over gentle heat; stir occasionally to break up any frozen lumps. When thawed, remove spinach from saucepan, drain well.

2. Heat the water in a saucepan, add the spring onions and cook until softened.

3. Combine the onions with the spinach, cheese, rice, lemon juice and nutmeg. Blend well.

4. Fold a sheet of filo pastry in half, widthwise. Brush lightly with milk.

5. Repeat with another 2 sheets of filo, stacking them on top of the first and brushing with milk between each sheet. You now have 6 layers of pastry.

6. Place a quarter of the filling along the edge of the pastry and roll up to encase the filling. Lift and tuck in the ends of the pastry before the last roll. This makes a neat parcel. Place seal-side down, on a lightly greased baking sheet.

7. Repeat Steps 4 to 7 to make 4 rolls.

8. Brush each roll with milk. Bake in a preheated oven for 15 minutes, or until pastry is crisp and golden.

To vary: Add 2 tbsp of pine nuts or chopped walnuts to the filling mixture.

To store: Keep cooked rolls, covered, in the refrigerator, for up to 3 days. If you wish to freeze them, bake for only 10 minutes at Step 8, or until pastry is palest gold. Thaw completely, reheat thoroughly at 180°C/350°F/gas 4 for 10 minutes.

Nutritional data per serving: 854 kJ (204 cal), Carbohydrate 31 g, Fat 3 g, Protein 15 g.

Preparation time: 45 minutes. Cooking equipment: medium-sized saucepan, baking sheet.

Oven temperature: 200°C/400°F/gas 6.

Conqueror's Curry Pie

Serves: 6

250 g (8 oz) potato, peeled and finely chopped

125 g (4 oz) parsnip, peeled and finely chopped

375 g (12 oz) carrot, finely chopped

125 g (4 oz) celery, finely sliced

2 onions, chopped

2 cloves garlic, crushed

500 g (1 lb) cooked brown rice

3 tbsp chopped parsley

3 tsp curry powder

375 ml (12 fl oz) Savoury White Sauce (page 177)

2 recipes Wholemeal Pastry (page 155)

Method:

1. Combine all the ingredients except the pastry. Mix together well.

2. Spray a shallow pie dish with non-stick cooking spray. Roll out pastry thinly; it should be double the size of the pie dish. Use half the pastry to line the pie dish.

3. Spoon in the filling and spread over the base of the pie shell. Cover filled pie with the remaining half of the pastry. Crimp the edges together round the edge of the pie dish and use a fork to pierce the top in a few places to let steam escape while the pie is baking.

4. Bake in a preheated oven for 15 minutes. Reduce oven temperature to 180°C/350°F/gas 4 and bake a further 20 minutes, or until pastry is golden brown.

5. Serve hot with a simple salad of sliced cucumber in Vinaigrette Dressing (page 181).

To store: Keep covered in the fridge for up to 2 days. Freeze the pie after it has been cooked.

Nutritional data per serving: 1,770 kJ (422 cal), Carbohydrate 67 g, Fat 15 g, Protein 9 g.

Preparation time: 55 minutes. Cooking equipment: 23 cm (9 in) pie dish.

Oven temperature: 200°C/400°F/gas 6.

QUICK TIP: Always have a container of cooked brown rice in the refrigerator for a quick carbohydrate addition to your meal.

Courgette Quiche

Serves: 6

2 tbsp water

1 medium onion, finely
   chopped

125 g (4 oz) courgette,
   sliced

1 recipe Wholemeal Pastry
   (page 155)

2 eggs

185 ml (6 fl oz) skimmed
   milk

60 g (2 oz) low-fat hard
   cheese, grated

ground black pepper

Although this recipe features courgettes, it also serves as an ideal low-fat quiche recipe just waiting for you to dream up variations. We have given a few alternatives.

Method:

1. Heat the water in a frying pan, add the onion and courgettes, sauté gently until the onion begins to soften.
2. Spray a quiche dish with non-stick cooking spray.
3. Roll out the pastry thinly and line the quiche dish. Set aside.
4. Beat together the eggs and milk. Add the cheese, courgette, onion and black pepper and combine well. Pour filling into the prepared pie shell.
5. Bake in a preheated oven for 5 minutes. Reduce heat to 160°C/325°F/gas 3 and bake a further 25–30 minutes or until the filling has set.
6. Serve quiche hot or cold, accompanied by a Mixed Green Salad (page 166).

Nutritional data per serving: 1,507 kJ (360 cal), Carbohydrate 37 g, Fat 19 g, Protein 11 g.

Preparation time: with pastry and courgette pre-prepared – 55 minutes.

Cooking equipment: frying pan, 23 cm (9 in) quiche dish.

Oven temperature: 220°C/425°F/gas 7.

Crab or Tuna Quiche

Instead of the courgettes, use 125 g (4 oz) of canned crab or tuna.

Potato Quiche

Replace the courgettes with 280 g (9 oz) cooked, sliced potato. Arrange the potato in concentric, overlapping circles in the pie shell. Beat together the eggs and milk. Add the cheese, onion and black pepper, combine well. Pour over the potato and bake, as above.

Mushroom Quiche

Replace the courgettes with 125 g (4 oz) of sliced mushrooms.

Spinach Quiche

Replace the courgettes with 250 g (8 oz) cooked spinach.

SALADS

Silver & Jade Salad

Serves: 4

2 cooked chicken breasts,
  chilled
125 g (4 oz) broccoli florets
125 g (4 oz) mangetout
250 g (8 oz) cooked plain
  fettuccine
250 g (8 oz) cooked spinach
  fettuccine
1 small green pepper,
  seeded and finely sliced
4 spring onions, cut into
  2.5 cm (1 in) pieces
1 recipe Ginger & Mustard
  Dressing (page 182)
2 tsp toasted sesame seeds

The white and green pastas and crisp, bright green mangetout combine with the other ingredients to make a dish that features colour, texture and flavour.

Method:

1. Finely slice the cooked chicken breasts.
2. *Blanch the broccoli and mangetout:* Two-thirds fill a saucepan with water and bring to a rapid boil. Meanwhile, prepare a large bowl of iced water. When the water boils, plunge in the broccoli and mangetout for 1 minute. Quickly drain the vegetables and immediately plunge them into the bowl of iced water. Drain once more.
  Microwave method: Place all the vegetables on a flat, microwave dish and microwave on 'high' for 2 minutes. Cool immediately, as above.
3. Combine the two kinds of cooked fettuccine. Arrange on a flat serving dish. Arrange the blanched vegetables, capsicum and sliced spring onion over the pasta. Top with the sliced chicken breast.
4. Just before serving, spoon over the Ginger & Mustard Dressing and sprinkle with toasted sesame seeds.

To vary: Use toasted slivered almond instead of sesame seeds.

To store: Prepare ingredients up to 24 hours in advance but keep them in separate covered containers in the refrigerator. Assemble the salad and add dressing at the last minute.

Nutritional data per serving: 786 kJ (188 cal), Carbohydrate 21 g, Fat 3 g, Protein 20 g.

Preparation time: chicken and pasta pre-cooked – 20 minutes. Cooking equipment: saucepan or microwave dish.

Whole fish looks grand but is easy to prepare: baby snapper, adorned with ingredients to make Whole Fish in Ginger (page 105), and backed up by crunchy Stir-fried Vegetables (page 88).

Mixed Green Salad

Serves: 4

8 *lettuce leaves (any*
  variety, or a mixture)
12 *cherry tomatoes*
1 *stick celery, sliced into*
  1 cm (¹/2 in) lengths
1 *carrot, cut into sticks*
12 *cucumber slices*
1 *small courgette, sliced*
8 *small broccoli florets*
8 *small cauliflower florets*
4 *French beans, topped and*
  tailed, cut in half
12 *mangetout, topped and*
  tailed

Dressing:
1 *recipe Vinaigrette*
  Dressing (page 181)
or
1 *recipe Yoghurt Dressing*
  (page 182)

Method:

1. Wash lettuce leaves, shake off excess water and tear into large pieces. Use to line a salad bowl.

2. In a separate bowl, combine the tomatoes, celery, carrot and cucumber.

3. *Blanch the remaining vegetables:* Two-thirds fill a large saucepan with water and bring to a rapid boil. Meanwhile, prepare a large bowl of iced water. When the water boils, add all the remaining vegetables and cook for 2 minutes. Drain the vegetables and immediately plunge them into the bowl of iced water. Drain again.
   Microwave method: Place all the vegetables on a flat, microwave dish and microwave on 'High' for 2 minutes. Cool immediately, as above.

4. Add the blanched vegetables to the fresh. Pour over Vinaigrette or Yoghurt Dressing and toss salad gently.

5. Spoon the dressed vegetables into the lettuce-lined salad bowl.

To store: Salad should be eaten on the day of preparation. If it has to stand for a few hours before serving, do not add the dressing. Store in an airtight container in the refrigerator until ready to serve.

Nutritional data per serving: 242 kJ (58 cal), Carbohydrate 9 g, Fat 0.25 g, Protein 6 g.

Preparation time: 10 minutes. Cooking equipment: large saucepan or microwave dish.

Meal-in-one Rice Salad

Serves: 6

375 g (12 oz) cold, cooked
brown rice
1 small green pepper,
seeded and finely
chopped
90 g (3 oz) mushrooms,
finely sliced
1 medium carrot, grated
90 g (3 oz) bean shoots
185 g (6 oz) corn kernels
125 g (4 oz) cabbage, finely
shredded
220 ml (7 fl oz) low-fat
natural yoghurt
1 tbsp lemon juice
white pepper

Method:

1. Combine the rice and all the vegetables.
2. In a separate bowl, blend the yoghurt, lemon juice and pepper.
3. Combine vegetables and dressing.
4   Chill in the refrigerator for at least 1 hour before serving.

Nutritional data per serving: 543 kJ (130 cal), Carbohydrate 25 g, Fat 1.3 g, Protein 6 g.

Preparation time: starting with cooked rice – 20 minutes; chill before serving – 1 hour.

Noodle & Poppyseed Salad

Serves: 4

2 oranges
315 g (10 oz) cooked
noodles (e.g. macaroni,
penne)
1 tbsp poppyseeds
1 tbsp snipped chives
1 tsp Vinaigrette Dressing
(page 182)

Method:

1. Using a small, very sharp knife, peel the oranges, removing the outer covering of membrane.
2. Carefully cut the oranges into individual segments, cutting off any remaining membrane at the same time.
3. Carefully toss the orange segments with the noodles, poppyseeds, chives and dressing.
4. Chill in the refrigerator for at least 1 hour before serving.

Nutritional data per serving: 495 kJ (119 cal), Carbohydrate 25 g, Fat 0 g, Protein 4 g.

Preparation time: 10 minutes; chill before serving – 1 hour.

Salad Niçoise

Serves: 2

4 large lettuce leaves

220 g (7 oz) canned tuna in
brine, drained

4 spring onions, finely
chopped

2 hard-boiled eggs, sliced

2 small potatoes, boiled,
chilled and sliced

1 large tomato, sliced

100 g (3½ oz) cooked
French beans

½ green pepper, seeded and
cut into strips

½ red pepper, seeded and
cut into strips

2 tbsp Vinaigrette Dressing
(page 181)

Method:

1. Tear well-washed lettuce leaves in half and use to line
    a salad bowl.
2. Carefully arrange all remaining ingredients on top of
    the lettuce.
3. Sprinkle over the Vinaigrette Dressing just before
    serving.

As an entrée: Divide salad ingredients between individual
plates and spoon dressing over each serving. Chill.

*Nutritional data per serving: 613 kJ (147 cal), Carbohydrate 11 g,
Fat 4 g, Protein 16 g.*

Preparation time: 20 minutes.

Four Seasons Salad

Serves: 6

1 lettuce, preferably cos or
    Continental variety
250 g (8 oz) cherry
    tomatoes or larger
    tomatoes cut into 8
12 button mushrooms,
    halved
1 medium cucumber, cubed
125 g (4 oz) cottage cheese,
    crumbled
½ clove garlic, crushed
30 g (1 oz) parsley, chopped
2 tbsp low-oil Vinaigrette
    Dressing (page 181)

Method:

1. Wash lettuce well and tear into bite-sized pieces. Place in the bottom of a salad bowl.
2. In a separate bowl, gently toss together all remaining ingredients, except dressing.
3. Pile salad ingredients on to the lettuce.
4. Just before serving, pour over the dressing and carefully toss the salad.

To store: Prepare and eat on the same day.

Nutritional data per serving: 128 kJ (31 cal), Carbohydrate 2 g, Fat 0 g, Protein 4 g.

Preparation time: 10 minutes.

Waldorf Salad

Serves: 6

2 red apples
125 g (4 oz) celery, diced
45 g (1½ oz) walnuts,
    chopped
1 tbsp lemon juice
185 ml (6 fl oz) low-fat
    natural yoghurt

Try adding 2 tbsp of stoned, chopped dates or sultanas.

Method:

1. Wash the apples and polish skins with a soft cloth. Core the apples and neatly dice the flesh.
2. Place the diced apple in a serving bowl. Add the celery, walnuts and lemon juice.
3. Add the yoghurt and lightly fold to combine ingredients.
4. Chill salad for at least 1 hour before serving.

Nutritional data per serving: 267 kJ (64 cal), Carbohydrate 7 g, Fat 3 g, Protein 4 g.

Preparation time: 10 minutes; chill before serving – 1 hour.

Tabbouleh

Serves: 4

75 g (2½ oz) burghul
  (cracked wheat)
250 g (8 oz) very ripe, fresh
  tomatoes or 250 g (8 oz)
  canned tomatoes
1 small white onion, finely
  chopped
60 g (2 oz) parsley, chopped
75 ml (2½ fl oz) Vinaigrette
  Dressing (page 181)
juice of 1 lemon

Method:

1. Place the burghul (cracked wheat) in a basin and cover with boiling water. Leave to stand for 2 hours.

2. *Using fresh tomatoes:* Place the tomatoes in a basin. Cover with boiling water. Leave to stand for 1 minutes. Pour off water. The skins will slip off easily. Finely chop the peeled tomatoes. Place in a colander and leave to drain.
   Using canned tomatoes: Chop finely and leave to drain in a colander.

3. Line a colander with muslin or paper towels and tip in the soaked burghul. Allow to drain – most of the liquid will have been absorbed by the wheat. Use both hands to squeeze the burghul, removing as much liquid as possible.

4. Place burghul in a large basin. Add tomatoes, onion, parsley, dressing and lemon juice. Combine thoroughly. Stand for at least 1 hour.

As a light meal: Serve with pitta (Lebanese) bread or on lettuce leaves.

As a casual but hearty meal: Split open a pitta bread to make a pocket. Place 2 or 3 small Chicken Balls (page 63) in the pitta bread, spoon in 2 tbsp of Tabbouleh. Top with low-fat natural yoghurt or Yoghurt Dressing (page 182).

To store: Keep covered in the refrigerator for up to 5 days.

Nutritional data per serving: 191 kJ (46 cal), Carbohydrate 6 g, Fat 1 g, Protein 3 g.
Preparation time: soaking cracked wheat – 2 hours; preparing salad – 15 minutes; standing time before serving – 1 hour, minimum.

Fast-slaw

Serves: 4

150 g (5 oz) cabbage, finely
  shredded
2 tbsp finely chopped green
  pepper
4 tbsp grated carrot
2 tbsp sultanas
2 tbsp chopped walnuts
2 tbsp Yoghurt Dressing
  (page 182) or low-calorie
  coleslaw dressing

Method:
1. Combine all ingredients.
2. Chill in the refrigerator for 1 hour before serving.

*Nutritional data per serving: 328 kJ (79 cal), Carbohydrate 8 g,
Fat 4 g, Protein 3 g.*

Preparation time: 10 minutes; chill time – 1 hour.

Marinated Bean Shoots & Mushrooms

Serves: 4

185 g (6 oz) bean shoots
90 g (3 oz) mushrooms,
  sliced
2 spring onions, finely
  sliced
½ green pepper, seeded and
  finely diced
1 tbsp soy sauce
1 clove garlic, crushed
ground black pepper
2 tbsp sesame seeds

Method:
1. Wash bean shoots well. Shake dry.
2. In a salad bowl, combine the bean shoots, sliced
    mushrooms, spring onions and capsicum.
3. Combine remaining ingredients and add to the
    vegetables. Toss gently.
4. Cover salad and chill in the refrigerator for 1 hour
    before serving.

To vary: You can also add half a stick of celery, finely
sliced, and/or 125 g (4 oz) mangetout, topped and tailed.

*Nutritional data per serving: 172 kJ (41 cal), Carbohydrate 2 g,
Fat 2 g, Protein 3 g.*

Preparation time: 10 minutes; chill before serving – 1 hour.

Sweet Potato & Banana Salad

Serves: 4

3 medium sweet potatoes

2 bananas

1 tbsp lemon juice

1 tsp curry powder

½ recipe Yoghurt Dressing
   (page 182)

2 spring onions, chopped

Method:

1. Peel the sweet potato and cut into neat, 2 cm (1 in) cubes.

2. Place in a large saucepan and barely cover with cold water. Bring to the boil, reduce heat and simmer for 10–12 minutes, or until potato is cooked through but still holds its shape.

3. Meanwhile, slice banana and toss in lemon juice.

4. Blend the curry powder with the Yoghurt Dressing.

5. Drain the cooked potato and allow to cool.

6. In a salad bowl, combine the potato, banana and spring onion. Pour over the dressing and toss gently.

7. Chill in the refrigerator for 1 hour before serving as an accompaniment to cold meat or poultry.

Microwave Method:

Cooking time: 5 minutes.

The microwave cooks the cubed sweet potato fast; so there is no chance of the cubes losing their neat shape and the lovely orange colour will be enhanced.

Prepare the sweet potato as described in the Method. Arrange the cubes around the edge of a large, shallow dish. Add 2 tbsp of water and cover with cling film. Microwave on 'High' for 2½ minutes, stir the potato and push back around the edges. Refresh the potato under cold running water. Proceed from Step 3 of conventional Method.

Nutritional data per serving: 665 kJ (159 cal), Carbohydrate 36 g, Fat 1 g, Protein 4 g.

Preparation time: approximately 20 minutes; chill before serving – 1 hour. Cooking equipment: large saucepan, mixing bowl.

Hot Potato Salad

Serves: 4

4 medium potatoes,
   scrubbed

2 hard-boiled eggs,
   chopped

2–3 spring onions, finely
   chopped

½ recipe Vinaigrette
   Dressing (page 181)

Serve this salad hot, with grilled fish or meat.

Method:

1. Cut the unpeeled potatoes into 2 cm (1 in) cubes. Place in a saucepan and add enough cold water to barely cover. Bring to the boil, reduce heat and simmer for 10–12 minutes, or until the potato is cooked through but holds its shape.
2. Drain the cooked potato and place in a salad bowl.
3. Add the hard-boiled eggs and spring onions to the hot potato. Pour over the Vinaigrette Dressing. Gently toss the salad.

Nutritional data per serving: 464 kJ (111 cal), Carbohydrate 18 g, Fat 3 g, Protein 5 g.

Preparation time: approximately 15 minutes. Cooking equipment: saucepan.

Creamy Potato Salad

Instead of Vinaigrette Dressing, use ½ recipe of Yoghurt Dressing (page 182).

Curried Potato Salad

Instead of Vinaigrette Dressing, use 125 ml (4 fl oz) Yoghurt Dressing (page 182) blended with 1 level tsp curry powder and ½ tsp caster sugar. Serve chilled.

Curried Chicken Salad

Serves: 2

2 small cooked chicken
   breasts, diced

1 large apple, diced

90 g (3 oz) sweetcorn
   kernels

2 tbsp sultanas

1 tbsp toasted pine nuts

2 tbsp low-fat yoghurt

½ tsp curry powder

Method:

1. Combine all ingredients in a salad bowl.
2. Chill salad in the refrigerator for 1 hour. Serve with hot baked potatoes in their jackets.

Nutritional data per serving: 1,423 kJ (340 cal), Carbohydrate 27 g, Fat 9 g, Protein 38 g.

Preparation time: 10 minutes.

SAUCES, DRESSINGS & GRAVIES

In this chapter you will find those delicious savoury liquids and toppings that so often add the final touch to a dish. Traditionally, these foods tend to include a high percentage of added fats in the form of butter and oil; this can present problems for those athletes trying to control fat intake.

We have developed these recipes, based on old favourites as well as some new ideas, so that you can still enjoy the pleasures of a sauce or gravy without radically increasing your overall fat intake. Several of these recipes include a high proportion of vegetable ingredients, thereby making the dishes even more nutritious.

Microwaved Sauces

Apart from the shortened cooking time, there are many other advantages to making sauces in the microwave. To begin with, many sauces can be mixed, cooked in the microwave and then served in the same dish. This reduces the risk of congealing or burning – and there are no saucepans to clean afterwards.

While different sauces require varying amounts of stirring, very few need to be stirred constantly. If you need to stir a sauce while it is cooking in the microwave, it is quite safe to open the oven and do so. Another advantage – the microwave reduces the risk of lumps forming in a sauce.

Hints for Cooking Sauces in the Microwave

- A container with straight sides allows liquids to heat faster than one with curved sides.

- Sugar heats up very quickly in the microwave, so sweet sauces microwave faster than savoury ones. Add sugar in the initial blending of the sauce.

- *For milk-based sauces:* Use a large, deep container as the sauce will rise to double its depth once it boils.

- *For egg-based sauces:* Prevent over-heating by stirring frequently during cooking. Stir from the outside into the centre. Remove sauce from the microwave just before it has thickened to the required consistency, a few minutes' standing time will allow for thickening.

- *For flour-based sauces:* These can be successfully reheated in the microwave. Thin sauces need 2 minutes on 'High' for every 280 ml (9 fl oz) and thick sauces need 3 minutes.

Sweet & Sour Sauce

Serves: 4–6

1 medium white onion

*2 medium carrots,
    scrubbed*

1 small red pepper, seeded

*1 small green pepper,
    seeded*

2 small courgettes

1 stick of celery

125 g (4 oz) mangetout

1 tsp grated fresh ginger

*1 clove garlic, finely
    chopped*

*250 ml (8 fl oz) tomato
    juice*

*250 ml (8 fl oz) canned,
    unsweetened pineapple
    pieces (juice included)*

1 tbsp soft brown sugar

*1 tbsp cornflour
    (cornstarch)*

1 tbsp vinegar

2 tbsp water

No fat, plenty of flavour and carbohydrate make this a sauce worth knowing about. Its piquant taste adds something special even to a simple bowl of boiled brown rice or noodles.

Method:

1. Slice the onion, carrot, pepper, courgette and celery into thin strips, about matchstick size. Top and tail the mangetout, but leave whole.

2. Lightly oil a wok or large frying pan and place over high heat until almost smoking. Add all the vegetables at once, including the ginger and garlic. Using a spatula, stir-fry, lifting and turning constantly, for 3 minutes.

3. Add the tomato juice, pineapple pieces and sugar. Bring to the boil, stirring constantly. Reduce heat and simmer for 3 minutes. Remove wok or frying-pan from the heat, but leave stove on at high heat.

4. In a small bowl, combine the cornflour, vinegar and water to make a thin paste.

5. Return wok or frying pan to the heat. Pour in the cornflour mixture. Bring to the boil, stirring gently but constantly, until the sauce thickens.

6. Serve hot or cold with grilled fish (page 104) or Skewered Lamb & Vegetables (page 125).

Nutritional data per serving: 361 kJ (87 cal), Carbohydrate 19 g, Fat 0 g, Protein 3 g.

Preparation time: 25 minutes. Cooking equipment: wok or large frying pan.

Classic Tomato Sauce

Serves: 4

2 tsp water

1 onion, finely chopped

440 g (14 oz) canned peeled
   tomatoes (reserve juice)

2 large mushrooms,
   chopped

good pinch of dried
   oregano or mixed herbs

¼ medium green pepper,
   seeded and diced

3 green olives, sliced

3 black olives, sliced

ground black pepper

Method:

1. Heat water in the saucepan until very hot. Add onions and sauté until soft.

2. Add tomatoes and simmer for 2–3 minutes.

3. Add mushrooms, oregano, capsicum, olives and black pepper to taste. Simmer for 2–3 minutes.

4. Add the reserved tomato juice. Simmer the sauce, uncovered, for 10–15 minutes, or until most of the liquid has evaporated. Pour hot over pasta.

To vary: To the completed sauce add: 2–3 anchovies, chopped, 3–4 tbsp of tuna, or cooked diced chicken.

To store: Covered, in the refrigerator, for up to 2 days.

Nutritional data per serving: 138 kJ (33 cal), Carbohydrate 8 g, Fat 1 g, Protein 2 g.

Preparation time: 20 minutes. Cooking equipment: saucepan.

Neapolitan Sauce

Serves: 2

2 tsp water

1 clove garlic, crushed

500 ml (16 fl oz) tomato
   purée

3 fresh basil leaves, finely
   chopped or good pinch of
   dried basil leaves

ground black pepper

2 tsp grated Parmesan
   cheese

This is an easy tomato and basil sauce for pasta.

Method:

1. Heat the water in the saucepan until very hot. Add the garlic and simmer until tender.

2. Add tomato purée, basil and black pepper to taste and stir. Simmer for 15–20 minutes, stirring occasionally.

3. Spoon the hot sauce over cooked plain or wholemeal spaghetti. Top with grated Parmesan cheese.

To vary: To the completed sauce add: 4 black olives, pitted and halved, 4 tbsp of tuna, or diced cooked chicken.

To store: Covered in the refrigerator for up to 3 days.

Nutritional data per serving: 290 kJ (69 cal), Carbohydrate 11 g, Fat 1 g, Protein 4 g.

Preparation time: 20 minutes. Cooking equipment: medium-sized saucepan.

Savoury White Sauce

Serves: 4–6

500 ml (16 fl oz) skimmed
   milk

1 onion, cut in half

1 small carrot, roughly
   chopped

1 stick of celery, roughly
   chopped

6 peppercorns

2 tbsp plain flour

Try adding 2 tbsp grated Parmesan cheese or 3 tbsp of grated, low-fat hard cheese at Step 3.

Method:

1. Pour the milk into a saucepan. Add the chopped vegetables and peppercorns. Bring mixture to the boil. Immediately reduce heat and simmer for 15 minutes.
2. Strain the milk into a bowl. Discard the vegetables and peppercorns. In a separate bowl, mix the flour with 2–3 tbsp of the warm milk. Stir to form a smooth paste. Gradually add the rest of the milk, stirring continuously.
3. Return the sauce to the saucepan. Bring to the boil, stirring constantly. Reduce heat and simmer gently for

Microwave Method: Cooking time: approximately 7 minutes.

Blend to a smooth paste the flour and 60 ml (2 fl oz) of the milk and set aside. In a casserole, blend the remainder of the milk with all the other ingredients. Cover with cling film, microwave on 'High' for 1–1½ minutes, stirring once during cooking.

Nutritional data per serving: 255 kJ (58 cal), Carbohydrate 10 g, Fat 0 g, Protein 5 g.

Preparation time: 25 minutes. Cooking equipment: medium-sized saucepan.

Satay (Peanut) Sauce with Chilli

Serves: 4

1 tbsp oil

1 small onion, grated

1 clove garlic, crushed

good pinch of ground chilli

250 g (8 oz) crunchy peanut
   butter

1½ tbsp sweet soy sauce or
   1 tbsp soy sauce plus
   2 tsp dark brown sugar

2 tbsp lemon juice

250 ml (8 fl oz) water

Method:

1. In a frying pan, heat the oil. Add the onion and garlic and sauté gently until soft and golden.
2. Add the ground chilli to the pan, stir in and fry for 1 minute over medium heat.
3. Add the peanut butter to the pan and stir well. Add remaining ingredients and stir well. Bring mixture to the boil, stirring constantly. Reduce heat and simmer gently for 1 minute.

Nutritional data per serving: 441 kJ (132 cal), Carbohydrate 18 g, Fat 3 g, Protein 2 g.

Preparation time: 20 minutes. Cooking equipment: frying pan.

Quick Vegetable Sauce for Pasta

Serves: 2

2 tbsp water

1 small onion, grated

½ green pepper, seeded and
  chopped

½ stick of celery, chopped

2 small courgettes, chopped

2 medium tomatoes,
  chopped

1 tbsp tomato paste

4 large mushrooms, sliced

1 clove garlic, crushed

½ tsp finely chopped fresh
  basil, or good pinch of
  dried

ground black pepper

Method:

1. Make the sauce while your pasta (e.g. spaghetti or shell noodles) is cooking. Heat the water in a saucepan, until almost boiling. Add the onion, capsicum and celery and sauté over low heat for 3 minutes, or until softened.

2. Add all remaining ingredients. Stir to combine. Cover saucepan and simmer gently for 10 minutes or until all vegetables are tender. Add the cooked pasta to the sauce and gently toss to combine. If necessary, briefly reheat. Serve.

Microwave Method:

Cooking time: 5 minutes.

If the conventional method for this sauce is quick, the microwave makes it even faster. Take care not to overcook the sauce or it will discolour.

Prepare the vegetables as described in Ingredients. In a large casserole, combine the water, onion, capsicum and celery. Cover with cling film and microwave on 'High' for 1–1½ minutes. Remove from oven and add all remaining ingredients, combine well. Cover with cling film and microwave on 'High' for 1½–2 minutes, stir, and then microwave a further 2 minutes. Remove from oven. Leave to stand, covered, for 1 minute before serving.

Nutritional data per serving: 201 kJ (48 cal), Carbohydrate 8 g, Fat 1 g, Protein 3 g.

Preparation time: 20 minutes. Cooking equipment: large saucepan.

Low-fat Cheese Sauce

Serves: 8

500 g (1 lb) cottage cheese

250 g (8 oz) ricotta cheese

125 ml (4 fl oz) skimmed milk

1 tbsp cornflour (cornstarch)

1 tbsp skimmed milk, extra

This sauce works well with a variety of savoury dishes. It is especially delicious with fish, vegetable or pasta dishes.

Method:

1. Using a blender or food processor, blend the cheeses and skimmed milk until smooth. (If you don't have a blender, use a wire sieve and rub the cheeses through. Then add milk and stir till smooth.)
2. In a saucepan, gently warm the cheese mixture, stirring constantly.
3. In a cup, blend the cornflour with the extra tablespoon of milk to form a smooth paste. Add to the saucepan and stir into the sauce.
4. Bring sauce to the boil, stirring constantly. Immediately reduce heat and simmer gently for 2 minutes, stirring constantly.

Microwave Method:

Cooking time: 5–6 minutes.

It's well worth preparing this sauce in the microwave: it will be smooth and creamy and you can cook and serve it in the same jug.

Blend the cheese and milk as in Step 1 of the conventional Method. Pour into a microwave-proof serving jug or bowl. In a separate bowl, blend the cornflour and extra tablespoon of milk to a smooth paste and then stir into the cheese mixture. Cover with cling film and microwave on 'High' for 5–6 minutes. Remove from microwave and allow 2 minutes standing time before serving.

To vary: For a more piquant sauce, add ½ tsp prepared English mustard and a pinch of cayenne pepper.

To store: The sauce will keep for up to 2 days in a sealed container in the refrigerator. Reheat thoroughly over gentle heat before use. Do not freeze.

Nutritional data per serving: 43 kJ (10 cal), Carbohydrate 3 g, Fat 0 g, Protein 2 g.

Preparation time: 10 minutes. Cooking equipment: blender, food processor or wire sieve, medium-sized saucepan.

Low-fat Gravy

Makes: 280 ml (9 fl oz)

250 ml (8 fl oz) prepared
stock (e.g. vegetable or
chicken)
45 g (1½ oz) carrot, finely
chopped
45 g (1½ oz) pumpkin,
finely chopped
1 large apple, finely diced
1 tbsp tomato paste
extra stock, as necessary

Method:
1. In a medium-sized saucepan, combine the stock, chopped vegetables and apple. Bring to a simmer and cook until completely softened.
2. Stir in the tomato paste.
3. Place the mixture in a food processor or blender – blend until smooth, or press mixture through a wire sieve.
4. If you find the gravy too thick, add more stock, a little at a time, until you have the desired consistency.
5. Serve with vegetables and grilled meats and poultry.

To store: Covered, in the refrigerator for up to 3 days.

Nutritional data per serving: 525 kJ (126 cal), Carbohydrate 29 g, Fat 0 g, Protein 4 g.

Preparation time: 25 minutes. Cooking equipment: medium-sized saucepan, blender, food processor or wire sieve.

Tartare Sauce

Makes: 250 ml (8 fl oz)

250 ml (8 fl oz) low-fat
natural yoghurt
2 tsp chopped capers
1 dill cucumber, chopped
3 tsp finely chopped fresh
parsley
1 tsp finely chopped mixed
fresh herbs – use a
mixture of 3 of the
following: basil, chervil,
rosemary, chives, fennel,
thyme, tarragon

Method:
1. In a small bowl, combine all the ingredients.
2. Chill in the refrigerator before serving.

To serve: Use as an accompaniment to grilled fish.

To vary: The use of different herbs will significantly change the flavour of the sauce. If liked, the capers and dill cucumber can be replaced with very finely diced celery and green pepper.

To store: Keep the sauce covered in the refrigerator for up to 2 days.

Nutritional data per serving: 678 kJ (162 cal), Carbohydrate 19 g, Fat 3 g, Protein 15 g.

Preparation time: 5 minutes.

Sweet & Sour Dressing

Makes: 250 ml (8 fl oz)

125 ml (4 fl oz) low-fat
   natural yoghurt
2 tbsp crushed pineapple
1 tbsp finely chopped
   gherkin
pinch of cayenne pepper

Use this sauce as an accompaniment to fish or as a dressing for potato salad.

Method:

1. In a bowl, combine all the ingredients.
2. Chill well in the refrigerator before use.

Nutritional data per serving: 430 kJ (103 cal), Carbohydrate 15 g, Fat 2 g, Protein 8 g.

Preparation time: 5 minutes.

Vinaigrette Dressing

Makes: 125 ml (4 fl oz)

1 tsp gelatine
60 ml (2 fl oz) cold water
2 tbsp wine vinegar
1 tbsp lemon juice
$1/4$ tsp dry mustard
1 tbsp chopped parsley
1 tbsp snipped chives
1 clove garlic, crushed
ground black pepper

Method:

1. In a small bowl, stir together the gelatine and the cold water. Place over hot water and stir until dissolved.
2. Pour dissolved gelatine into a jar with a tight-fitting lid.
3. Add the rest of the ingredients to the jar. Seal the jar and shake well to combine ingredients.
4. Store in refrigerator until required. Shake well before using.

To store: This dressing keeps well in the refrigerator and can be prepared and stored in larger quantities.

Nutritional data per serving: 25 kJ (6 cal), Carbohydrate 1 g, Fat 0 g, Protein 0 g.

Preparation time: 10 minutes.

Ginger & Mustard Dressing

Makes: 125 ml (4 fl oz)

3 tbsp lemon juice
3 tbsp water
2 tsp finely grated ginger
1 tbsp Dijon mustard
1 tbsp chopped parsley

Method:

1. Place all ingredients in a screw-top jar and shake well. Before serving, shake well again.

Nutritional data per serving: 25 kJ (6 cal), Carbohydrate 1 g, Fat 0 g, Protein 0 g.
Preparation: 5 minutes.

Yoghurt Dressing

Makes: 250 ml (8 fl oz)

250 ml (8 fl oz) low-fat
   natural yoghurt
1 tsp lemon juice
$1/4$ tsp prepared English
   mustard

Method:

1. In a bowl, combine all the ingredients.
2. Chill well in the refrigerator before serving.

As an appetizer or entrée: Use as a dipping sauce for fresh vegetables or for spicy, cold meat balls.

Seafood Dressing

Add 2 tsp prepared tomato sauce and serve as a dressing for cold, cooked seafood.

Nutritional data per serving: 674 kJ (161 cal), Carbohydrate 16 g, Fat 1 g, Protein 19 g.
Preparation time: 5 minutes.

Carrot Cake (page 205) iced with low-fat Cream Cheese Topping (page 198) (left), a stately plate of Drunken Pears (page 185) (back) and luscious Crème Caramel (page 199) garnished with blueberries (front).

DESSERTS, SWEET SAUCES & TOPPINGS

For athletes watching their fat intake, dessert may conjure up images of rich cream and sugar confections. Nevertheless, there is an enticing variety of fruit-based desserts, high in fibre, vitamin and minerals. Some of the traditional baked desserts have low-fat variations which can be a mouth-watering source of energy-giving carbohydrate.

The desserts in this chapter serve a double function: many of them, for instance Bread & Butter Pudding (page 195), make nutritious between-meal snacks, as well as providing the sweet end-note to a well-balanced menu.

Although many cooked desserts cannot be totally prepared in the microwave, it can make the preparation of some ingredients simpler, faster and with less mess. For instance:

- Where cooked or stewed fruit is used.
- Getting more juice from citrus fruit. Place whole, unpeeled oranges or lemons in the microwave and cook on 'High' for 1–2 minutes. Allow 30 seconds standing time before extracting the juice.

Dried Fruit Compote

Serves: 6

375 g (12 oz) dried fruits
  (e.g. prunes, apples,
  peaches, apricots)
750 ml (24 fl oz) cold water

This also makes an excellent breakfast dish eaten plain, with yoghurt, or with breakfast cereal.

Method:
1. Place the fruit in a bowl and add water. Cover and leave to stand overnight.
2. Drain the fruit. Serve with a topping of plain, low-fat natural yoghurt and a sprinkling of chopped nuts.

To vary: Alternatively, serve warm, with its cooking juices, plus an accompaniment of Cream Cheese Topping (page 198).

To store: Keep covered in the refrigerator for up to 4 days.

Nutritional data per serving: 438 kJ (105 cal), Carbohydrate 25 g, Fat 0 g, Protein 2 g.
Preparation time: soak overnight.

Drunken Pears

Serves: 4

4 firm fresh pears
   (e.g. Conference or
   Comice)
8 whole cloves
250 ml (8 fl oz) red wine
250 ml (8 fl oz) orange
   juice
½ tsp ground cinnamon
2 slices lemon
2 tbsp soft brown sugar
   (optional)
Garnish:
2 tsp slivered almonds,
   toasted

This elegant and delicious dessert is specially useful for the busy cook – it can be prepared up to 3 days before it is to be served. The alcohol in the burgundy evaporates in the cooking process, so you won't be breaking the Golden Rules.

Method:

1. Peel whole pears, leaving stems intact. Press 2 cloves into each pear.
2. Stand the pears upright in a saucepan just large enough to hold them.
3. Add wine, orange juice, cinnamon, lemon slices and sugar.
4. Bring to the boil, reduce heat and simmer gently for 45 minutes. Turn pears frequently as they cook, so they colour evenly.
5. Use a slotted spoon to lift out pears carefully. Remove cloves.
6. Bring the cooking liquid to a rapid boil. Boil till reduced by half to make a sauce.
7. Serve the pears warm or chilled, with the sauce poured over. Top with a sprinkling of toasted almond slivers. Accompany with Cream Cheese Topping (page 198).

To vary: Cut the cooked pears in half, lengthwise. Carefully scoop out the core, leaving a neat hollow. Use 4 tbsp of Cream Cheese Topping (page 198) to fill the pears. Sprinkle with toasted almond slivers. Serve accompanied by the sauce.

To store: Drunken Pears will keep well, covered and refrigerated, for up to 3 days.

Nutritional data per serving: 476 kJ (114 cal), Carbohydrate 28 g, Fat 0 g, Protein 1 g.

Preparation time: 1 1/4 hours. Cooking equipment: medium-sized saucepan.

Golden Syrup Dumplings

Serves: 4

2 tbsp butter or *margarine*

125 g (4 oz) self-raising
   flour

1 egg

125 ml (4 fl oz) skimmed
   milk

500 ml (16 fl oz) water

90 g (3 oz) caster sugar

1 tbsp golden syrup

This dish could be called 'Carbohydrate Heaven' – it has enough carbohydrate to keep even a marathon runner going. And it's sweet enough to satisfy even the sweetest tooth. For a change of flavour you can replace the golden syrup with honey or maple syrup.

Method:

1. Use your fingertips to rub 1 tbsp of the butter or margarine into the flour, until the mixture resembles fine breadcrumbs.

2. Lightly beat the egg and skimmed milk. Add to the flour mixture and blend well to make a stiff dough.

3. In a large saucepan, bring the water to the boil. Remove from heat and add the sugar. Stir to dissolve completely.

4. Add the remaining butter or margarine and the golden syrup. Stir well. Return to the heat and bring to the boil.

5. Break off small pieces of the dough and form into balls about the size of large marbles. Drop the dumplings into the boiling syrup.

6. Boil dumplings for 20 minutes, until light and fluffy.

7. Serve the dumplings immediately with the syrup spooned over. Hot or cold low-fat custard sauce or low-fat natural yoghurt make good accompaniments.

To store: Use freshly prepared. The dumplings will harden if left to stand.

Nutritional data per serving: 1,330 kJ (318 cal), Carbohydrate 54 g, Fat 10 g, Protein 6 g.

Preparation time: 40 minutes. Cooking equipment: large saucepan.

Baked Apples

Serves: 4

4 *small apples*

90 *g (3 oz) canned,*
unsweetened, apricots (or
peaches), drained and
chopped

2 *tbsp sultanas*

good pinch of ground
cinnamon

125 *ml (4 fl oz) water*

This time-honoured dessert is ideal if you are watching your calories.

Method:

1. Core the apples but don't peel them. Use a sharp knife to score skin of each apple around the middle.
2. Mix the apricots, sultanas and cinnamon.
3. Fill the centre of each apple with the apricot mixture. Place the apples in a baking dish. Pour the 125 ml (4 fl oz) of water around the apples.
4. Bake in a preheated oven for 30 minutes, or until apples are completely tender. You may need to baste them with their cooking liquid from time to time.
5. Serve hot or cold, with ice-cream, low-fat natural yoghurt or Baked Custard (page 193).

Microwave Method:

Cooking time: 8–10 minutes.

Using a microwave oven you can make this classic dessert in half the time, and the result tastes fresh and delicious.

Prepare ingredients as described in Steps 1–3 of the conventional Method. Arrange the apples around the edge of a plate and microwave on 'High' for 8–10 minutes. Leave to stand for 5 minutes before serving.

To vary: Add 1 tbsp chopped pecan nuts to the apricot filling mixture. To increase the carbohydrate, drizzle ½ tsp golden syrup over each apple before baking.

To store: Keep covered in the refrigerator for up to 3 days.

Stewed Fruit (in the Microwave)

For every 500 g (1 lb) of fruit, use 45 ml (3 tbsp) of liquid, such as water or wine. Add flavourings, such as spices, sugar or fruit peel, as desired. Core and peel the fruit and slice it thinly and evenly. Add the liquid and flavourings. Cover loosely with cling film. Microwave on 'High' for 6–8 minutes, or until just tender. Allow 2 minutes standing time before serving.

Nutritional data per serving: 231 kJ (55 cal), Carbohydrate 14 g, Fat 0 g, Protein 0 g.

Preparation time: 40 minutes. Cooking equipment: baking dish.

Oven temperature: 180°C/350°F/gas 4.

Fragrant Apple Rice Pudding

Serves: 4

220 g (7 oz) brown rice
125 ml (4 fl oz) water
375 ml (12 fl oz) apple juice
1 tsp ground cinnamon
good pinch of grated
   nutmeg
good pinch of ground
   cloves
250 ml (8 fl oz) skimmed
   milk
2 tbsp sultanas
1 tbsp desiccated coconut
sprinkling of ground
   cinnamon

If you love traditional rice pudding, this recipe will prove a wonderful surprise – it's rich in unrefined carbohydrate and is far lower in fat than most other recipes for this dish. You can take a slice of leftover pudding to training as a nutritious snack.

Method:

1. In a saucepan, combine the rice, water, apple juice, cinnamon, nutmeg and cloves. Bring to the boil.
2. Reduce heat and simmer very gently for 40 minutes.
3. Add milk and sultanas and stir.
4. Transfer mixture to a casserole. Sprinkle over the coconut. Bake in a preheated oven for 30 minutes.
5. Sprinkle over with ground cinnamon and serve hot or cold. Dried Fruit Compote (page 184) makes a good accompaniment.

To vary: Substitute the apple juice with unsweetened pineapple juice and omit the ground cloves. If desired, replace the sultanas with chopped, crystallized ginger.

To store: Keep covered in the refrigerator for up to 3 days.

Nutritional data per serving: 516 kJ (123 cal), Carbohydrate 26 g, Fat 1 g, Protein 3 g.

Preparation time: 1 hour 20 minutes. Cooking equipment: saucepan, casserole.

Oven temperature: 180°C/350°F/gas 4.

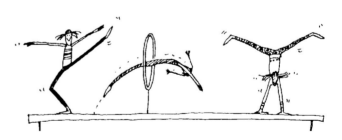

Banana & Pear Whip

Serves: 6

2 bananas, peeled

2 pears, peeled and cored

2 tbsp lemon juice

250 g (8 oz) ricotta cheese

4 tbsp low-fat natural
 yoghurt

grated nutmeg

A dessert athletes need in their repertoire — all the benefits of fresh fruit with a low-fat content, prepared in minutes.

Method:

1. Chop bananas and pears. Sprinkle with lemon juice.
2. Place the fruit in a blender with ricotta cheese and yoghurt. Blend till smooth and creamy.
3. Serve the Whip on the day of preparation. Spoon into individual bowls and chill for 1 hour. Before serving, dust with nutmeg and decorate with sliced fresh banana, sprinkled with lemon juice.

To vary: Swap banana for a large, ripe mango.

Nutritional data per serving: 370 kJ (88 cal), Carbohydrate 13 g, Fat 1 g, Protein 6 g.

Preparation time: 10 minutes; chill for 1 hour before serving.

Apple Filo Strudel

Serves: 4

6 sheets filo pastry

2 tbsp skimmed milk

4 apples, peeled and very
 finely sliced

4 tbsp sultanas

2 tbsp chopped almonds

1 tsp ground cinnamon

good pinch of ground
 cloves

2 tbsp soft brown sugar

Method:

1. Spread out 2 sheets of pastry on a kitchen work top. Brush lightly with milk.
2. Place another 2 layers of pastry on top. Again brush with milk. Repeat for remaining 2 sheets of pastry.
3. Sprinkle remaining ingredients over the pastry.
4. Prepare a baking sheet with non-stick baking spray. Carefully roll up the pastry. Place on a baking sheet, loose-edge down.
5. Brush strudel with milk. Bake in a preheated oven for 25–30 minutes. Serve warm, cut in thick slices.

Nutritional data per serving: 580 kJ (193 cal), Carbohydrate 37 g, Fat 4 g, Protein 3 g.

Preparation time: 45 minutes. Cooking equipment: baking sheet.

Oven temperature: 200°C/400°F/gas 6.

Yoghurt Cheese Velvet

Serves: 8

2 tbsp gelatine

125 ml (4 fl oz) cold water

45 g (1½ oz) almonds,
 finely ground

30 g (1 oz) wheatgerm

500 ml (16 fl oz) low-fat
 natural yoghurt

250 g (8 oz) cottage cheese

250 g (8 oz) ricotta cheese

4 tbsp clear honey

few drops of vanilla extract

rind of 2 oranges, finely
 grated

Garnish:

thin slices of orange

If your passion is for rich, baked cheesecakes, try this recipe. It is surprisingly low in fat, yet rich and creamy in texture and taste. You can make it the day before a dinner party, so it is a great addition to any busy cook's repertoire.

Method:

1. Sprinkle gelatine over cold water. Leave to stand until the gelatine has absorbed the water.
2. Stand bowl of gelatine mixture in a larger bowl of very hot water. Leave until the gelatine has dissolved. Allow to cool slightly.
3. Line a 20 cm (8 in) cake tin with foil, leaving enough extra foil overlapping the edge of the tin to help you to lift the Velvet once it is set.
4. Combine almonds and wheatgerm. Set aside 1 tbsp of this mixture for topping. Spread the rest over the base of the tin.
5. Beat yoghurt, cottage and ricotta cheese, honey, vanilla and orange rind together until smooth and creamy.
6. Fold gelatine into yoghurt and cheese mixture. Pour into the cake tin.
7. Chill in the refrigerator for 1 hour, or until firm.
8. Carefully turn out the set dessert on to a serving plate. Peel away the foil. Sprinkle over the reserved almond and wheatgerm mixture. Decorate with very thin slices of orange. Serve the dessert cut in wedges.

To vary: Use lemon rind instead of orange and decorate the dessert with a twisted slice of lemon in the centre.

To store: Keep covered in the refrigerator for up to 3 days.

Nutritional data per serving: 667 kJ (159 cal), Carbohydrate 18 g, Fat 4 g, Protein 13 g.

Preparation time: 20 minutes; chill for 1 hour, or till firm, before serving. Cooking equipment: 20 cm (8 in) cake tin.

SWEET FILLINGS FOR CREPES & PANCAKES

These delicious mixtures can be used to fill the crêpes and pancakes you make from the recipes on pages 159–60. Cooked crêpes and pancakes freeze well, so they are a great stand-by for desserts. They are great as a light meal after training, for a pre-event meal, or for breakfast. If you keep a supply in the freezer, you can simply take out a few crêpes and pancakes when you need them. Some of the fillings will also keep well for a couple of days when refrigerated.

Apple & Sultana Filling

Serves: 4 (allow 2 large pancakes/3 crêpes per serve)

4 apples, peeled, cored
   and sliced
2 tbs sultanas
½ tsp ground cinnamon
4 cloves
60 ml (2 fl oz) water
2 tbsp soft brown sugar
To serve:
8–12 pancakes or crêpes
   (pages 159–60)
Garnish:
ground cinnamon

Method:

1. Place all the filling ingredients in a saucepan. Cover and simmer for 10 minutes, or until apple is soft, but not mushy.
2. Remove cloves.
3. Fill and roll up the crêpes or pancakes *or*, if using crêpes, fill and fold in four, to make triangles.
4. Place the filled crêpes or pancakes, side-by-side, in a baking dish. Bake in a preheated oven for 10 minutes.
5. Serve hot, dusted with ground cinnamon. You can prepare the dessert in advance up to Step 3. Fill and reheat just before serving.

To store: The prepared filling will keep well for up to 3 days in the refrigerator.

Nutritional data per serving: 576 kJ (138 cal), Carbohydrate 35 g, Fat 0 g, Protein 1 g.

Preparation time: with pancakes/crêpes pre-prepared – 25 minutes. Cooking equipment: saucepan, shallow baking dish.

Oven temperature: 180°C/350°F/gas 4.

More Quick & Delicious Sweet Fillings for Crêpes & Pancakes

Some of these are great for breakfast, too!

Mixed Berries

Try fresh blueberries and raspberries, poached in a very little water with sugar to taste.

Fruit & Cheese

Cover mixed dried fruits with hot or cold water. Leave until softened. Use 1 tbsp of cottage cheese and 1 tbsp of fruit to fill each crêpe or pancake.

Apricot & Almond

Use stewed fresh or canned unsweetened apricots. Place 1–2 tbsp in each crêpe or pancake. Sprinkle with toasted slivered almonds. Roll up and serve hot or cold.

Apple Purée with Walnuts

Purée stewed, or canned, unsweetened apple. Combine with chopped walnuts and ground cinnamon to taste. Fill crêpes or pancakes and roll up or, if using crêpes, fill and fold in four, to make triangles. Serve hot, with maple syrup drizzled over.

Crêpes Suzette

Simmer fresh orange segments in a little orange juice. Drain. Set aside. Add 3–4 tbsp brandy to the orange segments and ignite. Allow flame to burn out. Fill crêpes and fold in four to make triangles. Add some grated orange rind and a little caster sugar to the reserved simmering juice; boil rapidly till reduced and thickened – serve as a sauce.

Special Fruit & Yoghurt

Chop up dried apricots, figs, prunes and dates. Soak in orange juice for 4 hours. Add toasted almond slivers or chopped walnuts and a sprinkling of cinnamon. Add just enough low-fat natural yoghurt or ricotta cheese to combine. Fill and roll up crêpes or pancakes or, if using crêpes, fill and fold in four, to make triangles.

Pawpaw (Papaya) & Cottage Cheese

Purée equal quantities of ripe pawpaw and cottage cheese. Stir in a little soft brown sugar and cinnamon to taste. Fill crêpes or pancakes, roll up or fold in four.

Use your imagination!

Baked Custard

Serves: 6

3 eggs

2 tbsp caster sugar

500 ml (16 fl oz) skimmed
   milk

few drops of vanilla extract

few drops of grated nutmeg

Method:

1. Lightly beat together the eggs and sugar.
2. In a saucepan, heat the milk until it begins to foam at the edges (scald).
3. Gradually add the scalded milk to the egg mixture, stirring constantly. Stir in the vanilla.
4. Pour mixture into the baking dish or dishes. Sprinkle over a little grated nutmeg.
5. Stand the baking dish(es) in a larger, ovenproof dish. Carefully pour enough hot water into the outer dish to reach two-thirds up the outside of the baking dish(es).
6. Bake in a preheated oven – 40 minutes for individual dishes, 50 minutes for one big dish – or until lightly browned and set in the centre.
7. Serve Baked Custard hot or cold. If you like, serve with Dried Fruit Compote (page 184).

Microwave Method:

Cooking time: 30 minutes.

Using single-serving microwave dishes, the microwave cooks this dessert in less than half the time of a conventional oven.

In a medium-sized bowl, lightly beat the eggs and sugar. Microwave the milk on 'Medium' for 2–3 minutes – this prevents it from becoming watery. Gradually add the scalded milk to the egg mixture, stirring constantly. Stir in the vanilla. Pour the mixture into six, individual dishes. Arrange the puddings in a wide circle in the microwave, to ensure even cooking. Microwave on 'Medium' for 8–10 minutes.

Nutritional data per serving: 355 kJ (85 cal), Carbohydrate 9 g, Fat 3 g, Protein 6 g.

Preparation time: 1 hour 10 minutes. Cooking equipment: deep pie/soufflé dish, or 6 ramekin dishes, and large ovenproof dish, big enough to hold the other dish(es).

Oven temperature: 150°C/300°F/gas 2.

Low-fat Peach Sponge

Serves: 4

250 g (8 oz) stewed or
   canned, unsweetened
   peaches
60 ml (2 fl oz) water
½ tsp ground cinnamon
2 eggs
4 tbsp sugar
few drops of vanilla extract
4 tbsp cornflour
   (cornstarch)
4 tbsp self-raising flour

Conventional wisdom has declared baked puddings high in fats. This dessert shows that you can still enjoy them, without fear of exceeding your fat allowance.

Method:

1. Spread peaches evenly over the base of a small, round or rectangular baking dish.
2. Pour over the water and sprinkle with cinnamon.
3. In a bowl, beat the eggs till frothy. Add sugar and vanilla and beat until sugar has dissolved and mixture is light and frothy.
4. Combine cornflour and self-raising flour. Gradually fold into the egg mixture, beating until smooth.
5. Spoon the batter over the peaches and spread evenly.
6. Bake in a preheated oven for 30 minutes, or until well risen and golden brown on top.
7. Serve hot, accompanied by hot or cold low-fat custard sauce.

To store: Keep covered in refrigerator for up to 2 days.

Nutritional data per serving: 614 kJ (147 cal), Carbohydrate 27 g, Fat 3 g, Protein 4 g.
Preparation time: 40 minutes. Cooking equipment: small baking dish.
Oven temperature: 180°C/350°F/gas 4.

Bread & Butter Pudding

Serves: 4

4 slices wholemeal bread

15 g (½ oz) butter

90 g (3 oz) raisins or
   sultanas

2 eggs

2 tbsp soft brown sugar

500 ml (16 fl oz) skimmed
   milk

few drops of vanilla extract

grated nutmeg or
   cinnamon (optional)

A well-balanced eating plan allows you to include a small quantity of fat in your diet. This dessert contains a little butter, along with plenty of carbohydrate and protein. Try a slice of cold Bread & Butter Pudding as a light lunch or as a snack after training.

Method:

1. Spread the bread thinly with butter. Cut each slice into 4 fingers or triangles.

2. In a small pie dish or casserole, arrange alternate layers of the bread (buttered side down) and raisins or sultanas.

3. Beat together the eggs, sugar, milk and vanilla. Pour over the bread. Leave to stand for 10 minutes.

4. Sprinkle with nutmeg or cinnamon. Stand the pudding in a larger, ovenproof dish. Carefully pour enough hot water into the outer dish to reach two-thirds up the outside of the baking dish.

5. Bake in a preheated oven for 1 hour, or until set and well browned on top.

6. Serve hot or cold.

To vary: Arrange very thin slices of apple between each layer of bread.

To store: Cover with cling film and store in the refrigerator for up to 2 days.

Nutritional data per serving: 1,068 kJ (255 cal), Carbohydrate 38 g, Fat 8 g, Protein 10 g.

Preparation time: 1 hour 20 minutes. Cooking equipment: small, deep pie dish or casserole, and large oven-proof dish, big enough to hold the pudding dish.

Oven temperature: 150°C/300°F/gas 2.

Creamy Rice

Serves: 6

50 g (2 oz) short-grain rice
750 ml (24 fl oz) skimmed
*   milk*
2 tbsp soft brown sugar
few drops of vanilla extract
grated nutmeg or
*   cinnamon*

This is one of those wonderful 'nursery' desserts appreciated by children and adults alike. It is also a delicious way to stock up on the energy-giving carbohydrates of rice and the protein and calcium found in skimmed milk – you might even try Creamy Rice for breakfast! With a microwave oven, the dessert can be prepared in less than a quarter of the time.

Method:

1. Wash the rice well. Drain and combine with the milk, sugar and vanilla.
2. Turn mixture into a casserole. Bake in a preheated oven for 2 hours, stir occasionally during the first hour.
3. Sprinkle the baked rice with grated nutmeg or ground cinnamon. Serve hot or cold as an accompaniment to Dried Fruit Compote (page 184).

Microwave Method:

Cooking time: 22 minutes.

In a large, microwave serving bowl, microwave the milk on 'Medium' for 3 minutes – this prevents it from becoming watery. Add the washed rice, sugar and vanilla to the milk and combine well. Microwave on 'High' for 6 minutes and then stir the mixture and give the bowl a half-turn. Repeat this process twice during the next 12–13 minutes. Allow 1 minute standing time before serving.

To vary: Add 1 tbsp of finely grated lemon rind at Step 1. Add 2 tbsp of sultanas at Step 1. Before Step 2, line the bottom of the casserole with slices of apple sprinkled with cinnamon, then spoon the rice mixture on top.

To store: Keep covered in the refrigerator for up to 2 days. Serve cold or reheat at 190°C/375°F/gas 5 for 20–25 minutes.

Nutritional data per serving: 300 kJ (72 cal), Carbohydrate 14 g, Fat 0 g, Protein 5 g.

Preparation time: 2 hours 5 minutes. Cooking equipment: casserole.

Oven temperature: 150°C/300°F/gas 2.

Fruity Crumble

Serves: 4–6

3–4 Granny Smith apples,
   peeled, cored and sliced

2 tbsp water

½ tsp ground cinnamon

Topping:

125 g (4 oz) Starter's
   Muesli (page 52) or other
   untoasted muesli

2 tbsp desiccated coconut

You can serve this recipe hot or cold. For a change, try replacing two of the apples with the same weight in fresh berries or apricots.

Method:

1. Place the apple in a saucepan. Add 1–2 tbsp of water. Sprinkle with the cinnamon. Gently simmer mixture until apple is tender, about 10 minutes.
2. Lightly grease a small casserole. Spoon in the cooked apple mixture and spread out evenly.
3. Combine the muesli and coconut. Sprinkle thickly over the apple.
4. Bake in a preheated oven for 30 minutes, or until topping is dark golden.
5. Serve hot or cold.

To vary filling: Add 2 tbsp of sultanas or raisins to the cooked apple.

To vary topping: Substitute for topping above:

30 g (1 oz) wholemeal breadcrumbs

45 g (1½ oz) rolled oats

45 g (1½ oz) desiccated coconut

150 g (5 oz) clear honey

Nutritional data per serving: 441 kJ (132 cal), Carbohydrate 18 g, Fat 3 g, Protein 2 g.

Preparation time: including baking – 40 minutes. Cooking equipment: saucepan, small casserole.

Oven temperature: 180°C/350°F/gas 4.

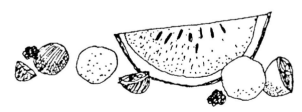

Cream Cheese Topping

Makes: about 250 g (8 oz)

250 g (8 oz) curd or ricotta
   cheese
2 tbsp skimmed milk
few drops of vanilla extract
2 tsp lemon juice
1 tbsp caster sugar

This is a wonderful protein-rich topping for fruit-based desserts as well as a low-fat icing for cakes and muffins.

Method:

1.   Combine ingredients. Beat until smooth and creamy.

As an accompaniment: Use as a topping with Dried Fruit Compote (page 184).

As an icing: It is also excellent as a low-fat icing for Carrot Cake (page 205).

To vary: Use the finely grated rind of 1 lemon instead of the lemon juice. Use clear honey instead of sugar and replace the lemon juice with the grated rind of an orange.

To store: Keep covered in the refrigerator for up to 2 days. Do not freeze.

Nutritional data per 125 g (4 oz): 1,483 kJ (354 cal), Carbohydrate 28 g, Fat 3 g, Protein 46 g.
Preparation time: 5 minutes.

Ricotta Fruit Topping

Makes: about 185 g (6 oz)

45 g (1½ oz) dried apricots,
   soaked in 250 ml (8 fl oz)
   warm water
125 ml (4 fl oz) soaking
   liquid from apricots
125 g (4 oz) ricotta cheese
pinch of cinnamon

Try this as a spread on hot wholemeal toast for breakfast. It's also delicious as a dip for fresh fruit.

Method:

1.   Purée the soaked apricots with 125 ml (4 fl oz) of their soaking liquid until smooth.
2.   Add ricotta cheese and cinnamon to the purée and blend until smooth. Chill the Topping until required and use as an accompaniment to Dried Fruit Compote (page 184) or stewed, fresh or canned fruit.

To store: Keep covered in the refrigerator for up to 2 days.

To vary: Instead of the apricots, combine the ricotta with: canned unsweetened peaches and a little of their juice; canned unsweetened or home-made stewed apple, puréed with a pinch of ground cloves and 1 tsp clear honey; the grated rind and juice of an orange; soaked and stoned prunes and their soaking juice.

Nutritional data per serving: 928 kJ (222 cal), Carbohydrate 17 g, Fat 11 g, Protein 15 g.
Preparation time: 5 minutes; apricots soaked overnight.

Crème Caramel

Serves: 6

Caramel:

60 g (2 oz) caster sugar

2 tbsp water

Crème:

2 eggs

2 egg yolks

1 tbsp caster sugar

500 ml (16 fl oz) skimmed milk

a few drops of vanilla extract

This popular dessert is not difficult to make. Read the recipe first to get the hang of what to do – the result is well worth the effort. If you like, sprinkle toasted flaked almonds or fresh blueberries over the finished dessert.

Method:

1. Spray a deep pie or soufflé baking dish with non-stick cooking spray.
2. In a small, heavy-based saucepan, heat the 60 g (2 oz) sugar and water, stirring until the sugar completely dissolves.
3. Bring to the boil. Boil, *without stirring*, until the mixture thickens (caramelises) and turns a deep amber colour. Be careful to remove the caramel from the hob. before it burns.
4. Immediately pour the hot caramel into the baking dish, or divide equally into individual dishes. Set aside.
5. In a mixing bowl, lightly beat the whole eggs, egg yolks and 1 tbsp sugar.
6. In a saucepan, heat the milk until it begins to foam around the edges.
7. Gradually add the heated milk to the egg and sugar mixture, stirring constantly.
8. Stir in the vanilla. Pour the mixture into the baking dish, covering the caramel.
9. Stand the baking dish in a larger, ovenproof dish. Carefully pour enough hot water into the outer dish to reach two-thirds up the outside of the baking dish(es).
10. Bake in a preheated oven for 40 minutes for individual dishes, 50 minutes for one big dish – or until lightly browned and set in the centre.
11. Remove from the oven. Leave to cool completely. If any skin forms on the top, you can carefully skim this away.
12. Gently turn out on to serving plate(s); the caramel now makes a sauce topping. Alternatively, do not turn out, but leave to chill in the refrigerator overnight. The caramel will dissolve, making more sauce when the pudding is turned out for serving.

Nutritional data per serving: 538 kJ (129 cal), Carbohydrate 17 g, Fat 5 g, Protein 6 g.

Preparation time: 1 hour 20 minutes. Cooking equipment: small, heavy-based saucepan, deep pie or soufflé baking dish or 6 ramekins, plus large ovenproof dish (big enough to hold the other dish(es).

Oven temperature: 150°C/300°F/gas 2.

BREADS, CAKES, BISCUITS, SCONES & MUFFINS

All breads are an excellent source of carbohydrate. They contain small but valuable amounts of protein and most breads are low in fat. Almost all commonly available breads are made from wheat or rye grains, as these contain gluten, which is essential if bread is to rise. Gluten is a protein which reacts with liquid to trap air in dough and produce a well-risen end result.

Wholemeal & Wholegrain Breads

These breads have several nutritional benefits not always present in the same quantities in refined or white flour products:

- In grinding wholemeal flours the *bran* (outer) layer of the grain is not stripped away. Bran provides the fibre to aid the digestive process. Bran is also rich in phosphorus, a mineral essential to the nervous system.

- Wholegrain flours include the *wheatgerm* part of the wheat grain. Wheatgerm is a rich source of all the B vitamins, protein, as well as essential Vitamin E and zinc.

Vary your diet by experimenting with the wide range of bread products available today, from the simple 'flat' breads of the Middle East, called pitta, pocket or Lebanese bread, to the dense rye flour and 'black' breads of Eastern Europe. In between, you may choose breads of all shapes and sizes containing all kinds of flavourings, including nuts, seeds, fruits and herbs.

If you have the time, there is nothing like freshly baked, home-made bread. This is not difficult, especially if you are using a recipe in which the dough requires no kneading, such as Quick Yoghurt Bread (page 204).

Breads that do not use yeast are particularly easy and quick to prepare. They often have a closer texture than yeast breads, but are equally delicious. Try the excellent Courgette Bread on page 203.

Pastries

Most traditional pastries are high in fat and therefore are not suitable as a regular food in your diet. Lower-fat pastries can be successfully made by reducing the amount of fat suggested in many recipes.

Try using filo, the very fine pastry originating from Greece. It contains very little fat. You can buy ready-made filo pastry at most supermarkets and delicatessens. There are an average of 25 sheets of pastry in a packet – more than adequate for most dishes. We use filo for several recipes in this book, such as Apple Filo Strudel (page 189).

Snack foods should be energy-packed and delicious: Muffins (page 211–12) and Energy Bars (page 67). A jug of fruit juice and mineral water offers vital fluids and carbohydrates.

Cakes & Biscuits

Commercially made cakes and biscuits can be high in refined carbohydrate, fat and additives. However, there are some nutritious wholemeal products available these days, especially from shops where baking is done on the premises.

On the whole, ensure that any cakes and biscuits you eat are included in your balanced daily diet and are not consumed as 'extras'. For example, in this chapter we include several muffin recipes that are excellent for breakfast, lunch-on-the-run, or for a snack in your daily diet plain.

Walnut Bread

Makes: 1 small loaf

150 g (5 oz) plain
   wholemeal flour
2 tbsp caster sugar
1 tsp baking powder
2 tbsp melted butter or
   margarine
1 large egg, beaten
125 ml (4 fl oz) skimmed
   milk
60 g (2 oz) walnuts,
   chopped and lightly
   toasted

Method:

1. Grease a small loaf tin. Set aside.
2. In a large bowl, combine the flour, sugar and baking powder.
3. Add the butter or margarine, egg and milk and stir in lightly but thoroughly until well combined.
4. Stir in the nuts. Spoon the batter into the greased loaf tin.
5. Bake in a preheated oven for about 40 minutes, or until a skewer comes out clean when inserted in the middle of the bread.
6. Serve sliced and spread with a little butter or margarine or try it with Cream Cheese Topping (page 198), or Ricotta Fruit Topping (page 198).

To vary: Replace walnuts with chopped pecan nuts, almonds, or a combination of nuts.

Nutritional data per loaf: 4,521 kJ (1,080 cal), Carbohydrate 159 g, Fat 38 g, Protein 34 g.
Preparation time: 40–50 minutes. Cooking equipment: small loaf tin.
Oven temperature: 180°C/350°F/gas 4.

Courgette Bread

Serves: 1 large loaf

---

30 g (1 oz) butter or
  margarine

2 tbsp oil

2 medium onions, finely
  chopped

1 tsp dried mixed herbs

250 g (8 oz) courgettes,
  coarsely grated

60 g (2 oz) pecan nuts or
  walnuts, coarsely
  chopped

125 g (4 oz) low-fat hard
  cheese, grated

315 g (10 oz) self-raising
  flour

3 eggs

60 ml (2 fl oz) low-fat
  natural yoghurt or
  buttermilk

3 tbsp finely chopped
  parsley

This may seem an unlikely bread recipe, but it is moist, fragrant with herbs and has a delicious savoury flavour.

Method:

1. Grease a large loaf tin. Set aside.
2. In a saucepan, melt the butter or margarine with the oil.
3. Add the chopped onion and sauté until transparent. Stir in the herbs. Set aside to cool.
4. In a large bowl, combine the fried onion, courgettes, nuts and grated cheese.
5. Sprinkle the flour over the courgette mixture.
6. In a separate bowl, beat the eggs. Add the yoghurt or buttermilk and the chopped parsley; combine well.
7. Add the egg mixture to the courgette mixture and combine thoroughly.
8. Spoon the mixture into the greased loaf tin and bake in a preheated oven for 40 minutes or until a skewer comes out clean when inserted in the middle of the bread.
9. Allow the bread to cool in the tin for 5 minutes before turning out on to a cooling rack.

To vary: Instead of courgettes, use the same quantity of grated carrot.

Nutritional data per loaf: 10,375 kJ (2,479 cal), Carbohydrate 283 g, Fat 112 g, Protein 100 g.

Preparation time: 50 minutes–1 hour. Cooking equipment: 1 large loaf tin, saucepan.

Oven temperature: 200°C/400°F/gas 6.

Quick Yoghurt Bread

Makes: 1 loaf

500 g (1 lb) wholemeal
   flour
2 tsp bicarbonate of soda
2 tbsp clear honey
500 ml (16 fl oz) full-cream
   natural yoghurt
1 tsp salt (optional)
1 tbsp sesame seeds
   (optional)

Method:
1. Place the wholemeal flour, unsifted, in a large bowl.
2. Add all remaining ingredients, except the sesame seeds, if using. Use a wooden spoon to mix lightly but well, until mixture is almost fluffy.
3. Spoon mixture into the greased loaf tin. Sprinkle with sesame seeds, if using.
4. Bake in a preheated oven for 50 minutes–1 hour, or until loaf sounds hollow when tapped.

To vary: Add 60 g (2 oz) roughly chopped pecan nuts or walnuts. Alternatively, try adding 60 g (2 oz) sunflower seeds or raisins.

Nutritional data per loaf: 9,022 kJ (2,155 cal), Carbohydrate 358 g, Fat 34 g, Protein 97 g.
Preparation time: Approximately 1 hour. Cooking equipment: loaf tin.
Oven temperature: 180°C/350°F/gas 4.

Rice Pie Shell

185 g (6 oz) cooked brown
   rice
1 egg, lightly beaten

Use this as a base for sweet or savoury pies which have baked fillings, for instance, pumpkin or custard.

Method:
1. Combine the rice and egg.
2. Spray a pie dish with non-stick cooking spray.
3. Firmly and evenly press out the rice mixture over the base of the pie dish.
4. Spoon in the filling of your choice and bake as directed in your filling recipe.

Nutritional data per pie shell: 1,152 kJ (275 cal), Carbohydrate 46 g, Fat 7 g, Protein 10 g.
Preparation time: 5 minutes. Cooking equipment: 20 cm (8 in) pie dish.

Carrot Cake

Makes: 10 thick slices

---

60 g (2 oz) margarine

60 g (2 oz) brown sugar

125 g (4 oz) golden syrup

2 eggs

juice and grated rind of
   1 orange

185 g (6 oz) carrot, grated

185 g (6 oz) canned
   crushed pineapple, well
   drained

60 g (2 oz) walnuts,
   chopped

½ tsp mixed spice

75 g (2½ oz) plain flour

75 g (2½ oz) self-raising
   flour

Topping:

100 g (3½ oz) light cream
   cheese

1 tbsp orange juice

150 g (5 oz) icing sugar

or

100 g (3½ oz) ricotta cheese

1 tbsp orange juice

1 tbsp clear honey

This superb cake is high in nutritional value but also fairly high in calories and fat so, if you are watching your weight, you should not eat very much of it. If you wish, you can use sultanas instead of walnuts in the recipe.

Method:

1. Cream margarine and brown sugar until light, smooth and pale.
2. Stir in the syrup. Add the eggs, one at a time, beating well after each addition.
3. Stir in the orange rind, grated carrot, pineapple, walnuts and mixed spice.
4. Combine the two flours. Stir the flours into the carrot mixture, a little at a time, alternating with orange juice.
5. Thoroughly grease a cake tin. Line the base of the tin with greaseproof paper.
6. Spoon in the cake mixture and bake in a preheated oven for 1 hour, or until a metal skewer comes out clean when inserted in the centre of the cake. Allow the cake to cool in the tin.
7. Prepare the topping. Beat together the cheese and orange juice. Add the icing sugar and beat until smooth. Ice the cake when completely cool.

To store: Best prepared the day before use. Keep in an airtight container for up to 4 days. To freeze the cake, wrap it securely in cling film; do not freeze with topping. Add topping only when cake has completely thawed.

Nutritional data per slice: 1,369 kJ (327 cal), Carbohydrate 53 g, Fat 11 g, Protein 6 g.

Preparation time: including baking – 1 hour 20 minutes. Cooking equipment: 20 cm (8 in) cake tin.

Oven temperature: 180°C/350°F/gas 4.

Boiled Fruit Cake

***Makes: 1 x 20 cm (8 in)
square cake***

45 g (1½ oz) butter
90 g (3 oz) caster sugar
*375 g (12 oz) mixed dried
    fruits*
*470 g (15 oz) can crushed
    pineapple*
2 eggs, lightly beaten
*125 g (4 oz) wholemeal self-
    raising flour*
*125 g (4 oz) plain self-
    raising flour*
1 tsp bicarbonate of soda

Here is a delicious cake packed with carbohydrate. The fat levels are reasonably high, so you'd need to limit the number of slices you eat. Fortunately, the cake stores well.

Method:

1. Place butter, sugar and dried fruit in a saucepan.
2. Drain the can of pineapple. Add the juice to the saucepan. Reserve the fruit.
3. Slowly bring the fruit mixture to the boil. Reduce heat and simmer for 15 minutes.
4. Remove from heat and allow the fruit mixture to cool completely.
5. Stir in the egg, both flours, bicarbonate of soda and reserved pineapple flesh.
6. Lightly grease a baking tin. Spoon in the cake mixture.
7. Bake in a preheated oven for 1 hour, or until a skewer comes out clean when inserted in the centre.

To store: Store the cake in an airtight container, preferably lined with waxed paper.

Nutritional data per cake: 11,753 kJ (2,808 cal), Carbohydrate 458 g, Fat 89 g, Protein 63 g.

Preparation time: 1 ½ hours. Cooking equipment: saucepan, 20 cm (8 in) square cake tin.

Oven temperature: 180°C/350°F/gas 4.

Oatmeal Cookies

Makes: 25

185 g (6 oz) rolled oats

90 g (3 oz) desiccated
  coconut

150 g (5 oz) stoned dates,
  chopped

250 g (8 oz) ricotta cheese

4 tbsp golden syrup

3 eggs

60 ml (2 fl oz) oil

2 large, ripe bananas,
  mashed

water

Method:

1. Combine the rolled oats, coconut and dates.
2. In a separate bowl, beat together the cheese, syrup, eggs, oil and mashed banana.
3. Add the banana mixture to the dry ingredients and stir until well combined. The mixture should hold together fairly well; if it is very crumbly, add water, a little at a time, working it in well after each addition, until it holds together.
4. Thoroughly grease a baking sheet. Drop tablespoonfuls of the mixture on to the baking tray leaving plenty of space between cookies. Use a fork to flatten the cookies slightly.
5. Bake in a preheated oven for 20 minutes. Leave the cookies to cool on the baking tray for 10 minutes, then remove and finish cooling on a wire rack.

To vary: Instead of dates, use the same quantity of soaked raisins, sultanas or chopped dried apricots. If you like, sprinkle some sesame seeds over the top of each cookie.

To store: Keep in an airtight tin for up to 10 days.

Nutritional data per cookie: 290 kJ (69 cal), Carbohydrate 8 g, Fat 4 g, Protein 2 g.

Preparation time: including baking – 30 minutes. Cooking equipment: baking tray, wire rack.

Oven temperature: 180°C/350°F/gas 4.

Basic Scones

This basic scone dough is ideal for a variety of sweet or savoury snacks. Scones are so simple and quick to make that even a busy athlete could manage to whip up a batch. Here are some of the secrets to making perfect scones every time:

- Keep the ingredients cool.
- Handle the dough as little and as lightly as possible – use your fingertips or a food processor.
- Bake near the top of a very hot oven – 220°C/425°F/gas 7.

Makes: 12 scones

250 g (8 oz) self-raising
   flour
1 tsp caster sugar
pinch of salt
1 tbsp margarine
185 ml (6 fl oz) cold milk

Method:

1. In a bowl, combine flour, sugar and salt, then – using your fingertips – rub the margarine into the flour until the mixture resembles fine breadcrumbs (a food processor does this very well).

2. Add the milk and use a knife to work the mixture until you have a fine soft dough. (If using a food processor, add the milk and process until dough forms.)

3. Turn the dough out on to a lightly floured board. Use your fingertips to knead the dough quickly and lightly until soft and smooth.

4. Gently flatten the dough, roll out to 2.5 cm (1 in) thick. Use a cutter or sharp knife to shape 12 scones. Avoid rolling or cutting dough more than once.

5. Place the scones on a lightly greased baking sheet. Leave a gap about half the width of a scone between each one. If you want the scones to brown on top, brush with a little milk.

6. Bake near the top of the preheated oven for 8–10 minutes.

7. Allow the scones to cool on a wire rack for at least 10 minutes before cutting open and spreading lightly with margarine. Accompany with jam or honey.

Nutritional data per scone: 400 kJ (96 cal), Carbohydrate 17 g, Fat 2 g, Protein 3 g.
Preparation time: including baking – 15 minutes. Cooking equipment: baking sheet, wire rack.
Oven temperature: 220°C/425°F/gas 7.

Special Scones

Makes: 12 scones

---

250 g (8 oz) self-raising flour – less 1 rounded tbsp

1 rounded tbsp gluten flour (available from health food shops and some supermarkets)

1 tsp caster sugar

½ tsp baking powder

pinch of salt

1 tbsp margarine

125 ml milk

125 ml (4 fl oz) natural yoghurt

Added flavour and texture make scones that would impress even a country grandmother!

Method:

1. In a bowl, combine the flour, sugar and salt. Use your fingertips to rub the margarine into the dry ingredients until the mixture resembles fine breadcrumbs.

2. Add the milk and use a knife to work the mixture until you have a fine, soft dough.

3. Turn the dough out on to a lightly floured board. Use your fingertips to knead the dough quickly and lightly until soft and smooth.

4. Gently flatten the dough and roll out to 2.5 cm (1 in) thick.

5. Use a scone cutter or sharp knife to shape 12 scones. Avoid rolling and cutting dough scraps more than once.

6. Place the scones on a lightly greased baking sheet.

7. To brown the scones on top, brush each one with a little milk and bake them near the top of the oven.

8. Bake in a preheated oven for 8–10 minutes.

Nutritional data per scone: 428 kJ (102 cal), Carbohydrate 18 g, Fat 2 g, Protein 4 g.

Preparation time: including baking – 15 minutes. Cooking equipment: baking sheet.

Oven temperature: 220°C/425°F/gas 7.

Wholemeal Scones

Replace half the flour with wholemeal self-raising flour (i.e. 125 g/4 oz of each). This will work for both the Basic and the Special Scone doughs.

Pinwheel Scones

Combine 2 tbsp of ricotta cheese, 1 tbsp of grated Parmesan and 2 tsp of finely snipped chives. Mix to a coarse paste. Roll the scone dough out to an oblong, 1 cm (½ in) thick. Spread with the cheese mixture. Moisten one of the long sides of the dough with water to make a sealing edge. Roll up the dough from the opposite (dry) long side, to make a sausage shape, gently pressing down the moistened edge to seal. Use a sharp knife to cut the dough into 2.5 cm (1 in) thick slices. Bake as for Basic Scone dough.

Cheese & Chive Scones

(Use either the Basic or the Special Scone dough.)

Leave out the sugar. After adding the milk at Step 2, add 2 tbsp of ricotta cheese, 2 tbsp of grated Parmesan and 2 tsp of finely snipped chives.

Fruit Scones

Knead 2 tbsp of sultanas, currants or chopped dates into the dough mixture at Step 3.

Curried Scones

After adding the milk at Step 2, add 2 tbsp ricotta cheese and ½ tsp of curry powder.

Scone Dough Specials

Scone Pizza Base

1. Prepare a Basic Scone dough (page 208), but omit the sugar.
2. Roll out the dough to 1 cm (½ in) thick. Lift the dough carefully and lay over an oblong baking sheet or pizza tin, if you have one.
3. Spread the dough with tomato paste or bottled pasta sauce.
4. Sprinkle over your favourite pizza toppings, such as thinly sliced onion rings, chopped fresh herbs, sliced red or green peppers, pitted and sliced olives, cooked seafood, strips of lean ham or grated, low-fat hard cheese.
5. Bake in a preheated oven at 220°C/425°F/gas 7 for 10 minutes, or until base is golden brown underneath.

Crusty Casserole Lid

1. Prepare a Basic Scone dough (page 208), but omit the sugar.
2. Roll out the dough to 1 cm (½ in) thick.
3. Spoon the hot, cooked casserole mixture (e.g. Hearty Beef & Vegetable Casserole [page 133]) into a pie dish.
4. Carefully lift the scone dough and lay over the casserole. Trim away any excess and neatly crimp the edge to seal.
5. Brush the dough with milk. Bake in a preheated oven at 220°C/425°F/gas 7 for 8–10 minutes, or until dough is well risen and golden brown.

Soup Dumplings

1. Prepare a Basic Scone dough (page 208), but omit the sugar.
2. Form the dough into small balls, about the size of walnuts.
3. Bring the soup to a simmer and drop in the dumplings. Simmer for 10 minutes before serving.

Seed Muffins

Makes: 16–18 muffins

250 g (8 oz) plain
   wholemeal flour
2 tsp baking powder
60 g (2 oz) brown sugar
3 tbsp butter or margarine
1 egg
250 ml (8 fl oz) buttermilk
2 tbsp sesame seeds
2 tbsp sunflower seeds
45 g (1½ oz) sultanas
2 tbsp chopped mixed nuts
   (optional)

Method:

1. In a large bowl, combine flour, baking powder and sugar.
2. Melt the butter or margarine. Cool slightly.
3. In a separate bowl, combine the melted butter or margarine and egg and mix well. Add the buttermilk to the egg mixture.
4. Add the liquid mixture to the dry ingredients. Stir lightly until combined. Stir in seeds, sultanas and nuts, if using. Spoon the mixture into greased muffin tins and bake in a preheated oven for 15–20 minutes.

Nutritional data per muffin: 485 kJ (116 cal), Carbohydrate 20 g, Fat 6 g, Protein 3 g.

Preparation time: including baking – 30 minutes. Cooking equipment: muffin tins. Oven temperature: 200°C/400°F/gas 6.

Banana Bran Muffins

Makes: 12–18 muffins

185 ml (6 fl oz) skimmed
   milk
60 g (2 oz) bran
3 ripe bananas, mashed
185 g (6 oz) plain flour
30 g (1 oz) sugar
4 tsp baking powder
pinch of salt
60 g (2 oz) soft butter or
   margarine
1 egg

Both the muffins on this page can be served warm or at room temperature with a sweet topping such as Cream Cheese Topping (page 198).

Method:

1. Combine the milk, bran and mashed banana. Set aside for 15 minutes. In a separate bowl, combine the dry ingredients.
2. Beat the butter and egg until well combined.
3. Add the banana mixture and mix lightly.
4. Add wet mixture to dry ingredients and stir lightly until just combined. Spoon into greased muffin tins. Bake in a preheated oven for 15–20 minutes.

Nutritional data per muffin: 489 kJ (117 cal), Carbohydrate 17 g, Fat 4 g, Protein 4 g.

Preparation time: including baking – 35 minutes. Cooking equipment: muffin tins.

Oven temperature: 180°C/350°F/gas 4.

Herb & Corn Muffins

Makes: 12 muffins

---

125 g (4 oz) plain flour

125 g (4 oz) cornmeal

½ tsp salt

2 tsp baking powder

1 tbsp melted margarine

250 ml (8 fl oz) low-fat
　milk

1 egg, beaten

good pinch of black pepper

½ tsp dried mixed herbs

2 tbsp grated low-fat hard
　cheese

These wonderful savoury muffins are great with corn or pumpkin chowder. Eat them fresh – they will not keep.

Method:

1. Sift flours, salt and baking powder into a bowl.
2. Mix margarine, milk and egg and add to dry ingredients. Beat until smooth.
3. Fold in seasonings and cheese and spoon mixture into lightly greased muffin tins.
4. Bake in a preheated oven for 15–20 minutes until golden brown.

Nutritional data per muffin: 471 kJ (112 cal), Carbohydrate 17 g, Protein 4 g, Fat 3 g.

Preparation time including baking: 30 minutes. Cooking equipment: muffin tins.

Oven temperature: 210°C/425°F/gas 6.

Blueberry Muffins

Makes: 12 muffins

---

150 g (5 oz) ripe blueberries

15 g (½ oz) brown sugar

250 g (8 oz) wholemeal
　self-raising flour

1 tsp baking powder

1 tsp ground cinnamon

1 egg

125 ml (4 fl oz) low-fat
　berry yoghurt

1 cup skimmed or low-fat
　milk

Method:

1. Wash blueberries and combine with sugar in saucepan.
2. Heat gently until juice just starts to run.
3. Sift flour, baking powder and cinnamon into bowl.
4. Mix egg, yoghurt and milk in a bowl. Add to flour and blend until smooth.
5. Gently fold blueberries into mixture.
6. Spoon mixture into lightly greased muffin tins, and bake in a preheated oven for 15–20 minutes until firm and very lightly browned.

Nutritional data per muffin: 486 kJ (116 cal), Carbohydrate 21 g, Protein 5 g, Fat 1 g.

Preparation time: 40 minutes. Cooking equipment: saucepan, muffin tins.

Oven temperature: 210°C/425°F/gas 7.

APPENDIX

Chart III — Energy Needs for Particular Sports (shown as kJ (cal) per minute)

Activity	50 kg (110 lb)		56 kg (123 lb)		62 kg (137 lb)		71 kg (157 lb)		80 kg (176 lb)		89 kg (196 lb)	
Badminton	13.8	(3.3)	22.6	(5.4)	25.1	(6.0)	28.9	(6.9)	32.6	(7.8)	36.0	(8.6)
Basketball	28.8	(6.9)	32.2	(7.7)	36.0	(8.6)	41.0	(9.8)	46.0	(11.0)	51.5	(12.3)
Boxing												
• in-ring	28.8	(6.9)	32.2	(7.7)	36.0	(8.6)	41.0	(9.8)	46.0	(11.0)	51.5	(12.3)
• sparring	46.5	(11.1)	51.9	(12.4)	57.8	(13.8)	66.2	(15.8)	74.5	(17.8)	82.9	(19.8)
Canoeing												
• leisure	9.2	(2.2)	10.4	(2.5)	11.3	(2.7)	13.0	(3.1)	14.6	(3.5)	16.3	(3.9)
• racing	21.8	(5.2)	24.3	(5.8)	26.8	(6.4)	30.5	(7.3)	34.3	(8.2)	38.5	(9.2)
Circuit training												
• hydra-fitness	27.6	(6.6)	31.0	(7.4)	34.3	(8.2)	39.4	(9.4)	44.0	(10.5)	49.0	(11.7)
• universal	24.3	(5.8)	27.2	(6.5)	30.1	(7.2)	34.8	(8.3)	38.9	(9.3)	43.1	(10.3)
• nautilus	19.2	(4.6)	21.8	(5.2)	24.3	(5.8)	27.6	(6.6)	31.0	(7.4)	34.3	(8.2)
• free weights	18.0	(4.3)	20.1	(4.8)	22.2	(5.3)	25.5	(6.1)	28.5	(6.8)	31.8	(7.6)
Cricket												
• batting	17.6	(4.2)	19.2	(4.6)	21.3	(5.1)	24.7	(5.9)	27.6	(6.6)	31.0	(7.4)
• bowling	18.8	(4.5)	20.9	(5.0)	23.4	(5.6)	26.8	(6.4)	30.1	(7.2)	33.5	(8.0)
Cycling												
• leisure (slow)	13.4	(3.2)	15.1	(3.6)	16.7	(4.0)	18.8	(4.5)	21.3	(5.1)	23.9	(5.7)
• leisure (moderate)	20.9	(5.0)	23.4	(5.6)	25.9	(6.2)	29.7	(7.1)	33.5	(8.0)	37.3	(8.9)
• racing	35.6	(8.5)	39.8	(9.5)	44.0	(10.5)	50.2	(12.0)	56.5	(13.5)	62.8	(15.0)
Dancing												
• aerobic (beginner)	21.8	(5.2)	24.3	(5.8)	26.8	(6.4)	30.6	(7.3)	34.3	(8.2)	38.5	(9.2)
• aerobic (advanced)	28.0	(6.7)	31.4	(7.5)	34.7	(8.3)	40.2	(9.6)	45.2	(10.8)	50.2	(12.0)
• ballroom	10.9	(2.6)	12.1	(2.9)	13.4	(3.2)	15.1	(3.6)	17.2	(4.1)	18.8	(4.5)
Football	27.6	(6.6)	31.0	(7.4)	34.3	(8.2)	39.3	(9.4)	44.4	(10.6)	49.0	(11.7)
Golf	18.0	(4.3)	20.1	(4.8)	22.3	(5.3)	25.1	(6.0)	28.5	(6.8)	31.8	(7.6)
Gymnastics	13.8	(3.3)	15.5	(3.7)	17.2	(4.1)	19.7	(4.7)	22.2	(5.3)	24.7	(5.9)
Hockey	17.6	(4.2)	19.7	(4.7)	21.8	(5.2)	25.9	(6.2)	29.3	(7.0)	33.1	(7.9)
Horse-riding												
• walking	8.8	(2.1)	9.6	(2.3)	10.5	(2.5)	12.1	(2.9)	13.8	(3.3)	15.1	(3.6)
• trotting	23.0	(5.5)	26.0	(6.2)	28.5	(6.8)	32.6	(7.8)	36.8	(8.8)	41.0	(9.8)
• galloping	28.9	(6.9)	32.2	(7.7)	35.6	(8.5)	40.6	(9.7)	46.0	(11.0)	51.1	(12.2)
Judo	41.0	(9.8)	45.6	(10.9)	50.7	(12.1)	57.8	(13.8)	65.3	(15.6)	72.8	(17.4)
Running/Walking	*see next page*											
Skiing												
• cross-country	34.7	(8.3)	38.9	(9.3)	43.1	(10.3)	49.4	(11.8)	55.7	(13.3)	62.0	(14.8)
• downhill (beginner)	18.4	(4.4)	20.5	(4.9)	22.6	(5.4)	25.5	(6.1)	29.3	(7.0)	32.6	(7.8)
• downhill (advanced)	29.3	(7.0)	32.6	(7.8)	36.4	(8.7)	41.0	(9.8)	48.9	(11.2)	52.3	(12.5)
Squash	44.4	(10.6)	49.8	(11.9)	54.8	(13.1)	63.2	(15.1)	71.2	(17.0)	79.1	(18.9)
Swimming												
• freestyle	32.7	(7.8)	36.4	(8.7)	40.6	(9.7)	46.5	(11.1)	52.3	(12.5)	58.2	(13.9)
• breaststoke	33.9	(8.1)	38.1	(9.1)	41.9	(10.0)	48.1	(11.5)	54.4	(13.0)	60.3	(14.4)
• backstroke	35.6	(8.5)	39.8	(9.5)	44.0	(10.5)	50.2	(12.0)	56.5	(13.5)	62.8	(15.0)
Tennis												
• social (doubles)	14.6	(3.5)	16.3	(3.9)	18.0	(4.3)	20.5	(4.9)	23.4	(5.6)	26.0	(6.2)
• competitive (singles)	36.8	(8.8)	41.0	(9.8)	45.6	(10.9)	51.5	(12.3)	58.6	(14.0)	65.3	(15.6)
Volleyball	10.5	(2.5)	11.7	(2.8)	13.0	(3.1)	15.1	(3.6)	16.7	(4.0)	18.8	(4.5)

Modified from Frank I. Katch, Victor L. Katch & William D. McArdle, *Exercise Physiology, Energy, Nutrition and Human Performance*, 3rd edition, Lea & Febiger, Philadelphia, 1991.

RUNNING/WALKING

How much energy you expend when running or walking depends on how far you run or walk and your body weight, rather than on speed. For instance, a 70 kg (154 lb) man will expend the same amount of energy whether he runs or walks 5 km (3 miles).

The surface on which you walk or run does not alter your energy expenditure much unless it is soft, such as sand. This latter surface can significantly increase your energy output.

Energy Expenditure Formula (Running/Walking)

Energy Expenditure (kJ/cal) = Distance travelled (km/miles) x Weight (kg/lb) x 4.2

For example, a 70 kg (154 lb) person who walked or ran for 5 km (3 miles) would have used 1470 kJ (350 cal).

Reference: K. Inge & P. Brukner, *Food for Sport*, William Heinemann Australia, Melbourne, 1986.

Ready Reckoner — Nutritional Content of Various Foods
(To help you with your Eating Strategy)

Food	Serving	Amount	Prot. g	Fat g	CHO g	Cal	kJ
Apple, raw	1 small	100 g (3½ oz)	0	0	12	49	207
Apricots	3 medium	90 g (3 oz)	1	0	7	34	140
Baked beans	Average	240 g (7½ oz)	12	1	24	155	648
Banana	1 medium	100 g (3½ oz)	2	0	20	86	358
Beef, corned	2 thin slices	60 g (2 oz)	14	7	0	115	482
Beef, lean (roast)	4 thin slices	120 g (4 oz)	32	6	0	182	761
Biscuit, wheatmeal (plain)	1 small	10 g (¼ oz)	1	2	7	45	188
Bread, multigrain	1 slice	27 g (1 oz)	3	1	11	63	262
Bread roll, wholemeal	1 average	90 g (3 oz)	9	2	39	215	900
Butter	1 tsp	5 g (⅛ oz)	0	4	0	36	152
Cabbage (boiled)	Average	50 g (2 oz)	1	0	1	8	33
Carrots (cooked)	Average	45 g (1½ oz)	0	0	3	12	51
Cauliflower (boiled)	Average	45 g (1½ oz)	1	0	1	9	36
Cereal, plain	Average	30 g (1 oz)	3	1	19	95	398
Cheese, Cheddar	1 slice	20 g (¾ oz)	5	7	0	81	337
Cheese, cottage	1 tbsp	20 g (¾ oz)	3	2	0	29	122
Cheese, cream (low-fat)	Average	220 g (7 oz)	33	2	0	217	906
Cheese, low-fat (18%)	1 slice	20 g (¾ oz)	6	4	0	56	236
Chicken, skinless (baked)	1 average fillet	120 g (4 oz)	34	6	0	189	792
Chocolate, milk	4 squares	30 g (1 oz)	3	9	18	159	664
Crumpet	1 whole	54 g (2 oz)	3	0	21	100	421
Dressing, Italian	1 tbsp	20 g (¾ oz)	0	7	1	66	275
Eggs	1 medium	50 g (2 oz)	7	5	0	75	316
Fish, fried (crumbed)	1 small fillet	70 g (2¼ oz)	15	6	5	134	563
Fish, white (steamed)	1 small fillet	70 g (2¼ oz)	17	2	0	87	365
Golden syrup	1 tbsp	27 g (1 oz)	0	0	21	82	343

(cont. over)

Food	Serving	Amount	Prot. g	Fat g	CHO g	Cal	kJ
Honey	1 tbsp	27 g (1 oz)	0	0	21	79	332
Ice-cream, vanilla	1 scoop	50 g (2 oz)	2	6	11	99	417
Jam	1 tbsp	27 g (1 oz)	0	0	19	72	301
Lemonade	1 glass	200 ml (7 fl oz)	0	0	26	101	421
Lentils (boiled)	Average	211 g (7 oz)	16	1	33	212	886
Margarine	1 tsp	5 g (¼ oz)	0	4	0	36	150
Milk, reduced-fat (2%)	1 glass	200 ml (7 fl oz)	9	4	12	112	468
Milk, skimmed	1 glass	200 ml (7 fl oz)	7	0	10	72	300
Milk, whole	1 glass	200 ml (7 fl oz)	7	8	9	134	559
Muesli, natural	2 tbsp	30 g (1 oz)	4	3	16	102	426
Muffin	1 whole	80 g (2¾ oz)	8	1	29	160	669
Nectarines	2 medium	140 g (4¾ oz)	2	0	11	52	218
Nuts, peanut (roasted)	10 nuts	8 g (¼ oz)	2	3	1	42	176
Oil, polyunsaturated	1 tsp	5 g (⅛ oz)	0	5	0	42	176
Orange	1 medium	122 g (4 oz)	1	0	10	45	190
Orange juice, 100%	1 glass	200 ml (7 fl oz)	1	0	15	71	204
Pasta, wholemeal (boiled)	Average	150 g (5 oz)	9	1	37	196	819
Peaches	1 medium	87 g (3 oz)	1	0	6	27	115
Pear	1 medium	150 g (5 oz)	1	0	23	93	390
Peas (boiled)	Average	44 g (1½ oz)	10	3	0	3	111
Pineapple, peeled (raw)	1 slice	80 g (2¾ oz)	1	0	6	30	126
Pitta (Lebanese) bread	1 round	50 g (2 oz)	5	1	26	134	561
Potato (boiled)	1 medium	145 g (4¾ oz)	4	0	19	94	394
Pumpkin (boiled)	Average	85 g (3 oz)	2	0	8	42	175
Rice, brown (boiled)	Average	180 g (6 oz)	6	2	57	271	1134
Salmon, canned in brine	Average	105 g (3¾ oz)	23	10	0	183	765
Spinach/Swiss chard	Average	44 g (1½ oz)	1	0	0	8	34
Steak, beef fillet (grilled)	1 small	100 g (3½ oz)	30	8	0	196	821
Sugar, white	1 tsp	4 g (⅛ oz)	0	0	4	16	67
Sweetcorn (boiled)	Average	80 g (2¾ oz)	2	2	21	106	442
Tuna, canned in brine	Average	95 g (3¼ oz)	24	2	0	95	492
Yoghurt, fruit (low-fat)	1 carton	200 g (6¾ oz)	10	0	26	151	630
Yoghurt, plain	1 carton	200 g (6¾ oz)	12	9	9	171	716
Yoghurt, plain (low-fat)	1 carton	200 g (6¾ oz)	14	0	12	120	502

INDEX